W9-BZK-240

THE RESISTANCE *versus* VICHY

THE RESISTANCE VERSUS VICHY

The Purge of Collaborators in Liberated France

by

Peter Novick

1968

COLUMBIA UNIVERSITY PRESS

NEW YORK

Published by
Columbia University Press
Myles Cooper Hall
440 West 110th Street
New York 10025

Library of Congress Catalogue Card
No.: 68-14772

Printed and bound in Great Britain

For my Mother and Father

PREFACE

THE failure of the French Resistance to carry out its program for Liberated France is the great cliché – and the point of departure – of all Fourth Republic historiography. For those who shared the dreams and the vision of the Resistance, this failure was the central tragedy of their political lives. It meant that the Fourth Republic would be little more than the continuation of the Third, not the "République pure et dure" for which they had fought. In their disillusionment, *résistants* frequently exaggerated the failure, and dismissed the really significant changes which had been effected.

In the postwar program of the Conseil National de la Résistance – the so-called "C.N.R. Charter" – the purge of Vichyites and collaborators was listed as the first task of the new Provisional Government. This priority did not reflect Resistance opinion on the relative importance of the purge as compared, for example, to social and economic reform. Rather, the purge was considered the necessary prerequisite for the "renouvellement de la France" – the removal of actual or potential impediments to the renovation and reconstruction of the nation. The desire for "renouvellement" underlay all Resistance plans, and not least on the subject of the purge. It is this desire which makes a coherent whole of plans for confiscating the press which appeared under the occupation, decreeing the future electoral ineligibility of those who voted full powers to Marshal Pétain in 1940, and visiting civic disqualifications on tens of thousands of Vichyites and collaborators. Other motives also played an important role. Punishment was an end in itself for those who desired revenge or "justice". In other cases personal or partisan advantage was the paramount consideration. Despite the complexity of motives – often coexisting within the same individual – it is the desire for "renouvellement" which seems to me to be at the center of the purge, and it is within this context that I have considered it.

I have accumulated many debts in the preparation of this study, and it is a pleasant duty to record them here, together with the expression of my warm appreciation and heartfelt thanks.

My research in France was facilitated by a French Government Fellowship in 1960-61 and a William Bayard Cutting Travelling Fellowship from Columbia University in 1962-63.

vii

The staffs of the following libraries have been extremely helpful: Bibliothèque de l'Assemblée Nationale, Bibliothèque de Documentation Internationale Contemporaine, Bibliothèque de "La Documentation Française", Bibliothèque de l'Institut National des Sciences Politiques, Bibliothèque de la Faculté de Droit de l'Université de Paris, Bibliothèque Nationale, Centre de Documentation de la Fondation Nationale des Sciences Politiques, Direction des Journaux Officiels, Musée de la Grande Guerre, Library of Congress, New Yord Public Library, and the Libraries of Columbia University.

Among those who generously gave of their time in order to make information available to me are: MM. André Boissarie and Raymond Lindon, ex-Procureurs-Général of the Cour d'Appel de Paris; M. Jean Robert, the present Procureur-Général, and M. Jean Tréglos of his office; President René Cassin of the Conseil Constitutionnel, Mme Alice Gorgeon-Demartres of La Documentation Française; Mme Marcelle Kraemer-Bach of "La France Combattante"; M. Christian Le Gunéhec of the Ministry of Justice; Senator Jean Odin, Secretary-General of "Les Quatre-vingts"; and M. Charles Veillon, Secretary of the Confédération Générale du Travail-Force Ouvrière.

The following scholars have made helpful suggestions: Mr Robert Aron; MM. Louis de Jong and Eduard G. Groeneveld of the Rijksinstituut voor Oorlogsdocumentatie (Amsterdam); M. Mattei Dogan of the Centre d'Etudes Sociologiques; M. Alfred Grosser of the Institut National des Sciences Politiques; M. Henri Michel of the Comité d'Histoire de la Deuxième Guerre Mondiale; Professor Robert Paxton of the State University of New York at Stonybrook; Mrs Dorothy Pickles of the London School of Economics; and Mr Philip Williams of Nuffield College (Oxford). Professor Shepard B. Clough of Columbia University gave me valuable advice on an earlier draft, and, together with Professors René Albrecht-Carrié, L. Gray Cowan, and Louis Henkin, made very useful comments on the version submitted as my dissertation.

Among those who have rendered assistance of various kinds are: M. and Mme. Raymond Jeanclos, Mrs Shirley Lerman, Mr Michael Novick, Mr Herman Roseman, M. Hans van Marle, Mrs Beatrice Waldman, Mrs Deirdre Wulf, and Mr Leon Wyszewianski.

It is particularly gratifying to be able to record here two very special obligations. For many years I have been inspired, encouraged, and assisted in countless ways by Professor Fritz Stern of Columbia University. It has been a privilege to be his student, an honor to have been granted his friendship. My wife Joan has given me new

PREFACE

insight into the psychology of the collaborationist by the way in which she has shamelessly and enthusiastically collaborated with this study —a brutal occupying power which has ruled our lives for so long.

PETER NOVICK

SOME IMPORTANT DATES: 1940-1946

June 16, 1940	Marshal Philippe Pétain replaces Paul Reynaud as Président du Conseil.
June 18, 1940	General Charles de Gaulle issues his appeal for continued resistance from London.
June 22, 1940	Franco-German Armistice signed at Rethondes.
July 10, 1940	National Assembly votes constituent powers to Marshal Pétain.
July 11, 1940	Vichy Regime established.
October 24, 1940	Marshal Pétain meets Adolf Hitler at Montoire.
October 30, 1940	Marshal Pétain publicly announces his willingness to "entrer dans la voie de la collaboration".
December 13, 1940	Pierre Laval dismissed from office by Marshal Pétain. (Triumvirate of Admiral François Darlan, General C.-L. Huntziger and P.-E. Flandin established.)
February 9, 1941	Triumvirate dissolved; Admiral Darlan rules alone.
June 22, 1941	Germany invades the Soviet Union.
April 18, 1942	Pierre Laval returns to office, replacing Admiral Darlan.
November 8, 1942	Allied landings in North Africa.
November 11, 1942	Germany occupies the "Free Zone".
December 24, 1942	Admiral Darlan assassinated in Algiers; succeeded by General Henri Giraud.
February 16, 1943	Service du Travail Obligatoire introduced.
May 15, 1943	Conseil National de la Résistance formed.
June 3, 1943	Comité Français de la Libération Nationale established; Generals Giraud and de Gaulle, co-presidents.
September 3, 1943	C.F.L.N. resolves to try Marshal Pétain and his ministers.
November 3, 1943	Assemblée Consultative Provisoire holds its first session in Algiers.
November 9, 1943	C.F.L.N. reorganized; General de Gaulle sole president.
December 21, 1943	C.F.L.N. arrests Pierre Boisson, P.-E. Flandin, Marcel Peyrouton.
March 20, 1944	Pierre Pucheu executed.

June 3, 1944	C.F.L.N. becomes Gouvernement Provisoire de la République Française.
June 6, 1944	Allied landings in Normandy.
August 15, 1944	Allied landings in Southern France.
August 25, 1944	Liberation of Paris.
October 23, 1944	Paris *cour de justice* opens; trial of Georges Suarez.
March 15, 1945	High Court opens; trial of Admiral Estéva.
April 29, 1945	Municipal elections.
May 7, 1945	Germany surrenders unconditionally.
August 15, 1945	Marshal Pétain sentenced to death by the High Court.
October 9, 1945	Pierre Laval sentenced to death by the High Court.
October 21, 1945	Constitutional referendum and election of First Constituent Assembly.
January 19, 1946	General de Gaulle resigns as president of the Provisional Government; replaced by Félix Gouin.
May 5, 1946	Constitutional referendum.
June 2, 1946	Election of Second Constituent Assembly.
July 26, 1946	P.-E. Flandin sentenced to five years' national degradation (suspended) by the High Court.
July 30, 1946	Strike of Communist jurors at the High Court.
October 13, 1946	Constitutional referendum.
November 10, 1946	Election of National Assembly.

ABBREVIATIONS

A.C.P.	Assemblée Consultative Provisoire.
A.M.G.O.T.	Allied Military Government of Occupied Territory.
A.N.	Assemblée Nationale.
A.N.C. (I)	(First) Assemblée Nationale Constituante [elected October 21, 1945].
A.N.C. (II)	(Second) Assemblée Nationale Constituante [elected June 2, 1946].
B.D.I.C.	Bibliothèque de Documentation Internationale Contemporaine.
C.D.L.	Comité Départemental de la Libération.
C.F.L.N.	Comité Français de la Libération Nationale.
C.F.T.C.	Confédération Française des Travailleurs Chrétiens.
C.G.E.	Comité Général d'Etudes.
C.G.T.	Confédération Générale du Travail.
C.G.T.-F.O.	Confédération Générale du Travail-Force Ouvrière.
C.G.T.U.	Confédération Générale du Travail Unitaire.
C.N.E.	Comité National des Ecrivains.
C.N.R.	Conseil National de la Résistance.
C.R.	Conseil de la République.
F.F.I.	Forces Françaises de l'Intérieur.
F.N.P.C.	Fédération Nationale de la Presse Clandestine.
F.N.P.F.	Fédération Nationale de la Presse Française.
F.T.P.[F.]	Francs-Tireurs et Partisans [Français].
G.P.R.F.	Gouvernement Provisoire de la République Française.
J.O.	Journal Officiel.
L.V.F.	Légion des Volontaires Français.
M.L.N.	Mouvement de Libération Nationale.
M.R.P.	Mouvement Républicain Populaire.
M.U.R.	Mouvements Unis de la Résistance.
O.C.M.	Organisation Civile et Militaire.
O.S.S.	Office of Strategic Services.
P.C.F.	Parti Communiste Français.
P.P.F.	Parti Populaire Français.
P.R.L.	Parti Républicain de la Liberté.
P.T.T.	Postes, Télégraphes et Téléphones.
R.H.D.G.M.	Revue d'Histoire de la Deuxième Guerre Mondiale.
R.G.R.	Rassemblement des Gauches Républicaines.

ABBREVIATIONS

R.P.F.	Rassemblement du Peuple Français.
S.F.I.O.	Section Française de l'Internationale Ouvrière [Parti Socialiste].
S.N.E.P.	Société Nationale des Entreprises de Presse.
S.S.S.	Service de Sondages et de Statistiques.
S.T.O.	Service du Travail Obligatoire.
U.D.S.R.	Union Démocratique et Socialiste de la Résistance.

LIST OF TABLES

CONTENTS

Chapter 1

LES DEUX FRANCES

You think that Hitler is another Wilhelm I, the old gentleman who
took Alsace-Lorraine and that was all. But Hitler is Genghis Khan.

> PAUL REYNAUD, at the cabinet meeting of
> June 12, 1940.[1]

Even if Germany wins the present war, France will, given the
strength and character of her people, and German weaknesses,
eventually be the dominating continental force. . . . A German
victory is really better for France . . . than a British victory.

> ADMIRAL DARLAN to H. FREEMAN MATTHEWS,
> December 1940.[2]

O N May 10, 1940, after eight months of "phoney war", Hitler
attacked in the West. By May 25 a number of leading figures
in the Government of Paul Reynaud – notably the new vice-
premier, Marshal Philippe Pétain, and the new Commander-in-Chief,
General Maxime Weygand – had become convinced that France had
no choice but to sue for an armistice.

For the next three weeks Reynaud fought – ineptly – a losing battle
against rising sentiment in his cabinet for negotiation with Hitler.
Proposals for the formation of a "Breton redoubt", or for a withdrawal
to French North Africa were dismissed by Pétain and Weygand as
militarily impractical – as perhaps they were. Reynaud at one point
demanded that, following the Dutch example, Weygand give the order
for a purely military surrender, with the Government carrying on from
abroad. This Weygand hotly refused as contrary to the honor of the
Army. Finally, on the evening of June 16, the exhausted premier submitted his resignation to President Lebrun, and recommended that
Marshal Pétain, the most prestigious of the partisans of an armistice,
be named his successor.[3] It was to be six more days before an armistice

---

1. Reynaud, *Au cœur de la mêlée: 1930-1945* (Paris: 1951), p. 852.
2. Telegram from Matthews (First Secretary of the American Embassy at
Vichy) to the Department of State, December 14, 1940, cited in William L.
Langer, *Our Vichy Gamble* (New York: 1947), p. 117.
3. In fact, on June 16 Reynaud probably still disposed of an anti-armistice
majority, though a dwindling one. On this disputed point see the tabular
presentation of different accounts of the line-up in Adrienne Hytier's *Two
Years of French Foreign Policy: Vichy 1940-1942* (Geneva: 1958), pp. 361-62.

was signed with Germany (formally it went into effect only on June 25), but the Battle of France was over.

The Armistice provided for the occupation of the northern half of France, plus the entire Atlantic coast. (The cost of the occupation was to be borne by the French Government.) The French Government could sit where it chose (in either occupied or unoccupied France), and would be responsible for the administration of the entire country, being pledged to cooperate with the German occupying forces in carrying out their decrees in the occupied zone. French armed forces, except for a small force to maintain order, were to be demobilized; war materials were to be either handed over or placed under guard; the fleet was to remain in the harbor of Toulon. French prisoners of war were to remain in captivity until the conclusion of peace. All French forces at liberty were forbidden to resume fighting against Germany. All German prisoners held by the French, as well as all other German nationals designated by Germany (i.e., anti-Nazi refugees) were to be handed over.

Later, many *résistants* were to see a plot of long standing in the negotiation of the Armistice. Allegations were (and are) made that Pétain had long been in secret contact with leading Nazis; that ever since the outbreak of the war in September 1939, he had been intriguing to gain power for the purpose of making peace with Hitler. These charges have never been substantiated. There remained, however, cogent reasons for *résistants* to view with suspicion the motives of those whom they referred to as "capitulards". There were, unquestionably, compelling military reasons for suspending the fighting in metropolitan France, but there appeared to be non-military motives at work as well.

For one thing, it could be observed that with very, very few exceptions, those who favored an armistice in 1940 had been *munichois* in 1938 and subsequently became *vichyssois*; while the opponents of an armistice had been among the opponents of Munich, and later of the Vichy Regime.[4] For another, it was clear that hysterical anti-Communism and fear of a "Bolshevik uprising" were prominent in the minds of

4. An exception to this general rule is the attitude of a number of leading French officials in North Africa – including General Noguès, Admiral Estéva and Marcel Peyrouton – who urged continued resistance from North Africa in June 1940 and who later became fervent supporters of Vichy. This reflected the general attitude of the European population of North Africa at the time, which in contrast to that in the metropole was stubbornly *résistant*, just as three years later it was stubbornly Pétainist at a time when metropolitan France was abandoning the Marshal. Perhaps the North African sun

at least some of the leading proponents of an armistice; many of the "capitulards" belonged to milieux whose motto had been "plutôt Hitler que le Front populaire". Finally – as subsequent events were soon to show – an even larger group of the "capitulards" were fundamentally hostile to the Republic, viewed the military collapse as a divine judgment on its sins, and took advantage of the defeat to strangle "the slut Marianne".

Even for those, like General de Gaulle, who did not explicitly embrace the view that the Armistice was the result of a plot,

> the principal offense of Pétain and his government was to have, in the name of France, negotiated the so-called "armistice" with the enemy.... All the offenses that Vichy was later led to commit: collaboration with the invaders; . . . battles against the resistance in cooperation with German police and armed forces; the handing over of French political prisoners, Jews, and foreigners who had found refuge among us . . . flowed inevitably from this poisoned spring.[5]

Whether in retrospect the Armistice is seen as a plot, a crime, an act of cowardice, an error in judgment, or a painful but necessary act of statesmanship, there can be no question but that in 1940 the overwhelming majority of Frenchmen considered it the last of these. Reeling under the impact of the German Blitzkrieg, virtually the entire nation rallied around the "Victor of Verdun" and accepted without question the correctness of his decision "with mixed sentiments of cowardly relief and shame".[6]

To the emotional impact of defeat was added what seemed the most obvious of military judgments: Germany had won the war; British capitulation could only be a matter of weeks. To believe otherwise – as did Paul Reynaud, Georges Mandel, Charles de Gaulle – seemed reckless bravado. To believe otherwise was even vaguely unpatriotic. As Paul-Marie de la Gorce wrote of Weygand:

> Like all military men of the generation that had been victorious in 1918, he could not imagine that any other army was comparable to the French, except the German Army. Since the German Army had just won a

---

simply breeds stubbornness, but concern with French prestige vis-à-vis the native population seems to have been important in both cases. Also, in both cases they were cut off from those experiences which moved opinion first one way, then the other.

5. *Mémoires de guerre* (Paris: 1954-59), III, 248-49.

6. Léon Blum used this phrase to describe his own reaction to the Anglo-French abandonment of Czechoslavakia in *Le Populaire*, September 20, 1938.

decisive victory in France, he could not imagine that any other power might match it in armed strength. Thus Germany had virtually won the war.[7]

(There was even some covert satisfaction that now Britain – which, in the view of many Frenchmen, had left France in the lurch by the Dunkirk evacuation – would feel the same onslaught that had overwhelmed France.)

For whatever motives, with whatever secret satisfaction or despair, the defeat and the Armistice were accepted as *faits accomplis*, and Frenchmen prepared to live, for an indefinite period, in Hitler's Europe.

For the Free French, the "regime of usurpation, capitulation and collaboration" came into being on June 16, 1940, at Bordeaux, when Marshal Pétain became the last premier of the Third Republic. But Bordeaux was in the occupied zone, and Pétain's Government, not wishing to operate under the shadow of German bayonets, settled in the resort town of Vichy, where the many great hotels permitted the installation of government offices. The Hôtel du Parc became Pétain's Elysée Palace. It was here that what post-Liberation legislation referred to as "l'autorité de fait se disant gouvernement de l'Etat français" – the Vichy Regime – came into being on July 11.

The Senate and the Chamber of Deputies had not met since late May, and the Armistice had been negotiated solely on the responsibility of the Cabinet. (Jules Jeanneney and Edouard Herriot, presidents of the Senate and Chamber of Deputies respectively, had sided with Reynaud.) Pétain could have continued indefinitely to rule without legislative sanction, using the system of decree-laws so widely employed during the 1930's to circumvent parliamentary paralysis. It was decided, however, that a formal break with the past should take place – that the Republic should cede to an authoritarian regime under the Marshal.

There were several reasons why such a course of action seemed desirable to the Pétain cabinet. For many of its members, long hostile to the Republic, the Armistice offered a unique opportunity to have done with the detested regime and construct a new one, either looking backward to a tradition of hierarchy and stability, or forward to a new order of corporatism and "the leadership principle". Others in the cabinet were convinced of the necessity for France to bring her political institutions into line with the principles of the "New Order" in

7. *The French Army* (New York: 1963), p. 299.

4

Europe.[8] Pierre Laval – who had entered the Cabinet on June 23 and was delegated by Pétain to engineer the operation – had personal motives as well. By presenting Pétain with absolute power he could gain the Marshal's gratitude, and, given the Marshal's age and political incompetence, become *dauphin régent*.

Laval was brilliantly successful. On July 9 he persuaded the Chamber of Deputies and the Senate to agree almost unanimously (395-3 and 229-1, respectively) to the principle of constitutional change. On the following day, by a vote of 569-80, the two chambers sitting together as the National Assembly voted not only full legislative, but constituent powers as well, to the eighty-four-year-old Marshal:

> The National Assembly grants all powers to the Government of the Republic under the authority and signature of Marshal Pétain, with a view to the promulgation, through one or more acts, of a new Constitution of the French State. This Constitution shall guarantee the rights of work, family, and native land. It shall be ratified by the nation and applied by the Assemblies which it shall create.[9]

Why was Laval so successful? Why did the Republic, which for seventy years had "governed badly but defended itself well", commit suicide on July 10, 1940? After the Liberation, this question came to be of more than historical interest, as the authors of the changeover, as well as those who acquiesced in it, were called to account for their actions.

Some, no doubt, were convinced by Laval's arguments of *Realpolitik*:

> Just as after 1918 Germany adopted the system of the victorious nations, so France must adapt her political institutions to those of her victors. . . . Parliamentary democracy whose greatest crime was to declare this war, lost the war; it must disappear and give way to an authoritarian, hierarchical, national and social regime.[10]

Anti-Republicans of various stripes – fascists, monarchists, miscellaneous authoritarians – needed no such arguments. Even among those

8. While the argument that France had to "align herself with the New Order" was frequently invoked, there is no evidence that any constitutional change in France was required or even desired by the Germans. Laval, in the apologia written shortly before his execution, wrote that "the immense majority of the deputies and senators realized that Hitler would be merciless [toward France] if he had to deal with certain French politicians. . . ." (*Laval parle* [Geneva: 1947], p. 48.) But the politicians who would strain the quality of mercy in the German Fuehrer were not in Pétain's Third Republic cabinet.

9. J.O., July 11, 1940.

10. Quoted in Vincent Auriol, *Hier . . . demain* (Paris: 1945), I, 107.

who were not hostile to the Republic in principle, there were many who thought the time ripe for sweeping changes. Throughout the 1930's men like André Tardieu and Gaston Doumergue had been urging constitutional revision in the direction of a stronger executive. The catastrophe of 1940 seemed to underline their arguments, and, as the votes of July 9 showed, there were few to be found in the summer of 1940 who would deny that some form of revision was called for.

In the case of some, threats and intimidation may have played a role. Léon Blum (who voted "no" on July 10) asserted after the war that

> the July 10 vote was a vote obtained under triple pressure . . . in the first place, Doriot's gangs in the street; in the second place, Weygand at Clermont-Ferrand, and, as I've said, the Germans at Moulins, fifty miles from Vichy. And the word that went around, the word that was passed along, was: "Those who don't vote [the right way] won't sleep in their own beds tonight." And in truth, not one of the men who voted "no" at Vichy was sure that he would depart a free man.[11]

No single factor was more important than the personal support of the proposal by Marshal Pétain. In a message read to the Assembly on the morning of July 10, he made acceptance of Laval's text virtually a vote of confidence in himself. Organized opposition all but collapsed following the reading of the letter. No French political leader in modern times – with the possible exception of General de Gaulle at the moment of Liberation – ever enjoyed such widespread confidence and support. Edouard Herriot, who had opposed Pétain over the Armistice, and subsequently abstained in the July 10 vote, nevertheless urged the deputies "to take care not to upset the accord which has been established under his authority".[12] Even those who were among the eighty "no-voters" were fulsome in their expressions of confidence in Pétain.[13]

There was, in the simplest terms, a "failure of nerve" on the part of French political leaders in July 1940. Stunned by the lightning German victory, overwhelmed by the extent of the catastrophe, they abdicated responsibility and handed over the destiny of France to an octogenarian soldier whose sole qualification to lead the nation was that he had carried out a successful defensive action a quarter of a century before.

11. Testimony in *Le Procès du Maréchal Pétain* (Paris: 1945), I, 243-44.
12. Edouard Herriot, *Episodes: 1940-1944* (Paris: 1950), pp. 136-37.
13. However, such statements probably say more about the atmosphere at Vichy than about the personal opinion of Pétain held by their authors. The opponents of Laval's text were practical politicians, and, at that time and place, a *pro forma* expression of confidence in Pétain had to preface any political pronouncement.

The abdication of responsibility was not unanimous. There were the eighty who voted "no"; there were seventeen others who abstained.[14] It is likely that most of those who had sailed to North Africa in June on the *Massilia* in order to carry on the fight would have swelled the ranks of the eighty, but at the time of the vote they were stranded across the Mediterranean.[15] Doubtless there were some among the other 150 deputies and senators who for one reason or another were absent from Vichy who would have joined the opposition.[16]

As it was, there was a good deal of activity on the part of the opposition. The so-called "Taurines proposal" would have given Pétain full decree-power, suspended the 1875 Constitution until the peace, and postponed definitive constitutional change until a free vote was possible. A resolution sponsored by Vincent Badie would likewise have given Pétain all the legislative power he needed, but it would have reaffirmed the Assembly's faith in the Republic and refused to vote its disappearance. All such efforts were in vain: the Taurines proposal was shunted aside by a legislative maneuver, Badie was shouted down when he attempted to speak for his resolution in the Assembly, and, of course, in the final voting the last-ditch republicans were swamped. On the day after the vote, the first "Constitutional Acts", beginning with the words "Nous, Philippe Pétain . . ." established the Vichy Regime.

Vichy resists brief definition: it was made up of so many different currents, its policy vacillated so frequently, its personnel and activities were so different at different epochs, that any summing-up is almost impossible. But if we are to understand the attitude of the Resistance toward Vichy – as well as the legislative and judicial consequences of that attitude – a few general remarks are necessary.

The ideology of the "National Revolution" was vague and never precisely defined. General Weygand has been described as having a political ideal "situated somewhere in the misty reaches of the Moral

14. Among the eighty were many of the leading figures of the Third and (as yet unimagined) Fourth Republics: Vincent Auriol, Léon Blum, Joseph Paul-Boncour, Marx Dormoy, Félix Gouin, Jules Moch, André Philip, Paul Ramadier. Well-known abstainers included (in addition to Herriot) Georges Monnet and Henri Queuille.

15. The *Massilia* passengers included André Le Troquer, Georges Mandel, Pierre Mendès-France, Tony Révillon and Jean Zay.

16. The Communist parliamentary delegation had by this time been expelled from the two assemblies. After the Liberation they naturally claimed that had they been present they would have been unanimously in opposition.

Order and the Orléanist 'République des Ducs' "[17]; this is perhaps as good a definition of Vichy ideology as any other. Charles Maurras was the unofficial court philosopher – at least of Pétain's immediate circle – but corporatism, technocracy, and other hobby horses found stable room at the Hôtel du Parc.

At first glance, many of the specific hallmarks of the Vichy Regime seem to be only a reflection of popular sentiment in 1940. Almost everybody in France believed that Germany had won the war and that France had to adjust herself to this state of affairs; the defunct Third Republic was almost universally unpopular; anglophobia was (briefly) general, violent anti-Communism had been widespread ever since the Russo-German Pact; almost all Frenchmen looked upon Pétain as the father and the saviour of France.

But at Vichy these widely held views were held with a difference. The men of Vichy did not just believe that German victory had to be accepted, but often cherished the conceit that by skillful collaboration and artful maneuver, the subtle French could "manage" the slow-witted Germans, and even take over from them the leadership of "the new Europe".

At Vichy the Third Republic was not just unmourned: a systematic effort was launched to extirpate every vestige of the despised "ancien régime". "Etat français" replaced "République française" and "Travail, Famille, Patrie" replaced "Liberté, Egalité, Fraternité" on coins, stamps, official documents and public buildings; busts of Pétain replaced those of Marianne. The changes were not all symbolic: thousands of civil servants, mayors, and municipal councillors were removed from office. Naval officers were often employed to replace dismissed officials; this practice became so widespread that Cardinal Lienart, archbishop of Lille, was prompted to speculate whether upon his demise there would still be an admiral left to replace him. A Supreme Court of Justice was established at Riom to try former ministers and high officials for actions connected with the declaration of war and its conduct. Léon Blum, Edouard Daladier, and General Gamelin were the principal defendants, but they were so successful in confounding their accusers – showing that Pétain and the General Staff were largely responsible for French unpreparedness – that the trial was adjourned indefinitely. It was a hollow victory: Blum, Daladier, and Gamelin; together with Georges Mandel, Reynaud, and other luminaries of the

17. Philip C. F. Bankwitz, "Maxime Weygand and the Fall of France: A Study in Civil-Military Relations", *Journal of Modern History*, XXXI, 3 (September 1959), 228-29.

Third Republic, remained in Vichy (later German) prisons for the duration.

Many Frenchmen resented the British evacuation at Dunkirk; an even larger number were embittered by the tragic events at Mers-el-Kébir, where on July 3 the British sank elements of the French Navy when their commanding officer refused to give satisfactory guarantees that the ships would not be eventually handed over to the Germans. But while for most Frenchmen resentment quickly turned to admiration for Britain's gallant resistance to Hitler, anglophobia at Vichy was deep-seated and often fanatical. Pierre Laval "hoped ardently that the English would be defeated", and his successor, Admiral François Darlan, was almost hysterical in his anti-British tirades.[18] Resentment over Britain's "treachery" was reinforced by scorn for Britain's liberal institutions. Anglophobia in France was traditionally both a right-wing and a Navy (as opposed to Army) phenomenon, and came to the fore in Vichy ruling circles.

The anti-Communism of Vichy was not the principled opposition to the Soviet system or the disgust with the acrobatics of the French Communists that was widespread in many quarters, including the Resistance. Rather it was an irrational, paranoid, and hysterical reflex: "la grande peur des bien pensants" in Georges Bernanos' phrase. French Communists were ruthlessly persecuted by the Regime, and Marshal Pétain, cool to any other form of French military collaboration with the Axis, endorsed the Légion des Volontaires Français, who fought on the Russian front in German uniforms.

The active supporters of Vichy did not just share in the almost universal respect for the Marshal and trust in his leadership; a cult was created around his person that attained ludicrous proportions. An adaptation of the Lord's prayer, addressed to Pétain, was circulated. *Bien pensant* historians took a leading role in the promotion of the cult: "During those years not a book appeared on Jeanne d'Arc, Henri IV, Louis XIV or Bonaparte in which the preface failed to point out the astonishing similarities between the hero of the work and the glorious Marshal".[19] As in Nazi Germany, army officers and judges had to take a personal oath to the Chief of State.

There were other prominent Vichy themes which happily were not reflections – however distorted – of widespread popular feeling. The Regime was officially and systematically anti-Semitic: a *numerus clausus*

18. Langer, pp. 83, 117.
19. Marc Pierre, Marquis d'Argenson, *Pétain et le pétinisme: Essai de psychologie* (Paris: 1953), p. 104.

was introduced in the professions, and Jews were barred from teaching, banking, the communications industry, and the civil service and were subject to a variety of other disabilities. A "Commissariat-General for Jewish Affairs" was established under the direction of virulent anti-Semites. Vichy administrative and police services cooperated with many of the German anti-Semitic programs in the occupied zone, but while the Germans were delighted with the ideological and program-matic support they received from Vichy, that regime's anti-Semitism was very much a native product.

As has been noted above, the Vichy Regime was initially supported by most of the population; nevertheless, there were some recognizable groups which came to be distinguished as particularly stalwart pillars of the Regime. Of course, there was no section of the national com-munity which was 100 per cent Vichyite. The Académie Française had its François Mauriacs and Georges Duhamels, the Army its Generals De Larminat and Catroux, the right-wing parties their Louis Marins and Georges Mandels. There were business leaders and monarchists, peasants and Cagoulards who were *résistants de la première heure.*

But only the most fanatical nominalist would dispute that the *bien-pensants*, the military, the Catholic hierarchy, the business community, high civil servants, the peasantry, and the various anti-parliamentary groups were almost unanimously *vichyssois.* To these should be added the bulk of certain "sub-groups" such as the anti-Communist-pacifist-*munichois* minorities of the Socialist Party (Paul Faure et Cie.) and the trade union movement (René Belin et Cie.).[20]

In the domestic field Vichy had almost no concrete achievements to its credit. There were a few abortive programs – an attempt at regional organization through the institution of "super-prefects", a modified corporatism embodied in the *Charte du Travail* – but little in the way of permanent accomplishment. This is perhaps natural. The Regime effectively controlled less than half of France (and after November 1942 not even that), and even in the "Free Zone" it was constantly subject to German blackmail. There were other reasons. Vichy, which was advertised as having put an end to the chaos and instability of the Third Republic, was hardly more stable than its predecessor. In the first year of Pétain's rule, there were four Ministers of Foreign Affairs, five Ministers of the Interior, five Ministers of Education, and six Ministers of Industrial Production. The atmosphere was that of a

20. A caveat: the groups mentioned here were united only in support of Vichy, not necessarily in favor of active collaboration, military or otherwise, with Germany.

Byzantine court, "headed by a feeble, frightened old man, surrounded by self-seeking conspirators".[21]

Apart from minor personnel shifts – a result of both court intrigues and changing winds from Berlin – there were a number of major reorganizations of the Government. Laval lost his position as *dauphin régent* on December 13, 1940. He was replaced by a triumvirate of Admiral Darlan, General Huntziger, and P.-E. Flandin. On February 9, 1941, Darlan ousted his colleagues, and proceeded to combine in his person the functions of Vice-President of the Council, Minister of Foreign Affairs, Interior and Information, in addition to the dauphinate. His reign lasted a little over a year: on April 18, 1942, Laval returned to power. The total occupation of France in November 1942, following the Allied landings in North Africa, did not produce any major change in the Vichy cabinet, apart from the defection of Admiral Darlan. Laval remained in office until the end, although the composition of the Government underwent a series of modifications in early 1944 when several of the Paris-based ultra-collaborationists entered the cabinet.

But throughout the various governmental crises and the changes in leadership at Vichy, the red thread of Vichy foreign policy remained unbroken from the summer of 1940 until the autumn of 1942, when Vichy lost its last shreds of independence and *raison d'être*.

From Vichy's point of view, there was, given Germany's might and the likelihood of her victory, one way and only one to improve France's lot, to obtain concessions which would alleviate her present miseries and to secure guarantees which would assure the future. One had to get along with the victor, to collaborate with him, however distasteful it might be. Collaboration, therefore, remained for two years the chief tenet of Vichy's foreign policy. It was the policy of Laval, it was the policy of Flandin, it was the policy of Darlan, it was that of the Marshal, it was that of his Ministers. To be sure, there were differences between the men and between their methods. Laval was more willing to prime the pump, Darlan more ready to make military concessions. Pétain, without whom there would have been no policy of collaboration, although his role in its application was not always very active, was more cautious and more responsive to public opinion than either Darlan or Laval.

... it seems likely that timely and generous concessions to them [from Germany to France] could have led them along much farther than they intended or wanted to go and that they could even have been drawn

21. Message from U.S. Ambassador William D. Leahy to President Roosevelt (November 22, 1941), cited in Langer, p. 194.

gradually into hostilities with England. . . . As things worked out, however, Vichy's German policy, because it failed to attain its chief objective, served France. It avoided direct German rule . . .[22]

In November 1942, the two principal justifications of Vichy's policy of collaboration, and of its very existence, collapsed. The first – to forestall total occupation – disappeared on November 11 when German troops crossed the demarcation line. The second – the wager on a German victory – dissolved as the tide of war shifted in favor of the Allies, in North Africa, in the Pacific, and at Stalingrad.

Paradoxically, collaboration increased in many respects after November 1942, when it had lost, or was swiftly losing, its justification. Moralists have sometimes pictured the evolution of Vichy as a classic case of the spiral staircase leading to hell. Concessions led inevitably to greater concessions; the first compromise of principle was the thin edge of the wedge, which made the next that much easier, and the next easier still; the initial step which departed by one degree from the narrow path of national honor eventually led, with geometric inexorability, miles away from it. The picture is not totally false, but there were less metaphysical forces at work.

Russian victories in the East led many fanatical anti-Communists at Vichy to second the German war effort in order to save Europe from "Bolshevization". Thus Laval's fateful remark: "I hope for a German victory, because without it, communism will reign throughout Europe".[23] Increased resistance activity led to more vigorous repressive action by Vichy – often in cooperation with the Germans. In this connection the evolution of the Légion des Combattants is instructive. Formed in 1940 as a consolidated veterans' organization, and perhaps as the nucleus of a Pétainist *parti unique*, in November 1941 the Légion incorporated Colonel de la Rocque's quasi-fascist Parti Social Français (the successor to the prewar Croix de Feu). In March 1942 a paramilitary Service d'Ordre Légionnaire was formed within the Légion. In January 1943 the Milice Nationale was created out of the S.O.L. The *milice* became a bloody instrument of repression, working closely with the Germans against the Resistance. Finally, those who in 1940-42 had been collaborators out of opportunism – personal or political – came to be replaced at Vichy by "principled collaborators": native fascists and zealous Germanophiles who had been waiting in the wings.

The Regime, which had been hoisted to power by the lightning

22. Hytier, pp. 358-59.
23. *Procès Pétain*, I, 559.

German entry into France in the summer of 1940, ended, appropriately, when the Germans, in the midst of an almost-as-hasty departure in August 1944, tucked Vichy under their arm and carried it off to Sigmaringen.[24]

But the story of Vichy is only half of the story of France from 1940 to 1944. At every juncture: in Reynaud's cabinet in June 1940, at Vichy the following month, and throughout metropolitan France and the French overseas possessions in the years that followed, there was another France.

There is no remark about French history which can compete for ubiquity and banality with the one that refers to "les deux Frances". The France of the *ancien régime* vs. the France of the Revolution; the "Party of Movement" vs. the "Party of Order"; the men of the Commune vs. the men of Versailles; *Dreyfusards* vs. *anti-Dreyfusards*; every epoch of French history has its "deux Frances". But never in French history have "les deux Frances" confronted each other with such prolonged and bitter antagonism, never have the lines been so sharply drawn, as during the four years of the German occupation and the Regime of Vichy.

The division of France in 1940-44 – as in all other periods – was far from total. We know very little about the state of public opinion in France in these years. The usual parameters – elections, a free press, polls – were totally absent. It appears likely that, as always, the bulk of the population passively accepted the *de facto* government, although with a degree of enthusiasm that constantly waned after the summer of 1940, and declined drastically after November 1942. But France in this period was a country in which politics were polarized, and the history of these years is the history of men who, with the inevitable shadings on each side – and occasionally with dramatic voltes-faces – came down decisively on one side or the other.

The "other France" went under various names: "La France Libre", "La France Combattante", "La France Résistante". Whatever name it went under – whether we are speaking of men who worked inside or outside metropolitan France – at bottom "La Résistance n'a été qu'un refus": a refusal to accept the Armistice, a refusal to accept the military verdict of 1940 as final, a refusal to accept the policy of collaboration, a refusal to accept Vichy as the legitimate voice of France.

24. Pétain and Laval protested their forcible emigration, and took no part in the puppet "government in exile" which was headed by Fernand de Brinon, and included Joseph Darnand, Marcel Déat and Jean Luchaire.

This refusal allowed us to look at a Russian, British or American soldier without blushing. . . . Never have so many men consciously run so many risks for such a small thing: a desire to bear witness. Perhaps it is absurd, but it was by such absurdities that we restored our dignity as men.[25]

There is no difficulty in dating the birth of the French Resistance: it began on June 18, 1940, when General Charles de Gaulle, broadcasting from London to his stunned countrymen, told them that "the flame of French resistance must not and shall not be extinguished".[26] De Gaulle was swiftly recognized by the British Government as the representative of "the Free French". During the next three months, a few French overseas possessions rallied to his cause, but the number of recruits who joined him in London was disappointingly small. Only three generals and one admiral joined the Free French before November 1942. A few French soldiers in Britain who had been evacuated from Narvik or Dunkirk joined De Gaulle; most chose repatriation to Vichy France. A few men from French colonies abroad, a few more who escaped from France in the midst of the catastrophe (but no one of real prominence) enlisted under his banner. For the next three years De Gaulle's committee in London was a symbol of the fact that not all Frenchmen had capitulated, but militarily it was insignificant, and politically it represented only itself. The Gaullist movement could have been – and for a time was – "swept into the dustbin of history" by its patrons, the British. That ultimately it was not, that eventually it became "The Provisional Government of the French Republic", was the result of quite independent developments inside France.

De Gaulle's appeal of June 18 had been addressed to French soldiers, sailors, technicians, and skilled munitions workers who either were in Great Britain or could come there. Subsequent talks and Gaullist publications made it clear that the Free French in London were neither calling for, nor expected, the widespread formation of underground groups in metropolitan France. In the following months attention was centered on the *ralliement* of the Empire. It was not until March 1941 that the London Gaullists made their first reference to resistance groups in the metropole. Long before this the first such groups had been born; indeed, by this time many had been decimated or destroyed by the German and Vichy police.

Before the summer of 1940 was over the nucleus of *Combat* had been formed at Lyons under Captain Henri Frenay; in Paris some young

25. Roger Stephané, "La Résistance n'a été qu'un Refus", *France-Observateur*, August 28, 1952.

26. Charles de Gaulle, *Discours de Guerre* (Fribourg: 1944-45), I, 13-14.

scholars at the Musée de l'Homme founded the Comité National de Salut Public. Before the end of 1940 resistance groups began to publish the first underground newspapers: *Quand Même, Pantagruel, L'Université Libre, Libération,* and many others. Other groups established contact with British Intelligence. But it was not in order to print newspapers, or transmit military information, that the Resistance came into existence; rather, it carried out these activities because it was in existence, and once organized, sought a practical *raison d'être.* The organizing impulse was not practical but moral: a compulsion to bear witness to "un refus".

It is because resistance was an *individual* phenomenon, based more often on temperamental than ideological considerations, that sociological or political generalizations about the Resistance are so difficult and tricky. In any case, Resistance "values" cut across traditional ideological lines. As Jean Bloch-Michel has pointed out, the ideals of the Left are liberty, justice, and peace; those who put the last of these first often wound up as collaborators. The ideals of the Right are nationalism and order; "many for whom the second was the strongest impulse wound up abandoning the Right's oldest fetishes – the uniform and the flag".[27] Usually the group with which an individual affiliated depended on chance and opportunity rather than political choice. The same *maquis* might contain "a Communist Parisian worker, a Catholic student, an officer returning to the struggle after undergoing a de-Pétainization cure, and a Socialist civil servant who *au fond* remained a pacifist".[28] The prewar political parties played a very subordinate role in the Resistance: their leaders were frequently in prison or under close surveillance; their members chose resistance, collaboration, or something in between on a personal basis (although the proportion who chose each varied greatly from party to party).

Despite the diversity of individuals and political currents in the Resistance, despite all the exceptions and qualifications which must be noted, it is not unfair to describe the Resistance as being "of the Left". There are many reasons for this. The wholesale enlistment of the Right under the banner of Vichy skewed the political composition of the Resistance "clientele". Lifelong anti-clericals reacted against the smell of incense that emanated from Vichy. (There were, of course, many Catholics in the Resistance, but these were frequently veterans of the struggles of "social Catholicism" against the Church hierarchy, or those who sympathized with them.) Industrial workers and left-wing

27. *Journal du désordre* (Paris: 1955), pp. 55-59.
28. Henri Michel, *Les Courants de pensée de la Résistance* (Paris: 1962), p. 6.

intellectuals found opposition to authority more congenial than did businessmen and *bien pensants*. There were material as well as temperamental motives at work. The working class was the worst sufferer under Vichy (and in 1943-44 was subject to conscription for forced labor in Germany) while many businessmen (and peasants) were prospering under the Occupation. Left-wing intellectuals lost their teaching positions and saw their journalistic outlets suppressed.

The orientation of the Resistance toward the Left had a self-reinforcing aspect. Unity was highly prized in the Resistance, and many right-wing *résistants* paid lip service to socialist ideals rather than cause internal dissension. Representatives of right-wing parties endorsed the "Charter" of the Conseil National de la Résistance, which, among other things, called for widespread nationalizations. After the Liberation, of course, this miraculous unity quickly dissolved, but not all conversions were temporary or based on expedience. Some (e.g., Emmanuel d'Astier, Claude Roy) moved from the extreme Right to the extreme Left under the impact of their Resistance experience. General de Gaulle, who came from a right-wing milieu, and who had respected the "Establishment", was forced to admit that

> with very few exceptions, not only was his appeal not heeded in [Establishment] milieux . . . but also that by and large they did not object to the policy of Vichy, which in his eyes was one of national shame. Not only that, but bishops, industrialists, leading writers and high officials approved [the policy of] collaboration with the enemy. On the other hand he saw the humble, men without rank – workers, clerks, minor civil servants – play a major role in the underground Resistance. He saw unknown men, left-wing politicians and trade unionists, rally to him. It was a wrenching experience and a revelation: the social hierarchy was not a hierarchy of merit.[29]

There is one element in the Resistance coalition that requires a special note: the French Communist Party. For years the Party leaders had been the most ferocious anti-fascists in France, the leading advocates of resistance to German aggression; on the eve of the war, immediately following the signature of the Russo-German Pact, they did an abrupt volte face, and denounced the "imperialist war".

Daladier's Government swiftly applied sanctions: the Party was dissolved, its newspapers were suppressed, its parliamentary representatives were expelled from the Assembly, and thousands of its militants were arrested and imprisoned. The government decrees were

29. *Ibid.*, pp. 98-99.

almost superfluous – the Party was completely demoralized. Militants of long standing left the Party in droves; a third of the parliamentary delegation – presumably the most disciplined elements in the Party – resigned. The Party was in shambles: some leaders, like Maurice Thorez, fled abroad[30]; those who remained went underground, and vainly tried to explain the reversal of policy (which they themselves found hard to swallow) to disillusioned members of the rank and file.

After the invasion in 1940 the first act of the French Communists vis-à-vis the Germans was to seek permission from them to publish *L'Humanité* openly. (It was refused.) Nevertheless, the underground *Humanité* continued to urge fraternization with the Germans, attack De Gaulle as a reactionary in the pay of British imperialists, and speak of Anglo-French war guilt. The Germans responded by releasing, during the first six months of the occupation, over 300 Communists who had been imprisoned by the French authorities.

Communist policy toward Germany was ambiguous: the Party was not pro-German; it was "anti-anti-German". Communist propaganda attacked "British imperialism" (occasionally, "the two rival imperialisms") and those Frenchmen who supported the British, but did not praise Germany, its political system, or its occupying forces.[31] Although clearly this policy "objectively" served German interests, the distinction is worth making: the Communists' reorientation after the German invasion of Russia on June 22, 1941, while dramatic, was not quite the volte face it is sometimes made out to be.

Toward Vichy – with its ferocious anti-Communism and thousands of Communist prisoners – the Communists were uncompromisingly hostile from the very beginning.

By their leap into Resistance activity after the German invasion of Russia on June 22, 1941, the Communists did much to wipe away the bitter memory of their behavior in the previous two years.[32] They were unquestionably the single most important element in the Resistance (though they were far from being a majority), and their losses were

30. Thorez had been called to active duty with his army reserve unit, from which he deserted.

31. At least I know of no such statements. While I have not examined all Communist propaganda in this period, it has been carefully sifted by researchers such as Angelo Tasca, who would certainly have brought to light any such material had they found it.

32. Some Communists had begun anti-German activity before the official change of line, either in the absence of contrary directives from headquarters, or in spite of them. It would be difficult to exaggerate the disorganized state of the Party during this period.

particularly severe. While the Communists in this period cooperated with all other Resistance elements (including repentant Vichyites), they were not hesitant about pointing out their own leading role. Their efforts in this direction were reinforced by German and Vichy propaganda which pictured all *résistants* as "Communist terrorists" or their tools. This propaganda was doubly valuable to the Communists, since it put non-Communist *résistants* on notice that by openly criticizing the Communists, and thus imperiling Resistance unity, they would be playing the enemy's game.

While before June 1941 the Communists coupled an ambiguous attitude toward the Germans with opposition to Vichy, most non-Communists in the metropole who were anti-German from the start had retained an ambiguous attitude toward Vichy for an even longer time. In May 1941 the underground newspaper *Liberté* noted that at Vichy, "side by side with the profiteers and the camp followers of the defeat, there are courageous and worthy men, seeking only to serve their country by . . . saving what can be saved". Four months later the newspaper projected its own hopes on to the population: "The acclaim which welcomes the Marshal during his travels testifies to the French people's hope that, contrary to [the wishes of] his ministers, the Chief of State is waiting for the right moment to act in accord with the unanimous wishes of the country".[33] By 1942 (especially after the events of November) both Communist and non-Communist *résistants* had adopted the attitude of double-barrelled opposition to both Vichy and Berlin that the Gaullists had had from the start, but neither had followed a straight line in getting there.

By the beginning of 1943 the London Gaullists and the Resistance inside France were united by more than common acceptance of common enemies. In 1940-41 De Gaulle had been, for the metropolitan Resistance, merely a symbol of resistance; the question of accepting his leadership simply did not arise. By 1942, as a concomitant of growing disillusionment with Pétain, the Resistance began to turn to De Gaulle as a leader, instead of merely a symbol.

Complementing the Resistance turn toward De Gaulle were the General's overtures to the Resistance, largely inspired by his need to strengthen his position with the Allies by demonstrating that his movement had broad support within France. Gaullist representatives were

33. No. 6 (May 30, 1941); No. 10 (October 1, 1941). For further citations evidencing a reluctance to disavow the Victor of Verdun, or doubt his anti-Germanism, see Michel, *Courants*, p. 160.

sent on secret missions to France in order to forge organic ties between London and the metropole; leaders of underground groups were invited to come to London and participate in the work going on there. Finally, in the spring of 1943 the Conseil National de la Résistance was established under the chairmanship of De Gaulle's representative, Jean Moulin.[34] The C.N.R. included representatives of all the major Resistance organizations, as well as delegates from the underground committees of the political parties and trade unions. It was the tangible evidence of the unanimous support for De Gaulle by all elements of the Resistance, from the pre-war Right to the Communists.

By 1943-44 the Resistance was a far cry from the small and uncoordinated collection of grouplets begun in 1940-41. While some small isolated units maintained an independent existence throughout the occupation, consolidation and coordination were the order of the day. Large organizations such as Combat, Libération, Front National, and the Organisation Civile et Militaire dominated the scene. There were specialized groups, such as Noyautage des Administrations Publiques, which colonized the civil service; *Combat* and *Défense de la France* had special services for producing false papers which between them supplied hundreds of thousands of forged documents to most of the movements in both zones, using thousands of different home-made stamps and seals; there were special sabotage and information-gathering groups which worked directly under the Intelligence Services of Britain, the United States, and the Free French; finally, the exactions of the Service de Travail Obligatoire [deportation of French workers to Germany] resulted in the flight of tens of thousands of young Frenchmen into the countryside where they gathered in guerrilla bands – the *maquis*. The underground press of 1943-44 bore little resemblance to the smudged mimeographed sheets circulated in tiny editions in 1940-41. There were over a thousand separate periodicals circulated secretly during the occupation, and while some had only a short life, others appeared regularly for years. Likewise, while some papers continued to be circulated in small editions, others attained a circulation of well over 100,000 (sometimes 200,000 or 300,000) well-printed and illustrated copies: *Combat, Défense de la France, Franc-Tireur, Populaire*.

In writing about *les deux Frances* of 1940-44, many writers have attempted to deliver a "verdict"; to determine which side served

34. Moulin was captured by the Germans shortly after the C.N.R. was formed, and died under "interrogation". He was succeeded by Georges Bidault.

France, which harmed her. From one point of view, Vichy was a self-sacrificing effort to save what could be saved, to limit France's material suffering by negotiation, compromise and accommodation; the Resistance – though it contained many men of courage and good intentions – harmed the nation by dividing Frenchmen among themselves and by provoking the Germans into committing terrible reprisals. There is merit in this point of view. It would be difficult to dispute the contention that on many points material advantages accrued to France from Vichy's negotiations with the Germans; above all, the existence of Vichy prevented, until November 1942, the total occupation of the country. And it is equally true that the very limited military contribution of the Resistance seems doubly insignificant when weighed against the deportations and massacres which it provoked.

From the diametrically opposed point of view, Vichy, though it included some well-meaning patriots, was a sink of shame and treason – a stain on the honor of France; the Resistance, and the Resistance alone, preserved the dignity and the traditions of France. This view also has much to commend it. The zeal of Vichy to collaborate with Germany bespeaks more than a caretaker role; without the efforts of De Gaulle and the Resistance, France could hardly have taken her place at the postwar conference table of the victors.[35]

The two views not only represent different evaluations, they are based on different yardsticks, and the debate is largely a *dialogue des sourds*. Material and moral factors cannot be totalled up in adjoining columns and a balance struck; the skills of the accountant or the "scientific historian" are of no use in delivering a "verdict" in the case of Vichy vs. the Resistance. But for the purposes of this study no "verdict" is required. The purge was the work of the victors – the Resistance – and, as always, at least in the short run, they wrote the history. The Armistice was a crime, the vote of July 10 a betrayal, Vichy a usurper-regime, collaboration a policy of treason: these were the historico-judicial postulates of the purge.

35. There is a third view, of which Robert Aron is the leading exponent, which sees the two camps as complementary – France's "sword and shield". Aron applauds the efforts of the bulk of those on each side, excoriating a handful of terrorists in one camp, a handful of traitors in the other. The motives of this variety of historiography – reconciliation – are as transparent as they are high-minded, but the characteristic result is the muddying of important distinctions and tendentious treatment of the facts to fit the system. Considering the way in which civil conflicts are generally treated with the passage of time, my guess is that it will before long be orthodox schoolbook history in France.

Chapter 2

THE REPUBLIC OF SILENCE

We were never more free than during the German occupation. We had lost all our rights, beginning with the right to talk; every day we were insulted to our faces and had to take it in silence; . . . and, because of all this, we were free. . . . Because an all-powerful police tried to force us to hold our tongues, every word took on the value of a declaration of principles; because we were hunted down, every one of our gestures had the weight of a solemn commitment.

JEAN-PAUL SARTRE[1]

FROM the very beginning, General de Gaulle and his colleagues in London laid the juridical foundation of the future purge by arguing that Vichy was both illegitimate and illegal. Concern with future punishment was limited at first, but grew as the course of the war brought an Allied victory closer. With the development of the Resistance inside France, blacklists were drawn up; sentences of death were not only pronounced, but executed. By the time of the Liberation there was broad agreement among *résistants* concerning both the sort of purge which was desired, and its place in their total plans for liberated France.

On June 19, 1940, the day after his first appeal for continued French resistance, General de Gaulle spoke again over the London radio:

At the present hour, all France understands that the ordinary forms of power have disappeared. In the face of the confusion in French hearts, in the face of the liquefaction of a government which accepts servitude to the enemy, in the face of the inability of our institutions to function, I, General de Gaulle . . . am conscious of speaking in the name of France.[2]

The first part of the statement was more than just a rhetorical prelude to the forty-nine-year-old Brigadier General's pretension to speak "in the name of France": it represented, in fact, De Gaulle's peculiar constitutional theory, which was to be the juridical foundation of the future Provisional Government, and, *pari passu*, of the purge.

From the first, De Gaulle was convinced of the "illegitimacy" of

1. "La République du Silence" [1944], reprinted in *Situations, III* (Paris: 1949), pp. 11-14.
2. Charles de Gaulle, *Discours de guerre* (Fribourg: 1944-45), I, 17.

Pétain's Regime, even before the signing of the Armistice and the assault on the Republic. Its very *raison d'être* – the solicitation of an armistice – was illegitimate, and this original sin was of infinitely greater significance than the formal legality of its investiture. Further- more, "the Government at Bordeaux [was] in immediate and direct dependence on the Germans and Italians . . ."; there was "no longer on the soil of France herself any independent Government capable of upholding the interests of France and the French overseas".[3] Finally, Pétain's Government was illegitimate because in accepting the Armis- tice it was accepting "not just capitulation, but reduction to slavery"; honor, good sense, and the higher interests of *la Patrie* demanded its rejection.[4] For De Gaulle, Pétain's Government was illegitimate be- cause it was betraying the national interest; De Gaulle himself, by cleaving to that national interest, automatically acquired legitimacy. Thus for De Gaulle, and later for the Provisional Government which he dominated, June 16, 1940, was the cut-off date: Pétain's Third Republic was as illegitimate as his tailor-made regime which followed; the Armistice which it negotiated was null; its servants, as well as those of Vichy, would later be called to account.

For over four months following the momentous vote of July 10, General de Gaulle virtually ignored the change of regime: his speeches contained oblique references to the "soi-disant gouvernement de Vichy" but concentrated on "the crime of the Armistice". There were, however, compelling reasons for the Gaullists to direct their attention to the events of July. Pétain's avowed break with the traditional regime underlined the Gaullist argument that Pétain did not represent the historic traditions of the nation. It enabled De Gaulle to assume the role of bearer of the republican as well as the national tradition. By arguing that the changeover (and thus the regime) was illegal, the Gaullists strengthened their own position. If Vichy was legal, De Gaulle was a seditionist; but if Vichy could be shown to be unconstitu- tional and illegal, not only were Frenchmen absolved of the duty of obeying its commands, but they could subsequently be prosecuted for obeying orders which violated Republican legislation. In a statement issued at Brazzaville on November 16, 1940 (the legal portion of which was the work of Professor René Cassin), General de Gaulle outlined what was to become the official position of the movement concerning

3. Speech of June 23, 1940, in Royal Institute of International Affairs (Margaret Carlyle, ed.), *Documents on International Affairs, 1939-1946*, Vol. II: *Hitler's Europe* (London: 1954), p. 166.
4. Speech of June 22, 1940, *Discours*, I, 18.

Vichy's legality; the case against Vichy was elaborated in an article by Professor Cassin in the following month.[5]

Cassin's charge can be reduced to three principal points. The first has to do with the circumstances of the meeting of the National Assembly, which, he alleged, were flagrantly irregular: it did not meet, as required by law, at Versailles; organized hooligan pressure intimidated the members of the Assembly; the circumstances of the occupation made a free consultation impossible. His second point was that the National Assembly alone held the right to revise the Constitution; it had absolutely no right to delegate (or abdicate) its constituent power to another party; acts by such a party are thus null. Cassin's final point was that Pétain's "Constitutional Acts", by abolishing the Republic, were in flagrant violation of the constitutional law of 1884 which denies even the National Assembly that right: the "Etat français" was thus illegal and unconstitutional.

Cassin's conclusions were officially adopted by the Gaullist movement; the metropolitan Resistance, though less concerned than London with Vichy's juridical status, later came to accept his thesis completely. All *résistants*, whether in London, the Empire, or in metropolitan France, were, eventually, united by their belief in Vichy's illegality and illegitimacy. They were to be equally united in their conviction that the men of Vichy should be called to account.

The foundation for the future punishment of the men of Vichy was laid, and the London Gaullists made it clear that one day it would come. But in the first months of their exile they had more urgent concerns. On July 13, General de Gaulle summed up what was to be the attitude of the Free French for many months: "To be sure, one day liberated France will punish those responsible for its disasters, the architects of its servitude. But for the moment, that is not what concerns us. Right now, what concerns us is doing everything possible, actively and passively, to see that the enemy is beaten."[6] He reiterated this theme a few weeks later, following Vichy's announcement of the Riom Trial, which would punish those "responsible" for the war and the defeat:

> The question of "responsibilities" is easily answered. Justice will be done when the masters of Germany and Italy, who unleashed this war,

5. Charles de Gaulle, *Mémoires de guerre* (Paris: 1954-59), I, 313-17; René Cassin, "Un Coup d'Etat: La Soi-Disant Constitution de Vichy", *La France Libre* (London), I, 2 (December 16, 1940), 162-76. Cassin's views on Vichy's legitimacy and legality, together with the opinions of other legal scholars, are discussed at greater length in Appendix A.

6. *Discours*, I, 39.

have been beaten. Justice will be done when the French leaders who have shown themselves unworthy of the name have been sentenced.... The punishment of the former and the punishment of the latter will take place simultaneously. Oh, not tomorrow, for justice moves slowly, but one day, without fail. For the world and for France, justice is as indispensable as sunlight. Justice will come; it will come with the victory.[7]

Thereafter, for a period of over two years, the theme of future punishment virtually disappeared from Gaullist propaganda.

In the early stages of the war, De Gaulle was more interested in wooing than in threatening followers of Pétain. When Charles Vallin, vice-president of Colonel de la Rocque's Parti Social Français (the successor to the Croix de Feu) and an erstwhile ardent supporter of Pétain's "National Revolution", defected to De Gaulle in the summer of 1942, he received a warm welcome. In a telegram to Adrien Tixier in Washington, De Gaulle informed his representative of his views on the *ralliement* of Vallin and similar personalities. Vallin's prewar opinions, or anyone else's, were of no importance. Vallin, like many others, was fooled by Pétain, but he had publicly confessed his error, which was sufficient. Men who collaborated with the enemy in official positions, *specifically including all members of Pétain's governments*, should be tried for "intelligence with the enemy". Those who had served Vichy as civil servants or soldiers without behaving scandalously with respect to the defense of the nation, or "what amounts to the same thing – toward us", were welcome. In practice, he noted, it would probably be best to use "public men" in a strictly military capacity.[8]

The metropolitan Resistance, too, was recruiting among former Pétainists; indeed, in 1940-41 many resistance groups in the occupied zone were still not unfriendly toward Vichy. The underground press in these first years contained little or no mention of a future purge. The Socialists, who later were to vie with the Communists in the severity of their attitude, made no mention of future retribution in their official underground press until 1943. Papers like *Défense de la France*, which later became ardent advocates of the purge, were at first Pétainist and distinctly cool toward De Gaulle.

Before the German setbacks in Russia and North Africa in late 1942 it was an act of faith to resist at all; to speak of punishing Vichyites and collaborationists after an Allied victory seemed pure bravado.

Nevertheless, the first calls for vengeance against collaborators, and the first demands for a future retributive justice, were sounded in the

7. *Ibid.*, p. 45.
8. De Gaulle, *Mémoires*, II, 374-75.

autumn of 1941. *Défense de la France* foresaw the day when "many would pay who had hoped to save their worthless lives".[9] *Libération (Nord)* considered preparing the punishment of traitors to be one of the three duties incumbent upon patriots, along with the formation of local groups and the distribution of the paper.[10]

Immediately following the German invasion of the Soviet Union, the Communists began to speak of future retribution. Their first fire was directed against the judges of the special Vichy court established to try Communists. The judges were reminded that "the Germans will not be in Paris forever", and readers were asked to keep records of the judges' names.[11] Happy to be relieved of the anti-national role assigned to them by the Hitler-Stalin Pact, they appealed to French revolutionary tradition:

> *Vive la Nation! Mort aux traîtres!*
> *Tel était le cri des volontaires de Valmy dont les Français viennent de célébrer brillament le cent cinquantième anniversaire. Et ils agissaient comme ils parlaient.*
> *Vive la Nation! Mort aux boches et aux traîtres!*
> *Tel est le mot d'ordre des patriotes en 1942. C'est lui qui doit guider tous nos actes.*[12]

It was a short step from general threats of vengeance to specific measures of preparation. In the fall of 1941 the Communists asked the population to begin drawing up "blacklists" of individuals to be

9. No. 3 (November 20, 1941).

10. No. 56 (December 28, 1941).

11. *Humanité (Nord)*, No. 126 (August 26, 1941).

12. *La Vie Ouvrière (Nord)*, Special Number of September 1942. While the Communists joined other *résistants* in looking forward to a day of reckoning, they were neither the most intransigent nor the most vocal group on this subject. On some issues (confiscatory nationalizations, their disregard for legal norms) the Communists were among the most implacable *épurateurs*; on others (the army purge in North Africa, parliamentary ineligibility for those who had voted for Pétain in 1940) they took a much softer line than the majority of their colleagues. Indeed, it is noteworthy that talk of vengeance and the ultimate punishment of collaborators and Vichyites has a very subordinate position among the themes in Communist newspapers and leaflets during the Occupation. Much more dominant were calls for more food, freedom for political prisoners (especially Communists) and the return of prisoners of war; exhortations to strike, carry out acts of sabotage, join the Front National or Francs-Tireurs et Partisans, and to avoid the forced-labor service; paeans to the Red Army, Stalin and Thorez. The official Communist press contained (so far as I have found) not one major article on the purge throughout the Occupation.

imprisoned or executed at the Liberation (or before). In October a Communist poster in Lyon urged citizens to draw up "dossiers of reprisals" against informers and collaborating policemen, judges, and journalists. Informers were threatened with the sentencing to death of five to ten members of their families.[13] An attractive lure was offered to peasants who established lists of collaborating or Vichyite landowners. They were promised that "the defeat of Hitler Germany will mark, for these bad Frenchmen, the hour of their arrest and the confiscation of their property, which will be divided among the peasants and agricultural workers".[14]

Similar in inspiration, although differing in execution, was the physical labelling of the homes of alleged collaborators. In September 1941, in the Bouches-du-Rhône, typewritten or mimeographed stickers announced "ICI HABITE UN PETAINISTE DONC UN AGENT DE HITLER / par conséquent / UN TRAITRE A LA FRANCE".[15] In the following month, at Dieppe, the Front National announced the institution of a secret tribunal which was to examine dossiers, and mark the doors of certain merchants with a "K" for "Kollaborateur".[16]

The idea of blacklists was quickly taken up by non-Communist underground newspapers. In March 1942 the Socialist *Franc-Tireur* (not to be confused with the Communist-dominated paramilitary organization Francs-Tireurs et Partisans Français, with which it had no connection) urged its readers to draw up blacklists for future use, giving detailed information on collaborators, informers, German propagandists, and especially merchants and manufacturers working with the Germans. *Populaire (Sud)* made a similar appeal in September.[17]

In 1943-44 the preparation and publication of blacklists became widespread. These lists had several aims. Of the greatest immediate and practical importance was warning the citizenry against informers

13. Reproduced in Angelo Tasca ["Rossi"], *La Guerre des papillons* (Paris: 1954), XXVIII, 3. This is the only example I have encountered of this sort of threat to families on the part of the Resistance.

14. Appeal to the peasants of France, dated September-October 1941 under the symbolic signature of Maurice Thorez, cited in Angelo Tasca ["Rossi"], *La Physiologie du Parti communiste français* (Paris: 1948), p. 193 n. 3. As with the previous Communist appeal cited, this example is the only one of its kind which I have come across, and like that one, may reflect the uncoordinated state of Communist propaganda in this early period.

15. Reproduced in Tasca, *Papillons*, XXVII, 2.

16. *Front National*, No. 6 (November 11, 1941).

17. No. 5 (September 15, 1942).

and provocateurs. This was principally the case with regional under-ground papers, such as *Combat du Languedoc*, which devoted its entire issue of July 1943 to a list of collaborators in the departments of Haute-Garonne, Ariège, and Gers. Sometimes such local lists could also serve as a boycott-guidebook, as in the case of *Le Patriote*, published in Le Havre, which advised its readers to consider as collaborationists all those shopkeepers who solicited business from the occupying forces by putting German-language signs in their windows.[18]

Another aim of the lists, sometimes avowed, sometimes not, was *pour encourager les autres*: a warning to officials and others that they were under observation, and that they would do well to mend their ways, lest they find their own names on the next list. Those who *were* listed, however, were often advised that it was too late, and that turning their coats at the last minute would gain them nothing. Most often, the lists were drawn up and published for morale purposes: to assure members of the Resistance that their day would come; to spread panic among the ranks of the collaborationists. The listing of prominent personalities tended to serve the former aim, that of *miliciens* and *petits fonctionnaires* the latter.

Many of the leading underground newspapers, *Libération* (both editions), *Populaire*, and *Résistance*, regularly printed the lists, some-times with capsule biographies, sometimes with the notation that "the dossiers have been sent to the competent authorities". They were not, however, generally found in the Communist press.[19]

Professional groups publishing their own journals often concen-trated their fire on their colleagues. Thus *Le Palais Libre*, organ of the Front National des Juristes, several times printed lists of collaborating judges and attorneys, *L'Université Libre* listed collaborationist profes-sors, *Police et Patrie* published lists of police officials who handed over members of the Resistance to the Gestapo.

Usually only the name, address, position, and perhaps a descriptive line or two were given, but on occasion a complete account of the activity denounced appeared. A typical example of this was the de-nunciation of a lycée directress by *Défense de la France* early in 1943.[20] She was accused of having expelled, and reported to Abel Bonnard,

18. No. 15 (February 1944).
19. In fact, I found no example of a blacklist as such in a Communist underground newspaper, although their own leading renegades were some-times mentioned. The files are incomplete, and I therefore hesitate to assert that there was no instance. Certainly it was not the rule.
20. No. 31 (April 20, 1943). See also No. 35 (July 5, 1943).

Vichy Minister of Education, a student found in possession of a Resistance leaflet. The student was arrested. The directress was told that her activities were now known to the newspaper's 100,000 readers.

Some papers let their enthusiasm get the better of them, publishing extravagant lists which lumped together the guilty, the half-guilty, and the innocent. The most notable example of this was the newspaper *Bir-Hakeim*, which began publishing long lists of prominent personalities in mid-1943.[21] On November 28, 1943, the Germanophile Vichy Minister of Information, Philippe Henriot, denounced the paper in a radio talk, and mentioned that among those on its blacklist was Maurice Sarraut, editor of the *Dépêche* of Toulouse.[22] Three days later Sarraut was assassinated (although not, as Vichy claimed, by the Resistance, but by Darnand's *milice*, which had its own scores to settle with Sarraut). The coincidence did not go unremarked by the Vichy press and radio, which charged that the paper was provoking indiscriminate terrorism. The B.B.C. at first claimed that Henriot had invented the list; then, when they received a copy of the paper, doubted its authenticity. *Bir-Hakeim* corrected the British broadcasters, pointing out that Sarraut had been on its list, and that while he had been killed by the *milice*, he had deserved his place on the list it had published.[23] In December 1943 the underground newspaper *Combat* warned its readers against believing that *Bir-Hakeim's* lists had been drawn up by the Resistance, but left it an open question whether provocation or ignorance was responsible. The Conseil National de la Résistance warned Frenchmen against

> the tendency of certain among them to believe that they have done their patriotic duty by disseminating inaccurate lists of "collaborationists," without discriminating between victims of the Pétain myth and the traitors in the enemy's pay. Such mistakes have not only been detrimental to the public interest but have compromised irreproachable men who could only have been denounced by *provocateurs*.[24]

The B.B.C. went further, and in the spring of 1944 denounced the paper as being of German or Vichy origin, a charge echoed by the

21. *Bir-Hakeim*, technically one of the best produced and one of the most widely distributed of underground newspapers, was named in honor of the battle in which Free French forces defended this hitherto unsung spot in Libya.

22. *News Digest*, No. 1304 (November 30, 1943).

23. No. 8 (December 31, 1943).

24. U.S., O.S.S., *Resolutions of the French National Council of Resistance* (Washington: 1944), pp. 23-25.

Resistance press.[25] (Suspicion of *Bir-Hakeim* was heightened by its attacks on some members of the C.F.L.N.) After the Liberation *Bir-Hakeim* was cleared of the charge.

The implicit warning to collaborators contained in the blacklists was made explicit in notices – mainly directed toward civil servants – which were distributed by underground newspapers, the C.N.R., and the Free French in London and Algiers. In November 1942, *Défense de la France* warned policemen that "their lives depended on their attitude", and two months later, in the same vein, they added: "Friends of Germany, be fearful and repent, if there is still time – the hour approaches ...".[26] *Libération (Nord)* warned of the punishment which would be visited upon those officials who cooperated with the new census, aimed at facilitating German recruitment of forced labor.[27] Similar warnings are to be found throughout the Communist and non-Communist underground press in 1943 and 1944.

The Conseil National de la Résistance seconded these unofficial warnings. Minor officials were cautioned that no excuse of "superior orders" would save them; after Darnand was named Secretary General for the Maintenance of Order, policemen were advised of their patriotic duty to disobey his orders or take the consequences; and members of the Vichy Courts-Martial which sentenced *résistants* to death were warned that participation in these bodies would bring the same penalty for themselves.[28] A C.N.R. leaflet addressed to provident family men warned them that "if any public employees are killed in the course of their service for the enemy, France will feel no moral or financial obligation toward their families – this is reserved for those who defend the country, not those who betray it".[29]

The C.F.L.N., in broadcasts from Algiers and London, took the same line. In June 1943 police officials were warned that there would be a settling of accounts for reprisals taken against the families of *résistants*. In an official declaration three months later, the Algiers Committee, after paying homage to those members of the administration who aided the Resistance, warned those officials who aided the Germans in any way; the Committee informed them of the great house-

25. *Lettres Françaises*, No. 14 (March 1944); *Libération (Nord)*, No. 174 (April 7, 1944).

26. No. 22 (November 11, 1942); No. 25 (January 1, 1943).

27. Leaflet attached to No. 117 (February 23, 1943).

28. *Populaire (Sud)*, No. 21 (February 1944); *Libération (Nord)*, No. 169 (February 29, 1944); *Populaire (Nord)*, June 15, 1944.

29. Undated mimeographed leaflet in the files of the B.D.I.C.: *Déclaration à propos de la campagne hitlérienne contre le "terrorisme"*.

cleaning that would follow the Liberation. After Mandel's assassination, Emmanuel d'Astier de la Vigerie, De Gaulle's Commissioner of the Interior, in a broadcast over the B.B.C., advised officials of the Vichy Government that those implicated in such affairs would be judged as murderers.[30]

Blacklists and warnings were, by their nature, basically preparatory measures, although they had (or were intended to have) immediate effect. There was, however, one form of pre-Liberation purge activity inside France which was definitive in the fullest meaning of the word. This was the summary execution of collaborators, informers, and others whom it was felt urgent to render *hors d'état de nuire*.

Individual acts of terrorism, at first directed against members of the occupying forces, were discouraged by London. For a time they were abandoned – at least by the non-Communist Resistance – because of the savage reprisals they brought. But as the struggle intensified in 1943 and 1944, attempts on the lives of collaborators as well as Germans, became common.

It was Vichy's custom to ascribe all acts of "terrorism" to the Communists, and the Communists gladly cooperated with Vichy in claiming credit for assassinations. It is hard to evaluate these assertions, whether they are put forward as indictments or as proud claims. There are, however, reasons for believing that Communists, and groups under their control, were particularly zealous in carrying out summary executions.

Many of those who broke with the Communist Party in 1939-40 followed Jacques Doriot (who had left the P.C.F. some years earlier) into his collaborationist Parti Populaire Français. Albert Clement, ex-editor of *La Vie Ouvrière*, and many others who followed this route were killed "by person or persons unknown" during the Occupation. Among the ex-Communists killed were some with no record of collaboration – perhaps victims of the "pitiless" struggle which Party members were ordered to carry out against renegades.[31] From at least 1942 French Communists were instructed "not to let any crime of the S.O.L. [Service d'Ordre Légionnaire], Légion Tricolore, or similar groups go unpunished, but to conduct vigorous actions against them to break the morale of their formations and spread panic in their ranks".[32] Volunteers in the Communist-led Francs-Tireurs et Parti-

30. *Libération (Sud)*, No. 32 (August 1, 1943); *Résistance*, No. 18 (October 13, 1943); *Populaire (Nord)*, No. 35 (August 15, 1944).
31. *La Vie du Parti*, August 1940, 16.
32. *Ibid.*, September 1942, 13.

sans Français signed an engagement not only to punish with death all informers but to consider likewise as a traitor, and deserving punishment as such, any individual who opposed this procedure.[33]

But the assassination of collaborators was advocated – and carried out – not only by the Communists but also by groups of quite different political coloration. *Combat* wrote that it was necessary for patriots to take justice into their own hands since

> if the traitors continued to get away with their crimes, they would be joined by other cowards and opportunists. Justice and public welfare demand that they be pitilessly punished. Those who strike them down are instituting a reign of terror only in the camp of the traitors. When France is liberated, and once more there is justice and the rule of law, they will retire.[34]

Résistants in the Haute-Loire were advised that

> there can be only one response to terror: a terror that is even more powerful and more implacable. Every assassination of a French patriot which is not immediately followed by the execution of its author, or one of his kind, is a dishonor for the Resistance. The best way to inspire in the enemy that fear with which he attempts to paralyze us, and at the same time preserve the support and confidence of the masses, is to carefully organize spectacular executions of well-known individuals who are universally known to be responsible for "legal" terrorism. The execution of mere accomplices often has an undesirable effect.[35]

The editor of *Défense de la France*, one of the most conservative in inspiration of all the leading underground papers, spoke, despite his avowed belief in the sacredness of human life, of the duty to kill.

> Kill the German in order to purify our land, kill him because he kills ours, kill him in order to be free.
>
> Kill the traitors, kill those who denounce, those who have aided the enemy. Kill the policeman who in any way at all has contributed to the arrest of patriots.
>
> Kill the *miliciens*, exterminate them, because they have deliberately chosen the road of treason. Strike them down like mad dogs. . . . Destroy them as you would vermin.

33. C.F.L.N., *Les Cahiers Français: Les Documents*, No. 39 (April 1, 1943), 55; Charles Tillon, *Les F.T.P.: Témoignage pour servir à l'histoire de la résistance* (Paris: 1962), p. 204.

34. No. 49 (October 15, 1943).

35. *Circulaire des groupes francs des M.U.R.* (n.p.: n.d. [1944], cited in Henri Michel, *Les Courants de pensée de la Résistance* (Paris: 1962), p. 338.

Kill without passion and without hate. Never descend to torture, to causing suffering. We are not butchers, we are soldiers.

Kill without pity or remorse because it is our Duty, an unhappy duty; *the duty of justice.*[36]

Often assassinations were preceded by secret "trials" and notification of the judgment to the accused. The announcement that one was slated for death sometimes took the form of simple notices sent to the person involved; on other occasions miniature coffins were sent.[37] Sometimes, however, the notification was formal in the extreme, and the reasons for the judgment given in detail. The best known example of this is the sentence pronounced against André Parmentier, the regional police prefect for Rouen, a copy of which was sent to all the prefects of France.

In the name of the French people, the Court Martial of the Resistance, acting in accordance with the rulings taken on behalf of the Committee of Action against Deportation . . .

Whereas Parmentier has taken a preponderant part in carrying out deportation measures in Rouen . . . has taken criminal measures designed to facilitate the capture of Frenchmen sought by the enemy . . . [various proofs are introduced, and the relevant sections of the Penal Code are cited] . . .

The Court Martial of the Resistance declares Parmentier guilty of attacks on individual liberty and of treason and condemns him to death.

Calls upon every patriotic Frenchman and orders him to seek out Parmentier, wherever he may be, and to carry out the present sentence.

Rendered in Paris, in a secret hearing, August 2, 1943.[38]

The executions accelerated as the hour of liberation approached. In Normandy, for example, there were nine executions noted in 1943, twenty-five in the first five months of 1944 (before the Allied landings),

36. No. 44 (March 15, 1944).

37. The sending of symbolic objects necessitated a change in articles 305 and 308 of the Penal Code, which punished threats of death only if they were made in speech or writing. These articles were modified to include threats made via "images, symbols or emblems" by the Law of December 21, 1943.

38. *Combat* (*Alger*), March 12, 1944; *Free France*, V, 11 (June 1, 1944), 403; Robert Aron, *Histoire de Vichy: 1940-1944* (Paris: 1954), pp. 595-596. The sentence was not executed. Parmentier was not legally tried until five years later; the High Court sentenced him to five years of national degradation, immediately suspended for acts of resistance.

and nineteen in the weeks between the landings and the liberation of the area.[39]

Most of the pre-Liberation executions were directed against *miliciens* and informers – individuals who were responsible for the arrest, torture and death of *résistants*: they were killed as a prophylactic measure, no less drastic measures being available to a state-within-a-state which had no prisons or internment camps at its disposal.[40] Informers were the most hated, and in the anti-purge and neo-Vichyite campaigns after the Liberation they had few, if any, defenders. Even during the occupation they were despised by the Vichyites and Germans who employed them.

On one dramatic occasion, however, the Resistance struck at the top, rather than at the bottom of the pyramid of collaboration. Philippe Henriot, Minister of Information in the Vichy Government and one of the leaders of the ultra-collaborationist circles in Paris, was condemned to death by the Conseil National de la Résistance and executed in a daring daylight raid on June 28, 1944. A detachment of *résistants* posing as *miliciens* presented themselves at Henriot's door, shot him down, and sped off.[41]

Henriot's assassination was widely hailed in the press of the Resistance. Typical was the comment of Christian Funck-Brentano in the Algiers edition of *Combat*:

> The art of war consists in striking at the best moment. Philippe Henriot's execution aids the offensive in Cotentin as much as the derailment of an ammunition train. For all of France, for all the world, it is a sign. . . . In the camp of treason they look uneasily at each other and panic spreads.[42]

Not all of the Resistance press approved of Henriot's assassination, however. *Le Français*, which had previously protested against the assault on the ex-Communist deputy Marcel Capron on the grounds that it would be better to wait until after the Liberation, attacked the shooting of the mayor of Pierrefitte on the grounds that it was "futile and useless", and condemned an attempt against Laval's life on the grounds that his successor might be worse, now protested Henriot's

---

39. Marcel Baudot, *L'Opinion publique sous l'Occupation: L'Exemple d'un département français (1939-1945)* (Paris: 1960), pp. 79-80.

40. There is one exception to this rule. In the redoubt of the Vercors *maquis* an internment camp was established in which *miliciens* and collaborators were held.

41. René Hostache, *Le Conseil National de la Résistance: Les Institutions de la clandestinité* (Paris: 1958), pp. 179-80; *Action*, September 22, 1944.

42. July 2, 1944.

assassination, not only on the grounds that he had a right to a trial, but on the singular basis that unlike Déat and Doriot, he was "sincere".[43]

For the most part, though, Resistance criticism of pre-Liberation executions was confined to those cases where it descended into indiscriminate terrorism, or where the Resistance was serving as a cover for banditry. *Résistance Paysanne* was voicing a widely shared anxiety when, while recognizing the need to execute traitors and informers, it inveighed against "punitive actions" carried out by individuals acting outside the departmental coordinating committees of the Resistance.

> If . . . discipline isn't observed, the most serious errors become possible, and the door is opened to individual vengeance and even the worst kind of simple banditry. Everyone should know that these bandits will sooner or later be identified and that they will pay with their lives for their thefts and ignoble crimes, just the same as the informers.[44]

How many cases were there of acts of individual vengeance masquerading as Resistance justice? For the occupation period, as for the Liberation and after, it is impossible to hazard a guess. Even the total number, "legitimate" and "illegitimate", both before and after the Liberation, is not known with certainty.[45] It is even unclear how many of those killed by the Resistance can be said to have been "executed", since, particularly in 1944, large *maquis* were frequently engaged in military action against *milice* formations.

The existence, in 1943-44, of units of the *maquis* numbering several hundred men also raised difficulties with respect to defining "banditry". The men had to be clothed and fed; raids on banks, warehouses and shops filled the role of paymaster and quartermaster corps in more regularly constituted formations. Sometimes these raids were carried out with the acquiescence, or even cooperation, of the personnel of the raided premises. The legal problems raised by these irregular requisitions were in part met by legislation of the Provisional Government on

43. No. 103 (April 21, 1943); No. 108 (May 19, 1943); No. 128 (October 8, 1943); No. 164 (July 5, 1944).

44. No. 2 (February 1944).

45. This question is examined at some length in Appendix C. While there were (proportionately) more pre-Liberation summary executions of collaborators in France than in the other occupied countries of Western Europe (with the possible exception of Italy), they occurred everywhere. According to Harold Flender, there were at least 170 in Denmark (*Rescue in Denmark* [New York: 1963], p. 229); Werner Warmbrunn reports 300 executions in the Netherlands in 1944 alone. (*The Dutch Under German Occupation: 1940-1945* [Stanford (Cal.): 1963], pp. 206-08.)

"the legitimacy of acts committed for the Liberation of France", but there were many borderline cases.[46]

The C.N.R. attempted to meet the problem by adopting the criterion of "necessity". In the case of executions, the criterion was not whether the collaborator's acts merited death, but whether they were sufficiently harmful to the Resistance to require it; the forced requisitioning of supplies became banditry when it was carried further than the needs of the unit involved demanded. Such activity (together, of course, with assassinations or looting for personal motives or gain) the C.N.R. not only disavowed and reproved, but punished. And, as in the case of those of their enemies whom it was necessary to put *hors d'état de nuire*, there was only one penalty available to them.[47]

At the same time that *résistants* were publishing blacklists of traitors, and settling their accounts in blood behind the backs of the German occupying forces, many of them were formulating their programs for the France of the future. No one who reads any appreciable portion of the underground press can fail to be amazed at the amount of space devoted to the sober consideration of postwar problems. The language of the underground journals was often violent, and never more than when they were discussing the purge. Extravagant rhetoric was both spontaneous (written under the impact of seeing friends and relatives tortured or killed); and calculated (intended to inspire awe in one camp, resolution in the other). But there was another side. Not only did general circulation newspapers devote considerable space to reflective articles and analytical studies, but a number of underground journals were entirely devoted to this task. These journals, like the rest of the underground press, were printed and distributed only with the greatest difficulty and at enormous risk.

It is difficult to generalize about *the* thought of the Resistance. As has been noted, the Resistance did not constitute a political or ideological community in the usual sense. While some groups concentrated

46. Ordinance of July 6, 1943 (J. O. [Alger], July 10, 1943, p. 23). The ordinance legitimized all acts, even if in violation of the Penal Code, committed since June 10, 1940, if they were committed for the Liberation. (A commission was set up to decide whether or not they were.)

47. For the relevant regulations of the C.N.R., dated February 3, 1944, see *Cahiers du Témoignage Chrétien*, XXVI-XXVII (May 1944); for the announcement of the execution of a *résistant* by the Resistance for "theft, looting and blackmail", see the poster of the F.T.P.F.-F.F.I. of Haute-Vienne, dated June 20, 1944, in the B.D.I.C., Dossier "France/Occupée/Résistance/Maquis".

on publishing pamphlets or newspapers, others – especially intelligence networks, sabotage groups, the *maquis* – did not generally make their thoughts public. And an organization's press did not necessarily reflect its members' views.

There was, nevertheless, a "Resistance point of view"; that which united the men of the Resistance was much stronger than that which divided them. The symbol of Resistance unity was the "Charter" of the Conseil National de la Résistance. The Charter proclaimed the determination of the Resistance to remain united after the Liberation in order to accomplish a broad program of political, social, and economic reform. Traitors were to be punished and their property confiscated; key industries were to be nationalized, the economy centrally planned, and workers assured a role in the direction of economic life; social welfare programs were to be greatly expanded, cooperatives promoted, and a "new deal" for farmers instituted; the colonial population was to be set on the road to self-determination; the press and the educational system were to be reorganized and reformed.[48]

The Resistance had no nostalgia for the Third Republic. The France for which it was fighting was not the *république des camarades*, but a new France, "pure et dure", with new institutions and a new spirit. And these could only be built by new men.

> France cannot hope to be restored or recover her traditional place in the world unless she achieves a social and moral revolution. . . . The revolution can be achieved only by entirely new men. The new France cannot entrust her destiny to those who were unable to save her in the past.[49]

It was frequently asserted that the "new men" would be found in the ranks of the Resistance.

> On the morrow of the Liberation, France will pose this question to each of her sons: what did *you* do during the years of shame and misery? And it is on the basis of their answer, without taking account of social class, party, or creed, that she will choose those who will have the honor of representing her.[50]

But before the new men could address themselves to the task of remaking France, the old occupants of the seats of power would have to

48. The C.N.R. Charter was unanimously adopted at a secret plenary session of that body on March 15, 1944. At the Liberation, the Charter became the symbol of the aspirations of the Resistance; later, for many, it became the symbol of the betrayal of those hopes. For this reason I have included a translation of the document as Appendix B.

49. *Résistance*, No. 6 (January 25, 1943).

50. *Combat*, January 1943.

be evicted. And this meant much more than merely removing (and punishing) the parvenus of Vichy; a "renouvellement" which limited itself to this would mean implicit acceptance of the status quo ante bellum.

The Resistance recognized at least three groups of men to be removed. *Défense de la France* listed:

> those who, uncaringly, allowed France to grow weak before the war; those who, in June 1940, doubted France, neglected her interests and soiled her honor; those who, since the Armistice, far from repenting, have each day sunk lower into treason by favoring the program of the enemy.[51]

The Organisation Civile et Militaire was the most conservative of the leading resistance organizations: its leaders were for the most part high civil servants, university professors, professional men, army officers, and business leaders. In the June 1942 issue of its *Cahiers*, this group defined the categories somewhat differently and detailed the treatment which should be accorded each. The O.C.M. found it virtually impossible to determine individual responsibilities among the prewar leaders of France, so a sweeping measure was proposed. All senators, deputies and high officials, as well as holders of semi-public positions (e.g., trade-union leaders) were to be declared henceforth ineligible to participate in public life. To the anticipated charge that such a wholesale approach would be inequitable, the organization replied that "in the case of the less-guilty (for there are no innocents), this [automatic] punishment is justified by the general interest; in the case of the really culpable, it is a light enough punishment". Exemptions from this sweeping decree of ineligibility would be granted only for those who had been active in the Resistance.

While recognizing that it was almost as difficult to assign individual responsibilities for the lack of military preparation and the errors committed during the campaign of 1940, the O.C.M. proposed that after the Liberation the dossiers prepared by the Court at Riom be reopened, and the trial concluded under civilian judges.[52] Punishing the third category of offenders – Vichyites and collaborators – was, for the O.C.M., as for other *résistants*, the most important task of all. These

51. No. 33 (May 20, 1943).
52. The study did, however, note the necessity of annulling the prejudgment of the trial pronounced by Marshal Pétain in October 1941. In the O.C.M.'s modified proposal seven months later, the idea of reopening the Riom Trial was repudiated. (*Résistance*, No. 6 [January 25, 1943].)

men were not to be merely removed, but, at least in the case of *vedettes de la trahison*, shot out of hand.[53]

For all their concern with removing unworthy carryovers from previous eras, it was, of course, the Vichyites and collaborationists who figured most prominently in the minds of *résistants* when they thought of cleaning house. As the O.C.M. study itself noted, this part of the task was politically the most urgent.

> Pre-war responsibilities are confused and attenuated by time. Even the errors committed during the war will [by the Liberation] have receded into the past. The acts of the occupation [period] will be the most recent. These are the ones which will have caused the most acute suffering and the cruelest humiliation to the people. Without doubt, the attitude of the population toward the new authorities will depend in large measure on the manner in which the crimes and misdemeanors committed during the foreign occupation are punished.[54]

But punishment was only to be a part of the great task of renewal. The purge was to be but one side of the coin, on the other side of which was the introduction of "new cadres". The confiscation of the collaborationist press was to be merely the prelude to the replacement of a corrupt journalistic establishment by an honest and dynamic one, just as the programs of confiscatory nationalizations and the purge of the judiciary were complemented by outlines of thoroughgoing "structural economic reforms" and elaborate plans for a new judicial machinery. For the Resistance, as for Bakunin, "destruction was a kind of creation". To be understood, the purge must be placed in the larger perspective of the *renouvellement des cadres* and the *renouvellement de la France*. This was why, in the C.N.R. Charter, the first task, after the installation of the Provisional Government, was defined as

> the punishment of traitors and the eviction from the administration and professional life of all those who have dealt with the enemy or have actively associated themselves with the policy of the governments of collaboration.[55]

53. In an interesting footnote, the study proposed a screening of the return to France of certain "émigrés" who had left France under less than honorable circumstances (a transparent reference to Maurice Thorez, who deserted his unit in 1940 and fled to Moscow). It went on to note that the release of unjustly imprisoned persons should not imply their rehabilitation, their right to be considered heroes, or the whitewashing of past errors, "particularly if they themselves avowedly favor the imprisonment of those who don't think as they do".

54. *Cahiers* [of the O.C.M.], June 1942.

55. See below, p. 198.

Résistants were agreed not only with respect to the priority to be given the purge, and the role it was to play in their overall plans for liberated France, but, in the main, on how it should be carried out. If the purge was to be effective, there were two necessary conditions: it must strike swiftly, and it must strike high. However, severe or moderate the purge desired by a given writer or group, all agreed that it should be swift.

Swift for some, in order to be done with an unpleasant task.[56]

Swift for others, because "the best parents are those who never let serious misbehavior go unpunished, but then wipe the slate clean".[57]

For others, because in the absence of prompt government action an outraged population would take matters in its own hands, with the anticipated result of widespread injustice and privately motivated crime.[58]

For some, because they feared that a government which failed to act decisively would be replaced:

> Danton wanted a political "terror", limited in its aims, its victims, its means. Robespierre and Saint-Just wanted on the contrary, to "totalize" the terror, make it daily, general. . . . Danton wanted severe and rapid justice . . . but because the moderates, the cowardly . . . criticized and opposed him, his sort of solution was bypassed ... and the Terror came. Because the Convention hesitated before Danton's plan, it later had to accept Robespierre's.[59]

For others, because it was necessary to act before the voices of timidity reasserted themselves.[60]

Finally, for all those *résistants* who had been frustrated and disillusioned by the snail's pace of the purge in liberated North Africa, and who were impatient to start building the new Jerusalem in the metropole.

Swift it must be, but even more important, it must strike the top, not just the bottom of the pyramid of collaboration: the ministers and prefects who ordered the repressive action, not just the *miliciens* who carried it out. "Lampiste" is a word that recurs again and again in Resistance discussions of the purge; it can be roughly translated as

56. Jacques Charpentier, *Au Service de la liberté* (Paris: 1949), pp. 223-24.

57. *Le Patriote*, II, 15 (February 1944).

58. *Libérer et Fédérer*, No. 12 (October 1943).

59. Boris Mirkine-Guetzévitch, "L'Indignité Nationale", *La République Française*, I, 8 (September 1944), 5-8.

60. *Au Service de la renaissance française* (Paris: n.d. [early 1944]), p. 26.

"fall guy" – the subordinate who is hanged from a lamp post while his boss gets away. The purge, they were unanimously determined, must not be an affair of *lampistes*. It was to be "inflexible for the *responsables*, moderate for the *lampistes*".[61]

61. *Ibid*. Or, in Pierre-Bloch's words, "nous frappons d'autant plus fort que les coupables seront plus haut" (*Fraternité*, December 26, 1943).

Chapter 3

NORTH AFRICAN REHEARSAL

In November 1942 we had a government opposed to any purge, in
June 1943 a government in which partisans and opponents of the
purge restrained and neutralized each other. Only since November
1943 has our government as a whole represented Fighting France,
and accepted the policy that General de Gaulle proclaimed. . . .
"National union can be established and can endure only if the State
knows how to recognize its faithful servants and punish the
criminals."

O. POZZO DI BORGO[1]

THE Allied invasion of French North Africa in November 1942
was heavy with consequences for the wartime history of France.
Within three days of the invasion German troops, in violation
of the Armistice terms, poured across the demarcation line into the
hitherto unoccupied portion of France; they met with no resistance
from Vichy's "Armistice Army". The political leaders at Vichy and
the naval establishment rejected both sending the fleet to North Africa
and allowing it to be captured by the Germans: the fleet was scuttled in
the harbor of Toulon. Vichy was transformed from a quasi-indepen-
dent state into a client and an instrument of the occupying power.

For many Frenchmen (and for the U.S. Department of State)
Vichy's existence had been justified, and the Regime worth supporting,
because it stood between the Germans and the total occupation of
metropolitan France. The concessions which Vichy made to the
Germans were justified – or at least explained – by the necessity of
giving the Germans enough to keep them on their side of the demarcation line. Continued success in this effort offered the only substantive
rewards of the so-called "double game". When this justification disappeared, there was little left.

Many who had been intoxicated by the aura surrounding the victor
of Verdun were sobered by the Marshal's refusal to heed the urging
of a number of his advisers and flee to North Africa after the Allied
landings. Many whose support of Vichy had been based on the calculation that an Axis victory was inevitable reconsidered their allegiance
when the total occupation of France coincided with a general turning

1. *Combat (Alger)*, December 30, 1943.

of the tide of war in favor of the Allies. And of great importance for "legitimists" was the establishment of an alternative center of loyalty in North Africa which was more than a committee of exiles existing by sufferance in London.

At first this center was loyal to the principles of the "National Revolution". Under the impact of events – some fortuitous, others calculated – it underwent a complete metamorphosis. This metamorphosis was in large part the result of the Gaullists' determination to punish the men of Vichy. Their ability to translate this determination into action was, in turn, a function of political developments in North Africa. It is with this reciprocal relationship that the present chapter is concerned.

On the morning of November 8, 1942, American forces made amphibious landings at several points on the coast of French North Africa. It had been hoped that the landings would be unopposed, or that, at most, token resistance would be offered by the French. To this end, long and involved negotiations had been undertaken with various military and civilian leaders in North Africa. General Henri Giraud, who, to Vichy's embarrassment, had escaped from German imprisonment at Koenigstein, was the American candidate for leadership in liberated North Africa. In the event, it was found that the attitude of French officials in North Africa "did not even remotely resemble prior calculations".[2] Local military and civilian leaders were found to be stubbornly loyal to Vichy and deaf to the appeals of the "dissident" Giraud. Fortune intervened. Admiral François Darlan, who after his fall from political power in April had been made Commander-in-Chief of the French armed forces, was in Algiers at the bedside of his son, who was believed to be dying. An agreement was hastily improvised between the Allies and Darlan, under which the Admiral assumed the role previously allotted to Giraud; on November 10 Darlan ordered a cease-fire. Unlike Giraud, Darlan stood above the local military chiefs in the chain of command, and he was obeyed. (The extent to which he was acting with Marshal Pétain's knowledge and consent was left unclear, and indeed remains unclear to this day.)

Under the agreement which Darlan concluded with General Eisenhower's deputy, Mark W. Clark, the Admiral became "High Com-

2. Message from General Eisenhower to the War Department (November 14, 1942), cited in William L. Langer, *Our Vichy Gamble* (New York: 1947), pp. 357-60.

missioner" of Algiers, Morocco and French West Africa. As one American historian has noted, from the political point of view,

the most important clause of the Clark-Darlan Agreement was that which left the Vichy administration in North Africa intact. Nowhere in the agreement could be found a stipulation which in the least implied that the French would be required to expunge Fascist elements from the governmental structure. If the High Commissioner chose to maintain in office the Vichy-appointed governors – Noguès, Boisson, and Chatel; if he kept anti-semitic laws patterned on Hitler's Nuremberg decrees in effect; or if he took no steps to liquidate the Service d'Ordre Légionnaire (S.O.L.), the North African version of the Schutzstaffel, there could be no justification for Allied interference unless it could be shown that such policies endangered military operations.[3]

In the words of Yves-Maxime Danan, it was "la substitution du vichysme sous protectorat américain au vichysme sous controle allemand".[4]

President Roosevelt, whose hostility to De Gaulle was both deep-seated and permanent, had insisted that the Gaullists be completely left out of Allied planning for the invasion; they received word of it on a radio news broadcast. Nevertheless, De Gaulle's headquarters was pleased about the news when it seemed that Giraud was the man of the hour. At the time of Giraud's escape from German imprisonment a few months earlier, De Gaulle had asked the British to invite Giraud (then in Switzerland) to London, and he had said that Giraud was the one man under whom he himself could work. After the landings in North Africa, De Gaulle immediately sought Allied permission to send a liaison mission to Giraud.[5] Then, on November 14, it was announced that it was Darlan rather than Giraud with whom the Americans would be dealing. The rage of the Free French knew no bounds. Not only had the *résistants de la première heure* been bypassed, but they had been bypassed in favor of a turncoat *de la dernière heure*. De Gaulle wrote to

---

3. Arthur Layton Funk, *Charles de Gaulle: The Crucial Years, 1943-1944* (Norman [Okla.]: 1959), p. 41. The governors mentioned were General Charles Noguès (Morocco), Pierre Boisson (French West Africa), and Yves Chatel (Algeria).

4. *La Vie politique à Alger de 1940 à 1944* (Paris: 1963), p. 346.

5. Charles de Gaulle, *Discours de guerre* (Fribourg: 1944-45), Vol. I, pp. 281-82; *Mémoires de guerre* (Paris: 1954-59), Vol. II, pp. 9-10, 45; George F. Howe, *Northwest Africa: Seizing the Initiative in the West* (Washington: 1957), p. 267; Langer, p. 279; "Colonel Passy" [André Dewavrin], *Souvenirs* (Monte Carlo: 1947ff.), Vol. II, p. 346.

Roosevelt's envoy, Admiral Harold R. Stark: "I understand that the United States buys the treachery of traitors, if this appears profitable, but payment must not be made against the honor of France."[6] The metropolitan Resistance – whose Pantheon did not include Talleyrand – was equally offended at the Allies' "temporary expedient". A number of leading resistance organizations published a communiqué which affirmed that General de Gaulle was "the uncontested head of the Resistance" and refused to consider the eleventh hour volte-face of "les responsables de la trahison militaire et politique" an excuse for their past crimes. This sentiment was echoed throughout most of the Resistance; the single exception was the Communist Party, which at first remained silent concerning the arrangement, then gave it qualified support.[7]

Resistance morale – both in the metropole and among the London Gaullists – was never lower than during the six weeks following the invasion of North Africa. Then, on Christmas eve, all previous calculations were altered when a young royalist, Fernand Bonnier de la Chapelle, assassinated Admiral Darlan. The "Conseil Impérial" which Darlan had constituted in November was hastily convened; on December 27 General Giraud, who had been commander of French ground forces under Darlan's brief regime, was named the Admiral's successor as High Commissioner, as well as head of all French armed forces in North Africa.

Had Giraud come to power in North Africa six months earlier, and had he been politically astute (the second hypothesis is more *outré* than the first – he might easily have won the backing of the metropolitan Resistance and gone on to become, in place of De Gaulle, the political leader of liberated France. At the time of his escape from Koenigstein, Giraud was hailed even more loudly by the Resistance in France than by the Gaullists. *Combat* wrote in May 1942:

> We don't know if Giraud is a republican, a royalist, a Bonapartist, a democrat, or if he dreams of autocracy, and that is of very little importance these days. For us, Giraud is an inflexible and unsullied soldier. He is free, having refused everything to the Germans. He has kept his sword immaculate for the service of France.

In the spring of 1942 the organizational ties binding the internal Resistance to De Gaulle were tentative and fragile; it is not inconceiv-

6. Funk, p. 44.
7. De Gaulle, *Mémoires*, Vol. II, p. 53; Henri Michel, *Les Courants de pensée de la Résistance* (Paris: 1962), pp. 611-12.

able that if Giraud had responded to the overtures made to him by the
Resistance he might have replaced De Gaulle as its leader.

But by the end of the year almost the entire Resistance had accepted
the organizational as well as the symbolic leadership of General de
Gaulle. Giraud still retained a certain popularity with the Resistance,
but his association with Darlan had dimmed his lustre, and his continuation of Vichy policies, and maintenance in office of leading Vichyites, was a constant irritant. In general, the attitude of the metropolitan
Resistance toward Giraud was a combination of very qualified support
and friendly criticism. They were, of course, enormously pleased to
see a French general in the Allied camp disposing of a real army instead
of the handful of volunteers that De Gaulle had mustered. At the same
time they were highly critical of Giraud's reluctance to break with
Vichy ideology and Vichy personnel. They looked forward to the unification of De Gaulle's forces with those of Giraud, and while awaiting
that day, urged Giraud to separate himself once and for all from Pétain
and his "National Revolution".

Unification finally came, but only after five months of involved and
frequently acrimonious negotiations. There were four parties to the
negotiations: all wanted unity, but each on different terms. American
policy, based on sponsorship of Giraud and hostility to De Gaulle,
favored the complete integration of the Free French forces into
Giraud's command, with De Gaulle himself being either completely
subordinated to Giraud or cast aside. The British, with a long-standing
commitment to De Gaulle, wished to see him enter North Africa on at
least an equal footing with Giraud, but feared to press too hard lest
their differences with the United States widen into a breach. Giraud,
the "simple soldier", was primarily interested in unification of their
respective forces for military purposes. He had no real political point of
view, though he shared the autocratic and hierarchical sympathies of
most army officers. In so far as he represented a political viewpoint it
was only as a mouthpiece for his Vichyite associates (who wanted to
maintain their positions) and the United States Government (which
wanted to block what they saw as De Gaulle's drive for power). De
Gaulle wanted at least equal authority with Giraud – probably recognizing that the politically naïve Giraud could then easily be outmaneuvered. He was also committed to a thorough housecleaning in
North Africa – not only a break with Vichy ideology, but the removal
from the administration of all Vichyite elements.

At the Casablanca Conference in January, Roosevelt attempted to

45

arrange a "shotgun wedding" between De Gaulle and Giraud. He informed Secretary of State Cordell Hull that he had

> produced the bridegroom, General Giraud, who cooperated very nicely on the proposed nuptials and was prepared to go through with it on our terms, I am sure. Our friends, however, could not produce De Gaulle, the temperamental bride. She has become quite high-hat about the whole affair and doesn't wish to see either of us, and shows no intention of getting into the bed with Giraud.[8]

Not only were the political terms – subordination to Giraud – unacceptable, but on the eve of the "nuptials" De Gaulle learned that another prominent Pétainist was joining Giraud's administration: Marcel Peyrouton, former Vichy Minister of the Interior, was named Governor-General of Algiers.

De Gaulle could afford to wait, because time was on his side. Giraud was under continued pressure from *les anglo-saxons* to at least appear to be a democrat; but every move he made in the direction of a break with Vichy and its supporters meant the undercutting of his position in North Africa, based as it was largely on the support of unreconstructed followers of the "National Revolution". His speech of March 14, in which he promised the annulment of Vichy legislation and the re-establishment of Republican legislation at the Liberation, led to the resignation of three of the "pure" Vichyites in his cabinet: General Jean Bergeret, Jean Rigault, and Jacques Lemaigre-Dubreuil. After the March 14 speech the Gaullists pressed the negotiations with renewed vigor, but did not soften their demands. A memorandum sent from London to Algiers in mid-April insisted on the total abolition of Vichy legislation (and the restoration of French citizenship to Algerian Jews), the dissolution of Vichyite groups such as the Légion des Combattants, and the dismissal from leading positions of "men who have taken personal responsibility for the capitulation and collaboration with the enemy".[9]

Gaullist sentiment was increasing in North Africa – not only among the civilian population, but among enlisted personnel in the armed forces as well; De Gaulle had many supporters in Tunisia, which finally fell to the Allies on May 12. Gaullist fortunes received their final boost when, on May 15, it was announced that the Conseil National de la Résistance, grouping all the leading resistance organizations, political parties and trade unions, had been formed in the metropole. The

8. *The Memoirs of Cordell Hull* (New York: 1948), Vol. II, p. 1207.
9. Jacques Soustelle, *Envers et contre tout* (Paris: 1947-50), Vol. II, p. 227.

C.N.R.'s first act was to issue a manifesto in support of General de Gaulle. On May 17 Secretary of State Hull cabled Robert Murphy in Algiers that

> reports reaching us during the past week . . . indicate that the delay in the meeting between Giraud and De Gaulle is working more and more to the latter's advantage. . . . The announcements concerning the French Council of Resistance . . . and the [Free French] National Committee's stand against [the disenfranchisement of Algerian Jews] . . . are cases in point. . . . We learn confidentially from members of Giraud Military Mission that Giraud sympathizers in Algiers report strong swing to De Gaulle among younger men both in and out of the army based largely on Giraud's failure to make adequate personnel changes particularly in the higher ranks of the armed forces and civil administration. In the circumstances we believe that there is no time to be lost, now that the Tunisian battle has been brought to a successful conclusion, in pushing forward long awaited reforms of a political character.[10]

Final arrangements for the delayed wedding were swiftly concluded between the groom and the no longer reluctant bride. The Free French National Committee dissolved itself; on May 30 De Gaulle arrived in Algiers.

General de Gaulle came to Algiers on the basis of a tentative agreement which called for a governing committee of which Giraud and himself would be co-presidents. Each was to nominate two other members; this six-man body would in turn choose further members. (Giraud nominated Jean Monnet and General Alphonse Georges; De Gaulle, André Philip and René Massigli. General Georges Catroux, the principal negotiator of unity, was a "neutral seventh" from the beginning.) However, no agreement had been reached concerning the action to be taken in the case of the Vichyite Governors-General (Peyrouton, Noguès, Boisson) and other "compromised" officials. On May 31, before the Committee was formally constituted, a long wrangle took place over this question. De Gaulle and Philip demanded the dismissal of the Vichyites as a condition of formal unity; Giraud, seconded by General Georges, defended them. Boisson's role in preventing the Germans from gaining control of West Africa was cited, while Peyrouton was defended on the basis of having helped depose Laval in December 1940, and because of his reputed skills as a colonial administrator. In response Philip pointed out the extent to which these men

10. *Foreign Relations of the U.S., Diplomatic Papers: 1943 II: Europe* (Washington: 1964), pp. 118-19.

symbolized collaboration to the Resistance in France. Giraud and Georges stressed the need for a broad front of anti-Germans; De Gaulle spoke of his responsibility to France to carry out a housecleaning. The meeting ended with De Gaulle stalking out of the room.[11]

On the following day Peyrouton, mistakenly believing that De Gaulle already shared command in North Africa with Giraud, submitted his resignation to both generals "in the interests of unity". De Gaulle (without authority) promptly accepted it, and told Peyrouton that he would grant his request to have his reserve commission activated. De Gaulle's usurpation of authority caused a renewed crisis, and it appeared possible that unity would be stillborn. General Catroux, seconded by Massigli and Monnet (who were less subservient to their respective sponsors than Philip and Georges), formed a moderate block which succeeded in persuading Giraud and De Gaulle to form the committee first and then deal with other questions. On June 3 the bicephalous Comité Français de la Libération Nationale was officially constituted. Peyrouton's resignation stood. A few days later Giraud consented to Noguès' replacement, and, before the end of the month, over Roosevelt's strenuous objections, Boisson too was removed.[12]

Giraud had lost the first battle with De Gaulle, as he was to lose the war. The apparent parity on the C.F.L.N. was an illusion: the ostensibly neutral Catroux was actually largely De Gaulle's man; Monnet moved into the middle. When subsequent appointments were made, De Gaulle's nominees formed a solid bloc of able politicians, while Giraud's – mostly technicians – were not equally loyal to their sponsor and voted individually according to the issue under discussion. Giraud, who had no real interest in political questions, came to concern himself exclusively with the military side; even in this area he found himself more and more subject to the control of an increasingly Gaullist Comité.

De Gaulle's entry into North Africa, his alliance with Giraud, and the dismissal of the leading Vichyites, were all hailed by the *résistants* of North Africa as well as those in France, but the Resistance was far

11. Catroux, *Dans la bataille de Méditerranée* (Paris: 1949), pp. 364-65; De Gaulle, *Mémoires*, Vol. II, pp. 105-06; Giraud, *Un seul but la victoire* (Paris: 1949), pp. 162-69.
12. Harry C. Butcher, *My Three Years with Eisenhower* (New York: 1946), p. 320; Catroux, pp. 366-69; De Gaulle, *Mémoires*, Vol. II, pp. 485-88; Funk, p. 127; Marcel Peyrouton, *Du service public à la prison commune* (Paris: 1950), pp. 231-34; Soustelle, II, 248-51.

from satisfied with the pace and scope of the housecleaning that they fervently desired. Even so loyal a Gaullist as René Capitant (later to become Minister of Education of the Provisional Government) took his chief to task for his laxity in this regard.[13] De Gaulle was urged to prosecute those guilty of intelligence with the enemy, and to waste no time in purging the administration of actual or potential fifth columnists.

In Casablanca, on August 8 and 10, General de Gaulle spoke out clearly for the first time on the subject of the punishment of Vichyites and collaborators. The union of all Frenchmen for the Liberation and Renaissance of France should not, he said, imply the blunting of the sword of justice as desired by some elements. On the contrary, enduring national unity could be forged only if the state knew how to recognize its faithful servants and punish the criminals. For the latter – the "capitulards" who used the excuse of defeat to strangle liberty, the men of Vichy who misled the French people, those who lined up with the enemy – for them there was only one term to apply: "treason"; one thing to do: "render justice". His remarks on the sort of purge he foresaw explained why he had delayed speaking of it until invested with state power.

> Nothing would be more lamentable from the point of view of the future of France – and everyone realizes this – than to make of the purge, which is a *question d'Etat*, a question of local battles. It is necessary to have enough self-mastery, be French enough, be great enough, to avoid this. Justice is an affair of state, at the exclusive service of France. The French want this state to be led by men who have the confidence of the masses. That being so, justice should be rendered solely in the name of the state. It is thus that the purge of which you speak will be carried out as it should be, normally, from on high, and under the authority and on the responsibility of those in charge. Nothing would be more unfortunate, with respect to the purge, than to allow the unleashing of local personal battles. This is what I want to say. A great many Frenchmen have been misled by the actions of the Vichy regime, endorsed by enemy propaganda. Nevertheless, despite everything, they too are Frenchmen. They are part of France. Naturally, those among them who have personally taken part in a disastrous policy should be dealt with as some already have been. Others still will be. But, I repeat, it is an affair of state.[14]

De Gaulle's supporters, while encouraged by these words, were not appeased. If the purge was to be an affair of state, then the state should

13. *Combat (Alger)*, July 24, 1943.
14. De Gaulle, *La France n'a pas perdu la guerre* (New York: 1944), pp. 257-59.

get on with it. On August 14, *Combat (Alger)* published a resolution of the Central Committee of La France Combattante in North Africa. It announced the formation of a Purge Commission made up of the organization's own members which would study various cases and advise General de Gaulle of its findings. Several cases which they regarded as flagrant affronts to patriots were cited – among them the continued freedom enjoyed by ex-Governor-General Chatel, Admiral Louis Derrien, who in November 1942 had allowed the Germans to enter Tunisia unopposed, and Pierre-Etienne Flandin, who had served as Foreign Minister under Vichy and was now in North Africa. Equally shocking to the authors of the resolution was the fact that ex-Vichy Minister of the Interior Pierre Pucheu was still only in *résidence surveilée*.

The same day that the resolution appeared, the C.F.L.N. decided that Pucheu would be tried before a military tribunal; he was arrested and imprisoned at Meknès in Morocco. Four days later the Committee, over the signature of its co-presidents, De Gaulle and Giraud, established a Purge Commission charged with suggesting measures to be taken in the case of

> all officials and civil servants who, since June 16, 1940, have by their acts, their writings, or their personal attitude, either encouraged enemy undertakings, or prejudiced the action of the United Nations and of Frenchmen who are resisting; or have interfered with constitutional institutions or basic public liberties; or knowingly derived or attempted to derive any direct material gain from the application of regulations enforced by the *de facto* authority contrary to the laws in force on June 16, 1940.[15]

The Commission was to distinguish between men who merely obeyed orders without having the authority necessary to dispute them, and those who, "going beyond their strictly professional obligations, knowingly associated themselves with an antinational policy". Composed of a president and four members to be appointed on the recommendation of the Commissioner of Justice and the Commissioner of the Interior, it had competence in the cases of all elected and appointed officials in the Government, armed forces, semi-public corporations, professional associations and the press. The Commission could subpoena both witnesses and documents. It could, after inquiry, recommend to the Ministries concerned that culpable officials be transferred, demoted or

15. J.O. (Alger), September 11, 1943, p. 116.

dismissed; where judicial action was, in its view, called for, it would hand over the dossiers to the regular court system.[16]

Two weeks later, on September 3, the C.F.L.N. took a more momentous step. It unanimously resolved

> To assure, as soon as circumstances permit, the operation of justice in regard to Marshal Pétain and to those who have taken part or are taking part in the pseudo-governments formed by him, who have capitulated, violated the constitution, collaborated with the enemy, handed over French workers to the Germans and compelled French forces to fight against the Allies or against those of the French who were continuing the struggle.[17]

The Committee was now formally committed – for the first time – to the punishment of Pétain, his Ministers, and his responsible subordinates. Pucheu, who had come to North Africa with a safe-conduct from Giraud – Peyrouton, who had come under American auspices – these and dozens of others were proscribed. The resolution was intended to squelch – finally and unambiguously – the rumors that secret contacts or agreements existed between the C.F.L.N. and Vichy, and that when France was liberated the Committee would come to terms with Pétain. The resolution served another purpose, unintended by at least some of its signers: it cut Giraud off not only from his ex-associates but from his current supporters, especially in the Army. The September 3 resolution, coming on top of the decision to set up the Purge Commission, was enthusiastically received by those who had been pressing for more vigorous action on the purge. *Liberté* (Communist) wrote:

> For the first time the Committee has officially proclaimed its unanimous determination to assure the action of justice in the case of the sinister Pétain and his odious accomplices, the traitors of Vichy. It is this which gives to all the decisions of the Committee a sense of unity, an air of force, an *esprit de guerre*, which it previously lacked.[18]

On September 17 De Gaulle and Giraud had signed an ordinance establishing a "Provisional Consultative Assembly to provide, insofar as present circumstances permit, the broadest possible expression of

16. The Commission's first president was William Marcais, Professor at the Collège de France; he was replaced in November by Charles Laurent, head of the Fédération des Fonctionnaires.
17. De Gaulle, *Mémoires*, Vol. II, p. 134.
18. September 11, 1943.

national opinion".[19] The Assembly was to be composed of representatives of the Resistance (52 seats), Third Republic senators and deputies (20 seats), and representatives of the *conseils généraux* of North Africa (12 seats). On November 3 the Assemblée Consultative Provisoire held its first session. The Assembly was overwhelmingly favorable to De Gaulle; with its support it was now possible for him to arrange Giraud's ouster from the C.F.L.N. All the members of the Comité resigned, in order to permit its broadening by the addition of *résistants* and representatives of the parties of the Left – a move urgently sought by the Conseil National de la Résistance. A committee chaired by De Gaulle was to draw up a new slate. On November 9 the new list was announced: many *résistants* and Third Republic politicians had been added; General Giraud, together with three of his principal supporters, had been dropped. From first to last, Giraud had been outmaneuvered by De Gaulle. The Communists, who had supported Giraud as a counterweight to De Gaulle, rallied 10,000 at a protest meeting. De Gaulle offered them the Ministries of Production and Public Health if he could name the Communists to fill them, but the Party refused, preferring for the time being to stay in opposition. Giraud threatened to resign as Commander-in-Chief of the Armed Forces, but was dissuaded by the Americans. Realizing too late the danger in which the new situation placed his late associates, Giraud tried to get a veto over purge trials in the Army, but was not successful. At a press conference on November 10 "a new General de Gaulle", showing "a sense of absolute confidence", explained that "the Committee was stronger, broader, and more sure of itself and would concentrate on purging collaborationists and on devising methods for the return of sovereignty to France".[20]

De Gaulle's statement of resolve notwithstanding, the delegates to the Consultative Assembly made haste to express their dissatisfaction with the course of the purge. Members of the Purge Commission complained of crippling limitations on their authority and the insufficient attention paid to their recommendations by the Ministry of Justice. Father Carrière, a delegate from the metropolitan Resistance, defined the present hour as "not that of pardon, but of God's justice". Indeed, one of the very first acts of the new body was to vote unanimously a resolution introduced by the Socialist Pierre-Bloch urging the Government to swifter and more resolute action.[21] They were

19. De Gaulle, *Mémoires*, Vol. II, p. 539.
20. Funk, pp. 193-94.
21. J.O., A.C.P. Debates, November 11 and 13, 1943.

willing, however, to heed André Philip's request not to give the impression of "pressuring" the Committee, and on November 15 rejected a proposal to hold an extraordinary session on the purge.[22]

But in the debate on the purge which took place two months later, the delegates were less inclined to excuse what they regarded as the shocking laxity of the C.F.L.N. A few days before the opening of the general debate on January 11, the Commissioner for Foreign Affairs had been attacked in the Assembly for continuing to employ "compromised" diplomats.[23] In the general debate as well, it was the question of a housecleaning in the administration that was most frequently and most passionately discussed. Charles Laurent, head of the Purge Commission, reported on what he considered nothing less than the sabotage of its work: the "loss" of letters in transit, the disappearance of dossiers, the failure of the authorities to hand over information to his group. He told the Assembly that of the over one hundred dossiers sent to the Justice Commission, action had been taken on only four or five. The reply of Commissioner of Justice François de Menthon – in which he disputed the picture drawn by Laurent – did little to curb the Assembly's indignation.[24] Not enough, at any rate, to prevent the Assembly from unanimously voting a resolution highly critical of the Government which called for greater powers for the Commission and a speed-up of juridical action.[25]

Concerning one aspect of the purge, however, the Assembly – and in particular the benches on the far left – were a good deal less zealous. This was the purge of the armed forces. In part, this reflected satisfaction with the job of housecleaning accomplished by the War Ministry under André Le Troquer. Of fifty-two cases sent him by the Purge Commission, he had acted in fifty-one, and in addition had taken sanctions against hundreds of others – a total of almost 1,500 cases.[26] Le Troquer had also created special regiments of men "not worthy to serve with good Frenchmen" but who should also "pay their blood debt". Many were shocked by the case of Captain Maurice Carré, whose internment had been ordered by the War Ministry. The

22. *Ibid.*, November 18, 1943, pp. 1-3.
23. *Ibid.*, January 8, 1944, pp. 8-12.
24. De Menthon claimed that 288 cases had been sent before the Army Military Tribunal (although none had as yet been heard). In the Justice Department, he continued, seventy-five magistrates had been punished by sanctions of various kinds, and in Algeria alone forty-eight out of fifty-three high officials had been removed from office.
25. J.O., A.C.P. Debates, January 15, 1944, pp. 1-12.
26. *Ibid.*, March 25, 1944, p. 15; January 22, 1944, p. 5.

Ministry was informed by his commanding officer that Captain Carré could not be interned because he had just died heroically at the head of his troops on the Italian Front, and that he was being recommended for the Légion d'Honneur.[27]

But second thoughts and reservations concerning a root and branch purge in the armed forces stemmed principally from fear that such a program would make it much more difficult to get France back into the war. To create divisions, to go back to the days of Dreyfus and the André Ministry, would be to jeopardize the chances of France finally finding a place in the first rank of the Allies. After the war was won, the agitation for a "Republican Army" was to begin again; many, the Communists in the lead, would organize a campaign to expose the French Occupation Army in Germany as a refuge for Vichyites. But in 1944, when the long-awaited Second Front was about to become a reality, many of the most implacable *épurateurs* trod lightly when it came to the Army. The Communist Fernand Grenier, C.F.L.N. Commissioner of the Air Force, one for whom no fault was too small or too long past to be raked up in other areas, expressed himself as follows on the question of the purge in his Ministry:

> The Resistance itself is not made up only of men who saw their duty from the beginning. We know the *silencieux* of 1940 and 1941, even the Vichyites of 1942, who became *résistants* only in 1943! If the avowed traitors should be punished, we must give those who were tricked and deceived the right to serve and redeem themselves. For me, the past is dead. I judge officers not on what they have done but on what they do today. . . . We are all the sons of the same mother, and we must make peace among ourselves. . . .[28]

Despite his success in eliminating Giraud, despite the unanimous support which he enjoyed from the Consultative Assembly and the C.N.R., De Gaulle was still far from being master in his own house. He was still dependent on the Allies for economic and military assistance, his regime was still not formally recognized by them, the spectre of an Allied Military Government imposed on liberated France still haunted him. The restrictions on his freedom of action were forcibly brought home to him when he made his first attempt to translate the September 3 resolution into action.

The resolution had committed the C.F.L.N. to the punishment of Pétain and his Ministers. The Marshal was, for the moment, beyond the reach of the Committee, but a number of his principal aides were

27. *The New York Times*, February 15, 1944.
28. J.O., A.C.P. Debates, May 13, 1944, p. 8.

not. On December 21 the C.F.L.N. authorized the arrest of Pierre Boisson, Marcel Peyrouton, and P.-E. Flandin. Within hours of the arrest Churchill cabled Roosevelt:

> I am shocked at the arrests reported this morning of Boisson, Peyrouton and Flandin. There are even rumours here that the first two at any rate will be shot. I consider I have a certain obligation as, in supporting your policy and that of General Eisenhower, I did undoubtedly in Algiers in February encourage these men to hold firm in their posts and aid us in our struggle for Tunis, saying also in that case, "Count on me." It seems to me the American obligation is even stronger because we were admittedly following (query) your general lines.[29]

The following day Roosevelt ordered Eisenhower to inform the C.F.L.N. that "in view of the assistance given to the Allied armies during the campaign in Africa by Boisson, Peyrouton, and Flandin, you are directed [sic] to take no action against these individuals at the present time".[30] Allied feeling on the question ran very high. Roosevelt "thought the time had come to eliminate De Gaulle".[31] Churchill wrote the American President that

> far above individuals, the whole question of our relations with France is raised. France can only be liberated by British and American forces and bloodshed. To admit that a handful of émigrés are to have the power behind this all-powerful shield to carry civil war into France is to lose the future of that unfortunate country and prevent the earliest expression of the will of the people as a whole. . . .[32]

Military conversations with the French were suspended, and a permanent rupture was threatened.

Roosevelt demanded, at a minimum, "formal assurance from the French Committee that no trials of these individuals will take place until the restoration of France is accomplished and then in accordance with the constitutional laws of the French Republic". On December 30 the American representative to the C.F.L.N., Edwin C. Wilson, "impressed upon [De Gaulle] that action on the very serious instructions which had been received could not be delayed much longer and urged him to give assurance in the sense desired".[33]

29. *Foreign Relations: 1943*, Vol. II, pp. 193-94.
30. *Ibid.*, pp. 194-95. Flandin had not, in fact, aided the Allies in Africa, but it may well have seemed to Churchill and Roosevelt that excluding Flandin from their protection would have been tantamount to throwing him to the wolves.   31. *Ibid.*, pp. 195-96.   32. *Ibid.*, pp. 196-97.
33. *Ibid.*, pp. 197, 199. There is no record of the exact nature of the "very serious instructions" alluded to, but they probably went to the point of a complete rupture with De Gaulle.

De Gaulle, although he avoided a public retreat, was compelled to give a verbal guarantee to the Allies. He stated, "speaking deliberately and measuring each word", that "the examining magistrate will not be able to assemble the necessary elements on which he would be in a position to decide whether or not a trial should take place until after the liberation of France". He further promised that the trio would not be subjected to a prison regimen, but would be placed in comfortable quarters. Wilson, his British opposite-number Harold Macmillan, General Eisenhower, and later Secretary of State Hull, considered these assurances satisfactory.[34] The assurances were honored by De Gaulle: the three men were moved to a villa outside Algiers, and were not tried until long after the Liberation.[35]

Allied pressure on behalf of Peyrouton, Boisson, and Flandin was no secret: it was discussed openly, and with a good deal of bitterness, in the Consultative Assembly. Emmanuel d'Astier de la Vigerie, speaking for the Committee, might declare that "neither the heavens nor Great Britain nor America will be able to prevent [the] purge";[36] his auditors knew that – at least for the moment – the boast was vain. But, as Albert Gazier remarked, although foreign intervention had taken place on behalf of some, there were others to whom this did not apply, and these could and should be tried and found guilty.[37] Foremost among those "others" in the minds of the delegates was Pierre Pucheu.

Ever since Pucheu's term of office at the Ministry of the Interior, he had been marked for future action by the Resistance. Even the B.B.C., which normally abstained from threats against Vichyites, singled out Pucheu early in 1942.[38] In May 1943, with the permission of General Giraud, Pucheu came to North Africa. Thereafter, calls for his prosecution multiplied. A few days after Pucheu's arrival, the French Parliamentary Group in London called for his immediate trial on the charge,

34. *Ibid.*, pp. 199-200.
35. Flandin, in 1946, was sentenced to five years of national degradation, the penalty being immediately suspended for acts of resistance. In 1948 Peyrouton was acquitted, becoming the first Vichy Minister whom the High Court did not automatically punish with national degradation because of his position in the Regime. Boisson died in 1948 before his case was heard by the High Court.
36. J.O., A.C.P. Debates, January 13, 1944, p. 13.
37. *Ibid.*, January 15, p. 1.
38. *Libération* (*Nord*), No. 59, January 18, 1942, while remarking on the lack of diplomacy implicit in the B.B.C. broadcast, endorsed its view that Pucheu should be punished, a task they would accomplish "without the help of the Intelligence Service or the G.P.U.".

among others, of selecting the hostages executed by the Germans at Châteaubriant in October 1941. During the summer the Comité Central de la Résistance in the north zone condemned him to death "in the name of the French people". In October the C.N.R. took the same action by mail ballot of its members. Understandably, since Pucheu's activities had in the main been directed against their ranks, the Communists took a leading role in the agitation for Pucheu's punishment. But the calls for his trial came from all quarters; in the Consultative Assembly the Socialist Pierre-Bloch urged Pucheu's execution as a salutary warning to officials in France which would "save thousands of lives".[39]

Pucheu's case was heard by the Army Military Tribunal, whose jurisdiction had been enlarged to cover crimes against the security of the state committed by cabinet ministers, high officials, and members of collaborationist groups such as the P.P.F. and the Phalange Africaine. His attempt to have his trial delayed on the grounds that necessary witnesses and documents were unavailable was not successful; however, during the pre-trial examination some of the charges, notably that of having collaborated with the Germans in selecting hostages for the Châteaubriant executions, were dropped from the indictment for lack of evidence.[40]

When the trial opened on March 4 Pucheu stood accused on fourteen counts, all relating to his ministerial activity. Pucheu immediately attempted to take the offensive – employing tactics which became almost a ritual after the Liberation. He began by attacking the competence of the Tribunal – a line later followed by Pétain among others. When the Presiding Judge began a discourse on the illegality of the Vichy Regime Pucheu reminded the judge that he himself had taken an oath to that Regime. Pucheu's attorneys devoted a large part of the time at their disposal to attacking Communist policy, of which they claimed their client was a victim. (Coming at a time when Communist participation in the C.F.L.N. was urgently being sought, and when the non-Com-

39. *France* (London), May 20, 1943; *Libération* (*Sud*), No. 37 (October 1943); René Hostache, *Le Conseil National de la Résistance: Les Institutions de la clandestinité* (Paris: 1958), pp. 179-80; the B.D.I.C. collection "Propagande communiste sous l'occupation allemande"; J.O., A.C.P. Debates, November 11 and 13, 1943, p. 7.

40. At every stage of the proceedings, in public and private, Pucheu denied any involvement in the selection of the hostages. After the Liberation Pucheu's denial was refuted by documentary evidence unearthed by the Ministry of Justice and published throughout the French press on October 20, 1944.

munist Resistance was particularly sensitive to Vichy's attempts to split their ranks, the tactic was poorly chosen.)

The first set of charges – plotting and carrying out the overthrow or illegal modification of the legal government – were extremely difficult to support in Pucheu's case; he had entered the Vichy Regime many months after the death of the Republic. The last two charges – personally directed arrests and violence – were found insufficiently supported by the evidence. The prosecution concentrated on the charges of intelligence with the enemy, favoring his projects, and enlisting Frenchmen in his service; for these there was ample documentary evidence. There were laws and decrees over Pucheu's signature setting up special tribunals to try "terrorists", circulars urging recruitment in the Anti-Bolshevik Legion (which fought on the Russian front) and similar documents. Pucheu was found guilty of these central charges and sentenced to death.

De Gaulle received a number of requests that the sentence not be carried out. Giraud asked that at least Pucheu not be executed until the return to France. De Gaulle reminded Giraud of his acceptance of the September 3 decision to try the men of Vichy, and replied that he would take no action. Just as Roosevelt's promises had led Peyrouton to Algiers, so Giraud's had brought Pucheu, and he felt a similar responsibility. But Giraud's cannons, unlike the American President's, were spiked. The judges themselves unanimously asked that their sentence not be executed, largely because of "le comportement du général Giraud à l'égard de Pucheu". De Gaulle rejected their plea on the grounds that to commute Pucheu's sentence would create a crippling precedent in the cases to come. To the appeal of Pucheu's attorneys, the General invoked the concept closest to his heart. He told them that he was personally persuaded that Pucheu, although he had done harm as a member of the Vichy Government, had acted in good faith and was sincerely anti-German. However, "in the tragedy in which we are participating, when the whole world is suffering, individuals do not count; our sole guide must be raison d'Etat". "Above all," De Gaulle wrote years later, "the state required a swift example." On the morning of March 20, after shaking hands with the firing squad, and himself giving the command to fire, Pucheu was executed.[41] The example was clear for all the world to see. A Minister of Vichy was convicted and executed, solely on the basis of his ministerial acts. The die was cast.

41. Giraud, pp. 265-80; G. Schmitt, *Toute la vérité sur le procès Pucheu par un des juges* (Paris: 1963), pp. 7, 162, 248-76; Paul Buttin, *Le Procès Pucheu* (Paris: 1948), pp. 231-33; De Gaulle, *Mémoires*, II, 179.

Pucheu's trial and execution effectively stilled most criticism of the Government on the question of the purge. There were still those who found the Government's pace unacceptably slow, but the Assembly debate in March reflected the relief of the delegates at seeing the machinery of justice in operation at last. That machinery was operating not just in the case of Pucheu but also with respect to many less prominent individuals in North Africa.

Even before Pucheu was tried, the Army Military Tribunal had heard the case of the "tortionnaires d'Hadjerat M'guil" – concentration camp guards who rivalled the S.S. in their treatment of prisoners. Four death sentences and several others to varying terms of imprisonment were pronounced. Shortly after the Pucheu case the Tribunal sat in judgment on members of the Phalange Africaine, French volunteers who had fought for the Germans against the Allies in the Tunisian campaign of 1943. Several members of the Phalange, including its leader, Colonel Christofini, were executed.

The trials in North Africa continued through the spring and summer. In May Vice-Admiral Derrien, who had ordered armed resistance to the Allies and allowed the Germans to enter Tunisia, was sentenced to life imprisonment by the Tribunal; in July another group of concentration camp guards was tried. The North African "rehearsal" had been something less than a brilliant success. Slow in getting under way because of Giraud's attitude, later braked by the Allies, it only began to operate effectively a few months before the Normandy landings. While the North African trials were still going on, American and British troops were establishing their beachhead in France. The Liberation had begun.

Chapter 4

JUSTICE AT THE CROSSROADS

L'ordre social, est-ce seulement la tranquillité des rues? . . . Nous avons tous l'impression pendant ces déchirants jours d'août que l'ordre commençait justement avec les premiers coups de feu de l'insurrection. Sous leur visage désordonné les révolutions portent avec elles un principe d'ordre. Ce principe régnera si la révolution est totale. Mais lorsqu'elles avortent ou s'arrêtent en chemin, c'est un grand désordre monotone qui s'instaure pour beaucoup d'années. . . . Nous sommes déterminés à rejeter pour toujours la célèbre phrase d'un faux grand homme et à déclarer que nous préférons éternellement le désordre à l'injustice.

Combat, October 12, 1944

ON the eve of the Allied landings in Normandy, General de Gaulle's principal problem was the establishment of his authority in the metropole. This authority faced a double challenge: from possible disorders provoked by the Resistance itself, and from the United States, which might decide to impose an Allied military government (A.M.G.O.T.), either because of civil disturbance or in spite of its absence. Elaborate precautions were taken to meet these eventualities, though in the event the C.F.L.N.'s fears proved somewhat exaggerated.

Before the landings the Allies had made no commitment to recognize the C.F.L.N. as the *de facto* government of France. By swift and decisive action the designated Gaullist authorities succeeded in presenting the Allies with a *fait accompli*. They either followed close in the wake of the advancing armies or emerged from the underground in the midst of the fighting; in both cases they had replaced the Vichy authorities and established themselves in the *mairies* and *préfectures* before the dust of battle had settled. Throughout Northern France the new regime assumed power and established its authority with a minimum of disorder; outbreaks of retributive violence against collaborators were relatively rare.

Affairs in the South of France were not as easily put in order. The imposition of an A.M.G.O.T. was not an issue: by the time that the southern beachhead was well established, De Gaulle had entered Paris in triumph and the Allies had abandoned whatever thoughts they might have entertained of supplanting him. But civil disorder – most notably the irregular and summary execution of collaborators – was a major problem. This was particularly true in those extensive areas liberated not by regular troops but by the metropolitan Resistance. The "test of strength" between the Gaullist authorities and Communist elements in the Resistance which some writers have described never took place. By determined and coordinated action the representatives of the central government succeeded without too much difficulty in repressing violence and disorder, although in some areas the process took several months.

Speaking of the future purge in August 1943, General de Gaulle had laid heavy stress on insuring that the purge did not degenerate into "the unleashing of local personal battles".[1] The metropolitan Resistance was in complete accord with the General on this point.[2] They were agreed, too, that one of the best ways to prevent spontaneous vengeance was for the C.F.L.N. to take a clear stand on future punishment and begin implementing it in North Africa.

But differences appeared on the question of what policy should be followed to limit popular violence in the metropole. Many *résistants* who were in general committed to the strictest adherence to legal norms regarded summary proceedings as desirable in some cases. *Résistance* considered that

> where treasonous conduct has been public and avowed the forms of justice should be reduced to the absolute minimum. The establishment of the individual's identity followed by the death sentence is the only form of justice possible for those who have become the agents or the recruiting sergeants of the enemy.[3]

Paul Rivet, Director of the Musée de l'Homme and an underground journalist, was of the opinion that

> when the armies of liberation land in France the people will already have begun their own liberation. . . . Paris will have rid herself of traitors without waiting for tribunals to be instituted. The wrath of the people is

1. De Gaulle, *La France n'a pas perdu la guerre* (New York: 1944), pp. 257-59.
2. See, e.g., *Populaire* (*Nord*), No. 31 (February 1943); *Libérer et Fédérer*, No. 12 (October 1943); *Résistance*, No. 18 (October 13, 1943); and Henri Michel, *Les Courants de pensée de la Résistance* (Paris: 1962), pp. 346-47.
3. No. 6, January 25, 1943.

always terrible, and I hope the people will not be guilty of injustice. But when the government arrives . . . it will find itself in the presence of an accomplished fact. Déat, Doriot, Laval, and even Marshal Pétain will have been liquidated, for this will not be a *revolution* but a *liquidation*. The French people are suffering physically. They are starving. There is no force on earth which will stop them from doing justice; the French people will execute the men who betrayed and sacrificed them.[4]

The conservative Organisation Civile et Militaire's position was that

the execution [at the Liberation], even without trial, of a small number of individuals – the *vedettes de la trahison* – can be considered a necessary police operation. It is of course not impossible that uncontrolled elements will have recourse to this procedure. But it is up to the authorities to demonstrate their capacity to keep order by severely limiting [*sic*] recourse to summary proceedings, and bringing the guilty before organized jurisdictions.[5]

In the eyes of their authors, the great merit of these proposals for "letting off steam" was that a greater explosion would thus be prevented.

This "permissiveness", no matter how high-minded its motives, was anathema to General de Gaulle. There could be no question of simply "limiting" summary proceedings. Justice, for De Gaulle, was "to be rendered solely in the name of the state". The purge would be carried out solely "from on high, and under the authority and on the responsibility of those in charge". It was, he constantly reiterated, solely "an affair of state". "There can be no public authority," he said, "except that which comes from a responsible power. Any artificial formation outside of the government would be intolerable and is

4. *Free France*, February 15, 1944, 156. (Italics in original.)
5. *Cahiers* [of the O.C.M.], June 1942. See also the interesting underground public opinion poll conducted in May 1944 by the Service de Sondages et de Statistiques on the subject of the anticipated popular justice in the first days of the Liberation. The sample was largely bourgeois; 19 per cent of the respondents were *résistants*, 60 per cent Resistance sympathizers and 21 per cent "neutrals"; for obvious reasons collaborationists were not polled. 44 per cent of the sample were for preventing popular justice; 28 per cent were for "braking and guiding" popular fury, which no power on earth could really prevent; 28 per cent were for allowing it free rein, to deal with the problem both effectively and expeditiously. No significant differences were found in the responses with respect to occupation, social class, or political leaning. Surprisingly, the young were most inclined to favor prevention. (*S.S.S.: Sondages*, No. 9 [July 6, 1944].)

condemned in advance."[6] He was resolved to so organize his assumption of power in France that no "artificial formations" would trouble public order.

De Gaulle had another and more urgent reason for paying careful attention to the problem of establishing a provisional administration in liberated France: it was far from clear that the United States would acquiesce in its installation. President Roosevelt's permanent hostility to De Gaulle led him to stubbornly resist accepting the C.F.L.N. as the only alternative to Vichy. Indeed, many *résistants* feared that Roosevelt would *not* seek an alternative to Vichy; there was considerable speculation that another "Darlan deal" might be in the offing. In fact, the American President had ruled out any deal with Vichy; he remained, however, inclined toward the imposition of a military government on France until shortly before the invasion. Finally – and reluctantly – he agreed to authorize General Eisenhower to make whatever arrangements he considered necessary with the C.F.L.N. But right down to D-Day the French Committee had no satisfactory assurance that an A.M.G.O.T. would not be imposed. As a consequence, its plans had to aim at the rapid installation of new authorities so as to present the Allies with a *fait accompli*.[7]

The organizational apparatus of the Liberation can be divided into three categories: the armed forces of the Resistance, which De Gaulle sought to unify and control; the departmental liberation committees, whose role he attempted to limit; and the *commissaires de la République*, the General's "intendants".

The Forces Françaises de l'Intérieur were organized early in 1944 and placed under the command of General Pierre Koenig. The F.F.I. was made up of the Armée Secrète – itself an amalgamation of various groups, the Organisation de Résistance de l'Armée – made up of *résistant* remnants of the dissolved Armistice Army, and the Francs-Tireurs et Partisans Français – military arm of the Communist Front National. Until D-Day the administration of these forces was under the Commission d'Action (COMAC) of the Conseil National de la Résistance;

6. De Gaulle, *France*, pp. 257-59; *Discours de guerre* (Fribourg: 1944-45), Vol. II, p. 213.
7. J.O., A.C.P. Debates, June 1, 1944, pp. 15-31; June 3, pp. 33-47; Harry L. Coles and Albert K. Weinberg, *Civil Affairs: Soldiers Become Governors* (Washington: 1964), pp. 661-70; Arthur Layton Funk, *Charles de Gaulle: The Crucial Years, 1943-1944* (Norman [Okla.]: 1959), pp. 198-99, 248-49, 265-72; Forrest C. Pogue, *The European Theater of Operations: The Supreme Command* (Washington: 1954), pp. 138-57.

after that date operational command was to pass to a hierarchy of "military delegates" of the C.F.L.N.[8] There was a *délégué militaire national*, two *délégués militaires de Zone* (North and South), and twelve *délégués militaires régionaux*. At the base of the pyramid, individual fighting units usually retained their separate (organizational) identity, but there was a certain consolidation of regional and departmental staffs.

The idea of constituting "Liberation Committees" (C.D.L.'s) in each department of France had been jointly conceived and agreed to by representatives of the C.F.L.N. and of the metropolitan Resistance in the summer of 1943. The committees were to consist of representatives of the leading resistance groups, political parties and trade unions in each department. From the standpoint of the C.F.L.N. these committes would serve the same function as the C.N.R. after which they were patterned: they would be a tangible demonstration to the invading Allies of the support which De Gaulle enjoyed from the population. But the "Statut des Comités Départementaux de la Libération" passed by the C.N.R. on March 23, 1944, foresaw a considerably wider role for the C.D.L.'s. It noted that while originally they were assigned only a consultative role, "today they appear to be – and should be – the heart and soul of their departments in the struggle for their liberation". The C.D.L.'s were told that they should,

> in order to facilitate the work of the future public authorities, infiltrate the administration and prepare immediate measures for the administrative purge and the neutralization of traitors. They shall make the necessary arrangements for the replacement of unworthy civil servants and study the question of installing provisional municipal governments.

At the Liberation they were to direct the armed struggle, see to the installation of new authorities and arrest traitors and suspects. On April 11 a C.N.R. circular empowered the departmental committees to proceed, at the Liberation, to the constitution of provisional municipal governments pending local elections. In those cases in which the prefect named by the C.F.L.N. failed to arrive, the presidents of the C.D.L.'s were to occupy his post until a substitute was officially designated.[9] By the spring of 1944 C.D.L.'s were installed in most of the departments of metropolitan France.

8. The COMAC came to have a Communist majority and developed some pretensions toward sharing operational command of the armed forces with De Gaulle's military delegates. It had no success in this attempt, outside of Paris itself, since it possessed no network of responsible subordinates.

9. René Hostache, *Le Conseil National de la Résistance: Les Institutions de la clandestinité* (Paris: 1958), pp. 300, 465-70.

General de Gaulle was not disposed to see such extensive powers entrusted to bodies which escaped his direct control; his principled objection to this prospect was not lessened by reports which he received from France advising him that the Communists were achieving a dominant position in several of the Committees.[10] On April 12 the C.F.L.N. adopted an ordinance which drastically curtailed the powers which the C.N.R. had – on its own authority – given to the C.D.L.'s. Instead of the provisional municipal governments foreseen in the C.N.R. directive, the 1939 municipal governments were to be reconstituted, minus those of their members who had shown themselves unworthy. If the municipal council as a whole had proved unworthy, a provisional council would be named by the prefect. The same procedure would be followed on the departmental level with respect to the *conseils généraux*. When these were reconstituted the C.D.L.'s would cease to exist; until that time they would play only a strictly consultative role.[11]

The principal agency upon which De Gaulle relied for the establishment of his authority and the maintenance of order was a new corps of "commissaires de la République" – eighteen "super-prefects", each with responsibility for the administration of a region. These *commissaires* – together with the departmental prefects under them – were nominated by a special C.F.L.N. commission inside occupied France which acted on the advice of the metropolitan Resistance: those named included teachers, trade unionists, engineers, deputies and lawyers as well as former members of the prefectoral corps.

Because of the anticipated breakdown in communications, which might prevent any reference to higher authority for many months, they were granted absolutely unlimited powers: they could legislate – or suspend existing legislation; they could create special judicial institutions at their discretion – or commute regular judicial sentences; they had complete administrative authority, including the right to remove the prefects under them and install new ones. They were, in short, a law unto themselves.

Among their duties, none was more important than the orderly management of the purge. Their enumerated tasks included the removal of compromised officials and the arrest of suspects. If it appeared desirable, they could organize courts-martial to try collaborators. All of this, however, was to be accomplished in an orderly fashion. They were to bear in mind that the public was "just as anxious to see life return to its normal course as to see that traitors were punished"; they

10. *Ibid.*, p. 305.
11. J.O. (Alger), April 22, 1944, pp. 325-27.

were reminded that "prolonged disorder would not only constitute a temptation for the Allied armies [to set up a military government] but would diminish the authority of the C.F.L.N. and compromise [the nation's] rebirth".[12]

By the end of May all arrangements had been made. The *commissaires* and prefects-designate were in place, ready to occupy the seats of power. On June 3 the C.F.L.N. adopted a new name which more accurately reflected its role: Gouvernement Provisoire de la République Française. Three days later the Liberation of France began.

The Allied campaign in Northern France was characterized by an agonizingly slow buildup of the Normandy beachhead, then a lightning drive to the German border. On July 24 (D + 48) the Allies held only the area whose liberation had been anticipated by D + 5. Then, from July 25 to 31, the breakthrough came at St Lô. Within less than a month Paris was liberated; by September 14 (D + 100), when the Allies had expected to be at the Seine, they were hammering at Hitler's West Wall.

12. "Circulaire du Délégué Général du C.F.L.N." [May 9, 1944], reprinted in *Les Cahiers Politiques*, No. 18 (February-March 1946), 23-26; cf. Commissariat à la Justice, *Instructions* (Algiers: 1944), pp. 5, 20-21. An insistence on orderly procedures was the invariable leitmotif of all Government instructions concerning the purge. Authors attempting to discredit the Resistance have made wide use of a "document" allegedly emanating from Emmanuel d'Astier de la Vigerie, C.F.L.N. Minister of the Interior. This "order of insurrection" called on local authorities to draw up lists of collaborators not for arrest, but for summary execution during the period "between the departure of the Germans and the arrival of the Anglo-Saxons". This procedure was to be followed in order to "assure in a few hours the revolutionary punishment of treason, conforming to the legitimate desire of the militants of the Resistance for reprisals". This, as well as similar actions, was "to give, by forcible and mass demonstrations, a popular and democratic base to the provisional government, and thus to assure the international recognition of the *de facto* government of General de Gaulle". The provenance of this "document", which contradicts every other instruction issued by the Provisional Government, is hardly reassuring. It appears for the first time in an article by Louis Rougier in *Ecrits de Paris*, No. 70 (August 1950), 104-23, and is quoted *in extenso* by Otto Abetz, the Third Reich's ambassador to occupied Paris, in his memoir *Histoire d'une politique Franco-Allemande: 1930-1950* (Paris: 1953), pp. 337-38. It is thus surprising to find it accepted and used uncritically by Alfred J. Rieber in *Stalin and the French Communist Party: 1941-1947* (New York: 1962), pp. 103-04. It is doubly surprising because Professor Rieber not only completely rejects the mythology constructed out of such "documents", but specifically discusses the doubtful origin and authenticity of purported calls to violence and insurrection (pp. 151-52 nn. 88-89).

The Provisional Government experienced no difficulty in establishing its authority. British and American military personnel did not share the antipathy to De Gaulle which permeated the White House and the Department of State. Once they had been given a free hand they were solely concerned with establishing a workable arrangement so that they could get on with the war. The Allied reaction to the Gaullist take-over in liberated Normandy is described by the Senior Civil Affairs Officer with the British Second Army, Brigadier R. M. H. Lewis.

> The first intimation I had of what amounted virtually to a coup d'état was when I found a French Colonel, stranded by the side of the road near Army Headquarters in a broken down car. When I asked him who he was, he informed me that he was the military commander for the French Military Region [Col. Pierre de Chevigné], and that the Civil Commissioner for the Region of Rouen was in Bayeux. At the same time almost, reports were received that General de Gaulle had landed, addressed a meeting in Bayeux and left a civil commissioner [M. François Coulet] behind to take charge of the civil administration. . . . A report was sent to London, but no answer, nor guidance was sent to me on this matter. Having found out that the Civil Commissioner was acceptable to the French, and that his first act was to dismiss M. Rochat, the Sous-Prefect of Bayeux, suspected of Nazi sympathies, I decided that I should accept him as the *de facto* civil authority for the Region of Rouen. I then arranged a meeting with M. Coulet, which was very cordial. . . .[13]

In July, Roosevelt reluctantly agreed to accept De Gaulle as the *de facto* authority for civil administration in France. In August, civil affairs agreements were finally signed with the Provisional Government, although formal *de facto* recognition was withheld until October.

In Northern France, during the weeks and months that followed the Allied landings, popular violence was most notable by its rarity. This did not prevent wild stories of revolutionary violence and terror from spreading. According to one authority, there were reports from Baud that the *tricolore* had been replaced by the red banner; that twenty Germans and six Frenchmen had been executed without trial; and that the *curé* and his vicar had fled fearing for their lives. When a Free French officer arrived he found that the red flag was indeed flying, together with the Union Jack and the American flag, by the side of the *tricolore*. Five, not twenty, Germans had been executed: they were sadistic prison guards who had been killed by their rioting prisoners. One Frenchman had been killed when he defended himself against

13. Coles and Weinberg, pp. 709-10.

arrest by throwing hand grenades at the arresting party. The *curé* and vicar were Breton autonomists who (correctly) feared arrest as collaborators.[14]

But not all the violence was exaggerated rumor. The occupation had given rise to hatreds and resentments that could not always be prevented from erupting into violence. While Northern France was for the most part spared the excesses of regions further south, there were killings here too. In Brittany, on the eve of the Liberation, German troops had massacred their French prisoners. At the Liberation, enraged Bretons shot several groups of Germans believed guilty of the murders together with a smaller group of collaborators. We are told that in Rennes, when the Americans drove out the Germans, two *miliciens* were hung; a third was burned alive.[15] The Allied armies frequently became involved in these affairs. In Normandy the commanding general of a Canadian division was asked by a departmental F.F.I. chief to step in and halt certain summary proceedings. H. Stuart Hughes reports that

> during the first days of liberation . . . [many] . . . American officers spent a large portion of their time in rescuing suspected collaborators from summary execution by their fellow citizens, French, Italian or German [?] as the case might be.[16]

More frequent than executions were the shearings administered to "horizontal collaborators". As much as the executions, these acts of minor violence responded to a deeply felt need for emotional release on the part of a population which for four years had been swallowing its resentment.

Father Bruckberger, an F.F.I. chaplain, later one of the chief apostles of forgiveness and reconciliation throughout the purge, had written in his diary of entering a café during the occupation that

> was full of German soldiers accompanied by French girls. As we came in, we saw one directly in front of us with a German N.C.O. I stared hard at her. She blushed to the roots of her hair. . . . Those girls could be dipped in tar and burned in the public square and it would affect me no more than a fire in the fireplace of a neighbor's house.[17]

14. Robert Aron, *Histoire de la Libération de la France: Juin 1944-Mai 1945* (Paris: 1959), pp. 216-19.

15. *Ibid.*, pp. 216-19, 325-26.

16. "The Problem of Limited Collaboration", *Confluence*, III, 2 (June 1954), 172.

17. Raymond Léopold Bruckberger, *One Sky to Share: French and American Journals* (New York: 1952), pp. 23-24.

It is more than likely that many girls who were shorn were, unbeknown to themselves or their barbers, the instrument of salvation for *miliciens* and collaborators who might otherwise have died to appease the rage of their fellow citizens.

Even where violence was repressed, there was fear on the part of the collaborators, suspicion and impatience on the part of the population at large, and a flood of denunciations pouring into the headquarters of the *gendarmerie*. The regional *commissaire* promised the population that justice would be done, and asked for an end to

> the shameful anonymous complaints that dishonored the Germans and the men of Vichy who initiated the practice. . . . We know the names of those who deserve punishment: none of them will escape. . . . They are a tiny minority among you, and we give you our solemn promise that the pitiless hand of France will strike them down. . . .[18]

In the North, which was liberated by the Allied armies, the population, while far from satisfied, was by and large willing to leave it to "the hand of France". In the South, where the Liberation was largely the work of the Resistance itself, there were many Frenchmen willing and anxious to put their own hands to the job.

A week before the Allied armies could reach Paris – and against the advice of General de Gaulle's delegate – the Resistance rose against the German forces occupying the city and seized most of the government offices. On August 25 General Leclerc's Second Armored Division entered the city as the Germans departed. General de Gaulle led a triumphal march down the Champs Elysées; the Provisional Government took over without difficulty or challenge. But the establishment of De Gaulle's Government in Paris did not automatically mean the effective extension of its authority throughout the country.

South of the Loire the Liberation proceeded very differently than it had in Northern France. On August 15 "Operation Anvil" was launched to support the southern flank of the Normandy invasion forces and provide Marseilles as a supply port: French and American forces made amphibious landings on the Riviera from Cannes to Cap Camerat. General Patch's Seventh Army and General de Lattre de Tassigny's First Army drove straight up the east side of the Rhône Valley: by August 26 they were north of Grenoble; by September 11

18. "Avis aux Populations Normandes", proclamation dated August 26, 1944, quoted in Marcel Baudot, *L'Opinion publique sous l'Occupation: L'Exemple d'un département français (1939-1945)* (Paris: 1960), pp. 264-65.

they joined forces with elements of General Patton's Third Army west of Dijon. From the Pyrenees to the Loire, from the Atlantic to the Rhône, the German forces occupying Southwestern France raced to the Northeast to escape the rapidly closing jaws of the Allied trap. Within this huge quadrilateral the Liberation was accomplished by the Resistance itself, as it harassed the withdrawing Germans and filled the vacuum of power which their departure created. There was no military reason to divert Allied troops from their strategic mission; as a result, in Southwestern France there were none of those regular forces which by their intervention – or simple presence – could have inhibited disorder. General de Gaulle realized that he

> could, of course, have provided those means [of keeping order] by re-assigning the forces from Africa to the interior of the territory. But that would have meant withholding the French Army from battle and thereby compromising our participation in the victory. I preferred to risk more or less violent explosions rather than make this disastrous renunciation.[19]

Having assumed power, the Departmental Liberation Committees and local Resistance leaders were not always happy about handing it over to parvenu Gaullist prefects "parachuted" in from Algiers. As has been noted, the instructions of the National Resistance Council to the C.D.L.'s assigned them much broader powers than were allowed by the Ordinance of April 21. Before the arrival of the new prefects, many C.D.L.'s had seen only the former instructions and were carrying them out in good faith.[20] In addition, the Resistance – and not just its Communist members – often had a revolutionary and rather romantic view of the Liberation; *résistants* much preferred to see it directed by committees of "sans-culottes" rather than by double-breasted appointees from Paris.

For a brief period the C.D.L.'s in some areas seemed to be aspiring to a sort of "dual power". An official surveying the situation in the Southeast reported that "for the C.D.L.'s it isn't the government . . . which sends its orders to the departments . . . [but] the C.D.L.'s which inform the government of their desires". Their pretensions, the report went on, extended to decreeing a general salary increase, a fifty per cent rise in family allowances, and "legislating" the confiscation of illegal profits and fines for black marketeers.[21]

19. *Mémoires de guerre* (Paris: 1954-59), Vol. III, p. 9.
20. Hostache, p. 314.
21. "Report to General de Gaulle from a high civil servant on mission in the Southeast" [September 28, 1944], De Gaulle, *Mémoires*, Vol. III, pp. 316-18.

The arrogation of state authority by the Resistance was most frequently seen – and most tragic in its consequences – with respect to the purge. There were understandable reasons for this. The instructions of the C.N.R. to the C.D.L.'s, while stressing the importance of avoiding injustice due to hasty action, assigned these committees an important role in dealing with collaborators: this role frequently overlapped that of the Government.[22] The tolerant attitude toward a certain amount of "crossroads justice", which had been adopted by even conservative resistance organizations, was surely a factor. And finally, the habit learned in the underground days of personally settling accounts with collaborators and *miliciens* was not readily set aside after the Liberation.

At least four and a half thousand summary executions took place in France in the months following the Liberation.[23] The geographic incidence of summary executions is not known with any precision, but appears to have been very uneven. American civil affairs officers reported a reign of terror in Nice which produced an estimated one hundred summary executions in two days; noting rumors of unrest in Toulouse, another officer reported his conclusion that "considering the times there is a high degree of order here and that there are no valid grounds for rumors of violent struggles". In the Dordogne there were reports of a reign of terror which lasted three months; in an area of the Drôme which was liberated by the Communist F.T.P., Emmanuel Mounier noted "l'absence de la phobie des suspects, la fièvre chaude de ce genre de crises". While government representatives usually preached tolerance to the Resistance, in the Côte d'Or the *commissaire de la République* had to warn the F.F.I. that they were adopting an over-friendly attitude toward Vichyites.[24] The only valid generalization that can be made about the Liberation is that there are no valid generalizations.

Sometimes the executions followed drum-head trials which were

---

22. *Cahiers du Témoignage Chrétien*, Vols. XXVI-XXVII (May 1944); Hostache, pp. 300, 465-70; Michel, *Courants*, pp. 335-37; United States, Office of Strategic Services, *Resolutions of the French National Council of Resistance* (Washington: 1944), pp. 51-53.

23. The evidence concerning the number of summary executions, being too involved and contradictory to be examined within the compass of a footnote, has been made the subject of a special section. See Appendix C.

24. Coles and Weinberg, pp. 764-65; Aron, *Libération*, pp. 569-72; *Bulletin des Amis d'E. Mounier*, Nos. 7-8 (December 1955), 4; Maurice Lombard, "Les Maquis et la Libération de la Bourgogne", R.H.D.G.M., No. 55 (July 1964), 48.

held discreetly ("pour éviter le spectacle") but whose results were posted publicly afterwards "to show that [the F.T.P.'s] justice is implacable but fair".[25] (According to Government estimates, roughly one-quarter of the post-Liberation summary executions were preceded by a *de facto* trial.[26]) Sometimes a *milicien* was simply shot out of hand when his identity was discovered. There were unquestionably executions that were carried out "in good faith" but in error – on the basis of insufficient or inaccurate information. At the same time many executions seem to have been committed for private gain; criminal elements sometimes infiltrated the F.F.I. or masqueraded as *résistants* to cover their lootings and murders. In other cases, partisan political advantage or revenge seems to have been the motive for assassinations. Most executions, however, were the result of either spontaneous and uncontrollable outrage, or frustration at the slowness of official justice.

The new *commissaires* and prefects did their best to appease popular anger by the rapid institution of courts-martial.[27] But when, as frequently happened, the *commissaires* commuted death sentences pronounced by the tribunals, violence often flared anew. When it was learned in Alès that the death sentence handed down against the former mayor of the town had been commuted, the local Liberation Committee led a march of protest to the *sous-préfecture*. Fearing for the life of their prisoner, the police spirited him away toward Montpellier. The outraged mob went to the prison anyway, stormed it, and lynched four of its inmates who were under sentence of death. In Montpellier, just as the police car carrying the ex-mayor was passing in front of the Palais de Justice another car blocked its way, the prisoner was abducted and shot.[28]

Some features of the Liberation have led to speculation concerning the existence of a Communist plot to seize power. The "dual power"

25. Letter from the F.T.P. leader "Doublemètre" to a subordinate commander (August 11, 1944), quoted in Aron, *Libération*, pp. 568-69.

26. J.O., A.N. Debates, November 9, 1951, p. 7835.

27. The courts-martial, which were under the direct authority of the *commissaires* and prefects (they appointed their personnel and determined their competence and procedure) should not be confused with the military tribunals, staffed with regular French Army personnel, which could be established by the *délégués militaires*.

28. *Combat*, December 30, 1944. Reporting to De Gaulle on the incident, Adrien Tixier, Minister of the Interior, noted that the crowd had been "spontaneously and sincerely exasperated by delays in trials and punishment and by the commutation accorded [the mayor] who was certainly an abominable collaborator". (De Gaulle, *Mémoires*, Vol. III, pp. 422-23.)

represented by the C.D.L.'s, and the Communist attempts to dominate those bodies, have stimulated analogies with Petrograd in 1917; overdrawn pictures of general disorder and inflated estimates of summary executions, the extravagant rhetoric of many *résistants* and the difficulty experienced by the Provisional Government in establishing its authority – all these have led to retrospective anxiety about a Communist revolution in France in the fall of 1944. Robert Aron alleges that the F.T.P. of the Dordogne received orders to proclaim "la République des Soviets du Sud de la France", and coyly withholds judgment as to whether this represented official Communist policy.[29] Herbert Luethy goes further, and talks about the establishment of "revolutionary Soviet republics" at Limoges, Toulouse, Montpellier and Nice.[30] Clearly there was no Communist revolution, but was this just luck (or De Gaulle's skill)? Was it, as Denis Brogan would have it, quoting the Duke of Wellington on Waterloo, "a close run thing"?[31] Or, as Pierre Hervé has suggested, is the speculation "haute fantaisie", advanced "pour mieux glorifier la politique de ceux qui auraient conjuré le péril".[32]

Whatever the motives of those who have stressed the danger, it was indeed "haute fantaisie". The possibility of a Communist takeover could have really existed only if virtually every factor in the situation had been different.

First of all, the "objective conditions" for revolution were not present. One factor is of obvious and overriding importance: the presence of hundreds of thousands of American and British troops sprawled across Northern France and all along the Rhône Valley. These forces could hardly have been expected to stand aside in the presence of a Communist uprising. Also, the Communists did not dispose of forces capable of mounting an insurrection aimed at the seizure of political power. The size of the Communist-dominated resistance organizations is deceptive. The fact that some C.D.L.'s were dominated by Communists – and they were a minority – usually meant no more than that some of the Committee members had succeeded in masking their true allegiance. The mainly political Front National and its military arm, the Francs-Tireurs et Partisans Français, were indeed tremendous groups, among the largest in all of the Resistance. But these groups were as large as they were precisely because the Communists, by play-

29. *Libération*, p. 594.
30. *France Against Herself* (New York: 1955), p. 102.
31. *Citizenship Today* (Chapel Hill [N.C.]: 1960), p. 59.
32. *France-Observateur*, June 11, 1964.

ing the patriotic card, had been able to attract enormous numbers of non-Communist – and even normally anti-Communist – recruits.[33] If the Communist leadership of these groups had tried to carry their troops with them into direct and armed opposition to the Provisional Government the troops would have melted away (as indeed they largely did when their leadership later went into peaceful and tentative opposition).

But uprisings are not the automatic result of even favorable objective conditions and physical resources: they must be willed, they must be carried out. The French Communist Party willed nothing of the sort. In 1939, faithful to the demands of Soviet foreign policy, they had deafened themselves to patriotic appeals and undermined the war effort. In 1944 the same fidelity demanded that they become the most ferocious of "French patriots", that they second the efforts of the Red Army by doing nothing to disrupt the French war effort, nothing that could result in a diversion of Allied troops from the western front, nothing to embarrass the wartime coalition. They could not have done otherwise and remained Communists.[34]

Nor did Communist practice support the contention that they planned a bid for power. Henri Michel notes that

> the Communists often scolded the Socialists for excessive preoccupation with postwar problems in the middle of battle. For them, the war was not over with the Liberation of France. . . . It was vital to avoid putting forward any opinion that could compromise the achievement of the common task.[35]

There is abundant testimony to the assistance given by Communists to the Provisional Government in its task of re-establishing order.

> M. Bourdeau de Fontenay [commissaire de la République at Rouen] declared that the Communists carried out his orders "blindly". . . . [Another commissaire] indicated that the Communist Party was a staunch defender of the central government, and the prefect of the department of Creuze reported that the Communist Party, "more than the S.F.I.O.

33. E.g., François Mauriac and Georges Bidault were on the executive committee of the Front National. By dispersing their militants throughout these broad fronts the Communists were deprived of even their normal disciplined action groups.

34. For an extraordinarily frank statement of the bases of Communist policy in 1944 see Benoît Frachon's speech, Confédération Générale du Travail, 26ème Congrès National [1946] (Paris: 1946), pp. 141-42.

35. Courants, p. 682.

poses as the defender of the provisional government. . . . They do not even demand a structural reform." According to another prefect, the Communists in the department of Eure-et-Loire manifested "a great patriotic discipline". In fact, in some places the Party was so outspoken in its support of the provisional government that the population, which demanded more action from Paris, turned against it.[36]

And it was the same when Communists themselves held temporary positions in the prefectoral corps. De Gaulle himself complimented Maurice Thorez' work in helping to restore order, although in terms that the Communist leader would hardly appreciate: "So far as his party's harsh and secretive rigidity allowed, he opposed the attempted abuses of the Committees of Liberation and the acts of violence over-excited groups tried to commit".[37]

The Communists' support of the Government, their eschewal of revolution, did not prevent them from taking political advantage of the opportunities offered by the disorders and fears of the Liberation. A signature on a membership application, or a sizable contribution to the Party, sometimes became " 'the best soap' for whitening a collabora-tor".[38] In many towns a leading position in the local Liberation Com-mittee was parlayed, through a timely "purging" of the local officials, into a permanent political fiefdom.[39] Jacques Debû-Bridel, who be-lieved that summary executions were excusable, "even in their errors

36. Rieber, pp. 170-71, citing Ministère de l'Intérieur, Service Central des Commissariats de la République, *Bulletin sur la situation dans les régions et les départements* Nos. 48, 49, 57, 64, 69.

37. *Mémoires*, Vol. III, p. 101. Opinion in the councils of the Party was not, however, unanimous with respect to exactly how far the Communists should go in accomodating themselves to De Gaulle and agreeing to the dissolution of "sources of revolutionary energy". A 1952 purge of the P.C.F. leadership revealed that André Marty and Charles Tillon among others thought that the Party was going further than necessary along that road. In the fall of 1944, when the Marty-Tillon group was presumably in the ascendancy, the Party protested De Gaulle's dissolution of the *milices patriotiques* – resistance auxiliaries which had been consistently supported by the Communists as a necessary security measure against "the fifth column". After Thorez' return from Moscow at the end of November the protests ceased.

38. Jacques Debû-Bridel, *Les Partis contre Charles de Gaulle* (Paris: 1948), p. 57. The Marquis d'Argenson notes a number of cases in which men badly compromised by their wartime records sought to "devenir rouges pour se faire blanchir". (*Pétain et le pétinisme: Essai de psychologie* [Paris: 1953], p. 137.) Cf. Baudot, p. 212.

39. "Report . . . from . . . the Southeast", De Gaulle, *Mémoires*, Vol. III, p. 318; Baudot, pp. 211-12.

and excesses, when they were spontaneous", reports that "too often, particularly in the Midi and Central France [they served] as the vehicles for Communist Party political vengeance. One saw *résistant* policemen pursued and sometimes shot for having arrested Communist deserters in 1939."[40] There is a certain amount of evidence which suggests that this sort of thing was not uncommon;[41] it is not clear, however, to what extent such executions represented local initiatives or general Party policy. (George Marrane, a leading Communist member of the Paris Liberation Committee, saw to the release of a number of Trotskyists whom some over-zealous Communists had arrested as part of the Paris round-up.)[42] Political motives are frequently alleged when ex-Communists were the victims of summary executions. However, since a number of former Party members became ferocious collaborators, and, in cooperation with German forces, ruthlessly tracked down their ex-comrades, the dominant motive of these executions, even when it is clear that they were carried out by Communists, must remain obscure.

Even if the threat posed to public order by summary executions was not evidence of a Communist bid for power, it had to be dealt with. And to deal with the threat, more than the normal administrative routine was required. While giving a dinner for the new British consul in Lyons, Commissaire Yves Farge learned that a mob was storming the prison where his Vichy predecessor, Alexandre Angeli, whose death sentence had just been overturned by the Court of Appeals, was being held. Also in the prison was René Cussonac, the ex-*intendant de police*, whose death sentence had not yet been carried out. Hurrying to the prison, Farge arrived to find the crowd knocking the prisoners about. The *commissaire* spoke to the crowd at length, rejected a deal which would have saved Angeli and Cussonac in return for handing over another hated prisoner, and finally talked its members into leaving.[43]

40. *Op. cit.*, pp. 56-57.
41. Cf. *Histoire du P.C.F.* (Paris: 1960-62), II, 89-90; Angelo Tasca ["Rossi"], *Les Communistes français pendant la drôle de guerre* (Paris: 1951), pp. 21, 254ff., 263.
42. Henri Denis, *Le Comité Parisien de la Libération* (Paris: 1963), p. 137.
43. Yves Farge, *Rebelles, soldats et citoyens* (Paris: 1946), pp. 241-45. (Cussonac was executed legally a few days later.) On another occasion Farge found his rhetoric futile. After commuting the sentence of an alleged *milicien* he organized a meeting at which he explained his decision to the population. On leaving the meeting he learned that as he had begun speaking the man whose sentence he had commuted, together with four others, had been forcibly taken from the prison and executed. (*Ibid.*, pp. 229-31.)

There were those, like Farge, who were energetic not only in dealing with attempted lynchings as they occurred but also in disarming "all those who were playing at being characters in *romans policiers*".[44] But many local officials displayed what Minister of the Interior Tixier called "an excessive docility" toward resistance groups.[45] In addition to being undermanned and underarmed, the *gendarmerie* and *gardes mobiles* were, as De Gaulle remarked, "morally inhibited by the use which Vichy had made of them".[46] By shake-ups in the new prefectoral corps, by the issuance of unambiguous orders for the repression of lynchings and summary executions, by De Gaulle himself going on tour "to give the government machine a start in the right direction", the violence and disorder were brought under control.[47]

In January 1945 the Government, by a symbolic act, made it clear that it would tolerate no yielding before the threat of violence. The previous October, in Maubeuge, an angry mob had stormed the local prison demanding the execution of two collaborators whose death sentences had been commuted by General de Gaulle. The mob threatened to massacre all the other inmates of the jail if it did not receive satisfaction; the three F.F.I. officers in charge did as the mob demanded. Brought to trial in Paris, the three officers were sentenced to prison terms of five to seven years.[48]

Numerous other arrests of *résistants* for unauthorized executions took place during early 1945;[49] while many of them were either released or pardoned after a short time, a considerable malaise was created in Resistance circles, particularly on the Left. Pascal Copeau wrote, apropos the arrests:

> During four terrible years the best of the French learned to kill, to assassinate, to sabotage, to derail trains, sometimes to pillage and always to disobey what they were told was the law. . . . Who taught these Frenchmen, who gave them the order to assassinate? Who if not you,

44. *Ibid.*, p. 223.
45. De Gaulle, *Mémoires*, Vol. III, p. 422.
46. *Loc. cit.*, p. 9.
47. *Loc. cit.*, pp. 8-10, 418-19, 422-23, 579-80; Emmanuel d'Astier de la Vigerie, *Sept fois sept jours* (Paris: 1947), pp. 200ff.; J.O., A.C.P. Debates, February 20, 1945, p. 126.
48. *Monde*, January 13, 1945.
49. See the official Government statement concerning mass arrests in Béziers, quoted *in extenso* in Aron, *Libération*, pp. 609-11. For the Government's criterion in defining culpable and non-culpable "acts of resistance", see the statement of Minister of Justice Pierre-Henri Teitgen in the Assembly. (J.O., A.N.C. [I] Debates, December 27, 1945, p. 425.)

mon général? If not you, M. Maurice Schumann, La Pasionaria of the microphone? If not you, Georges Bidault, president of the C.N.R.?[50]

There were a few further lynchings, notably at Gap in February, where twelve *miliciens* and *doriotistes* were forcibly removed from prison and the bodies of ten of them found the next day.[51] Isolated assassinations of suspected collaborators continued for a few months, then petered out.

The Liberation had been costly for *résistants* and "collabos" alike. Thousands of *résistants* never lived to see the Liberation for which they had fought: they lie in graves on the Vercors and the Plateau de Glières; their sacrifice is commemorated on plaques which begin: "Ici est tombé, le 24 août, pour la Libération de Paris . . .". Thousands of their enemies were summarily executed, either with no trial at all or after a simulacrum of a trial. Alleged collaborators were often deprived of the fair hearing and due process which democracies must grant even – or especially – to those who deride or destroy them. No doubt many of those executed were innocent; certainly most would not have been executed under regular procedures given the trend of verdicts later on. It is tempting to say that they died for nothing. Yet it may be that without the release of accumulated tensions by the blood-letting of the Liberation the regular trials would not have been as lenient as they often were. The collaborators who were killed in the first days may have been, like the girls who submitted to the shears, the sacrificial offering that purchased leniency for many of their colleagues.

50. *Action*, January 19, 1945. Agitation for the release of imprisoned *résistants* was not, however, restricted to the extreme left. (See, e.g., *Monde*, March 30, 1945, and the resolution of the League for the Rights of Man, *Cahiers des Droits de l'Homme*, June 1945, 2.) After the pardon accorded the three F.F.I.'s in May, a "National Committee for the Liberation of Imprisoned Patriots" was formed to agitate for further acts of clemency. It had the endorsement of the M.R.P., S.F.I.O. and P.C.F.

51. *Combat*, February 8, 1945. See also *Aurore*, February 17 and Aron, *Libération*, pp. 609-11.

Chapter 5

THE NEW BROOM

> The Government intends to proceed to the necessary eliminations and reforms in recruitment . . . but does not intend to discharge the great majority of state employees, most of whom have sought only to serve the nation during the terrible years of the occupation and the usurpation. It is easy to denigrate this or that individual or category of individuals in the administration – easy, but often unjust or exaggerated. In any case, governments have the kind of servants that they deserve; it is when the public authorities themselves give an example of competence, impartiality and responsibility that they have the best chance of being served as they should be.   GENERAL DE GAULLE
> July 25, 1944[1]

THE first part of the Provisional Government's program for the "renouvellement" of France to be put into effect was the purging of the administration. Before the police could effectively maintain order, collaborationist policemen had to be removed. Before the magistrature could – with any semblance of moral authority – judge collaborators, judges who had been zealous Vichyites had to be eliminated. As with other programs for Liberated France, detailed plans had been made in Algiers for the criteria and procedures to be adopted. According to one account, General de Gaulle's first question to the provisional police prefect of Paris on the day of that city's liberation was: "How is the purge going in your department?" When told that the planned committees were being organized he urged the official to move quickly, stressing the necessity of finishing with the task within a few weeks.[2] The concern with speed in the purge of the administration was shared by all groups and parties. While De Gaulle's optimistic estimate of the time within which it could be accomplished was not met, the bulk of the task was completed within a relatively brief period – long before the purge in other areas.

The attitude of the Provisional Government concerning the administrative purge was similar in some respects to that adopted toward Vichy legislation. The Government could declare that "in law the Republic has never ceased to exist" and, as a corollary, that all acts of

1. *Mémoires de guerre* (Paris: 1954-59), Vol. II, pp. 583-84.
2. Robert Aron, *Histoire de la Libération de la France: Juin 1944-Mai 1945* (Paris: 1959), p. 441.

79

the Vichy Regime were null and void. In practice it recognized that Vichy had legislated on thousands of matter-of-fact questions; to sweep away four years of Vichy enactments would have produced chaos. Accordingly, De Gaulle's Government was selective, striking down Vichy's more noxious enactments (racial laws, etc.) while provisionally keeping most in force.

The same kind of discrimination had to be exercised in purging the administration. While there had been many new appointments in the upper levels of the civil service under Vichy, the overwhelming majority of *fonctionnaires* in office at the Liberation were prewar appointees, and they had all, to some extent, "served Vichy" and "collaborated with the Germans". Just as the Government kept most of Vichy's decrees in force because they were politically innocuous, so the vast majority of those who administered them would be kept in office, and on the same grounds. The recommendations of the underground Comité Général d'Etudes and De Gaulle's own wishes on the subject were in accord: no radical purge of the civil service.[3]

But rejection of a root and branch purge did not mean no purge at all. Both the Resistance and the Provisional Government were committed to a housecleaning of the administration. In September 1943 the Algiers Committee had enacted legislation for a purge of the French administration in North Africa. The definition of punishable offenses in the Ordinance of June 27, 1944, which instituted the administrative purge in the metropole was almost exactly identical with that of the previous September. It included any act, writing, or personal attitude which aided the enemy, harmed the French or Allied war effort, or jeopardized constitutional institutions or fundamental public liberties, as well as any attempt to draw material advantage from new Vichy regulations.[4] (In practice this last was extended to include German regulations.)

At the same time, the definition of punishable offenses in the Ordinance of June 27 was very close to those kinds of behavior juridically characterized as constituting "national indignity" in the Ordinance of August 26.[5] The administrative purge was, indeed, to be a rapid procedure for ridding the state service of those who were "indigné" in the same way that the *chambres civiques* were to remove them from public

3. *Cahiers Politiques*, No. 2 (July 1943); De Gaulle, *Mémoires, loc. cit.*
4. Cf. the September 1943 text quoted above, p. 50, and that of the June 27 Ordinance, J.O. (Alger), July 6, 1944, p. 536.
5. See below, pp. 147-48. The inclusion of "personal attitude" was, however, peculiar to the Ordinance of June 27.

life in general. The definition of offenses was in both cases broad because of the endless variety of ways in which one could be guilty of antinational acts. In neither case did the legislator want to allow an unworthy Frenchman to be able to hide behind the letter of the law.

The scope of the June 27 Ordinance extended not only to members of the regular administrative machine, but included the traditionally "irremovable" judiciary, the armed forces, and employees of semi-public, state-subsidized or state-chartered corporations. While the Ordinance did not set up the actual procedural mechanism of the administrative purge – this was left to individual ministerial decrees – it did authorize immediate suspension of all suspect employees at half pay while awaiting a final decision, and laid down certain procedural guarantees for the accused which the ministries were obliged to follow in their individual decrees.[6] The range of administrative sanctions which could be imposed ran the gamut from an official reprimand or loss of an honorific title to dismissal without pension. If the competent ministerial body found evidence of misconduct warranting judicial action, it was to forward the dossier to the State prosecutor.

Frequently the same individual was subject to the jurisdiction of both an administrative purge commission and a *cour de justice* or *chambre civique* – the bodies set up to try cases of collaboration or "national indignity".[7] A conviction by either of these latter institutions made any administrative sanction nugatory since it carried with it automatic dismissal from any state employment without pension (the maximum penalty which could be inflicted administratively).[8] On

6. The principal procedural requirement was that no sanction might be applied unless the accused had been first informed of the charges aaginst him and afforded an opportunity to answer them, either orally or in writing. Any suspended employee subsequently adjudged blameless would, upon his reinstatement, receive the half of his salary which had been withheld.

7. These jurisdictions are discussed in Chapter VII.

8. There were, however, a number of cases in which, even after an individual had been automatically excluded from public employment by such a verdict, a separate and deliberative administrative purge measure was taken. The ministries concerned may have acted to prevent a subsequent amnesty of the penal sanction reintegrating the individual in the administration. (In the event, the three major amnesty laws affected both administrative and judicial action.) As a result of the coexistence of these two quite independent but overlapping ways of losing state employment, it is quite impossible to have any idea of the total number of state employees who lost their jobs through the operation of the purge in all its separate areas and manifestations. In the few cases where available data allows me to indicate the number of *épurés* in a given branch of government I am, unless otherwise indicated, speaking solely of those hit by purely administrative sanctions.

the other hand, an acquittal before either of these courts, before or after an administrative hearing, was not binding on a purge commission.

Events outran the preparations of the Provisional Government, and the first steps in the administrative housecleaning of France were carried out before the Ordinance of June 27 was promulgated. The new *commissaires de la République* who replaced the Vichy Regional Prefects began to purge local administrations immediately following the Allied landings. The new authorities did not operate in a legislative vacuum. The ordinances which created the *commissaires* and provided for the naming of a completely new set of prefects under them simultaneously removed from office all Vichy prefects. They also empowered the new regional administrators to suspend from office whichever local officials it seemed desirable to remove. The handing over of authority from one set of prefects to another was accomplished in various fashions. On one occasion, we are told, the old prefect lent his uniform to his replacement, with the helpful suggestion that he might want to replace the buttons, which bore the Vichy *francisque*. In a few departments Vichy prefects were shot by *résistants* during the Liberation.[9]

Local civil servants were generally not severely hit by the administrative purge. Pre-Liberation instructions to the new prefects, while giving them full powers in this regard, suggested that the functioning of local services demanded "a certain indulgence" with respect to the purge.[10] The C.F.L.N. further suggested that

the criterion [should be] public scandal . . . the impossibility of maintaining an individual in office in the face of hostile criticism from the population. . . . Obedience to legislative measures, weakness of character,

9. Aron, *Libération*, pp. 96-97; Pierre Henry, *Histoire des préfets* (Paris: 1950), pp. 343-45; Brian Chapman, *The Prefects and Provincial France* (London: 1955), p. 59. After hearings before the Ministry of the Interior's purge commission, 60 members of the prefectoral corps were dismissed (with or without pension), some were put on half pay, others received lesser sanctions. (Report of Minister of the Interior Adrien Tixier to the Consultative Assembly, J.O., A.C.P. Debates, December 27, 1944, pp. 604-07; Chapman, pp. 60-61; Henry, pp. 345-49.) Jules Moch suggested that in principle prefects should be removed and subordinate members of the corps (*sous préfets, chefs de cabinet*) retained; exceptions should of course be allowed in the case of *résistants* in the first category and ardent Vichyites in the second. (*Le Parti socialiste au peuple de France* [Paris: 1945], p. 66.) In general, this policy seems to have been followed.

10. "Circulaire du Délégué Général du C.F.L.N." [May 9, 1944], reprinted in *Les Cahiers Politiques*, No. 18 (February-March 1946), 23-26.

lack of courage – these are all regrettable, but should not by themselves be the cause of suspensions.[11]

Commissaire Yves Farge, in his first proclamation to the liberated population of Lyons, reminded them that most civil servants had behaved loyally, and pointed out that to do so they had had to disguise their true feelings.[12]

The other local housecleaning chore assigned to the new prefects concerned mayors and municipal and departmental councillors. They were to remove all elected local officials who had favored the Germans or Vichy. The vacancies were to be filled by the prefect, on the advice of the Departmental Liberation Committee. The new appointees were to be named from among

> Frenchmen and Frenchwomen having actively participated in the "resistance" against the enemy and the usurper, taking account, on the one hand, of the majority expressed at the last . . . election, and on the other of the tendencies that have appeared . . . since the Liberation.[13]

In fact, the Councils were rarely fully reconstructed until after the local elections in the spring of 1945.

Once the Provisional Government was installed in Paris the purge began in earnest. The original target date for the end of the purge in the central offices of the ministries was February 15, 1945, and for other levels a month later. In the event, while the bulk of the cases were disposed of quickly, some proceedings dragged on for years.

The police purge was, of course, of particular importance. For reasons of security it was necessary to remove unreliable elements; since policemen were particularly "visible" members of the administration, failure to purge policemen with a collaborationist reputation would discredit the Government in the eyes of the Resistance and the population at large. In Paris the police had played a major role in the August insurrection which preceded the entry of Leclerc's troops – indeed it was their strike which triggered the rising. The strike did a good deal to save their reputation; by their leading role in the insurrection they partially erased popular resentment over the role they had played during four years of German and Vichy repression. Even so, almost 700 Paris policemen, including many high officials, were arrested within two weeks of the Liberation.[14] By the end of the year the Government

11. G.P.R.F., Commissariat à la Justice, *Instructions* (Algiers: 1944), pp. 14-17.
12. Farge, *Rebelles, soldats et citoyens* (Paris: 1946), pp. 189-92.
13. Ordinance of April 21, 1944, J.O. (Alger), April 22, 1944, pp. 325-27.
14. *Combat*, September 7, 1944.

reported that 5,000 had been suspended from the various police forces throughout France.[15]

Another critical problem – and consequently one of the first state corps to be dealt with – was the magistrature. Without a trustworthy judiciary the entire program for the punishment of collaboration and "antinational behavior" could not be carried out. At the same time the problem of purging the magistrature was an extraordinarily delicate one.

Many of the problems faced by the French magistrature during the years of Vichy were common to other state corps. Jews, Freemasons and other suspect individuals were removed from their ranks; faithful supporters of the "National Revolution" were brought in to replace them. But there were significant differences. Unlike ordinary civil servants, the magistracy was required to take a special oath of allegiance to the "Chef d'Etat" – similar in inspiration to the "Fuehrer Oath" exacted by Hitler. More important, the French judges, the traditionally independent guardians of justice, were made the instruments of policies that were not only partisan and flagrantly irregular but frequently murderous as well.

The oath had been refused by only one judge in all of France, and thus was hardly useful to the Provisional Government as a criterion in evaluating judicial conduct under the Vichy Regime.[16] In any case, the Free French in London and some (but not all) resistance organizations had counselled acceptance of the oath, since the alternative was to see captured *résistants* come before a judiciary even more Pétainized than it already was. After the Liberation, Justice Minister Pierre-Henri Teitgen pointed out this fact, and maintained that, by taking it, the magistracy had been enabled to save thousands of lives. He also held that the oath was null because obtained under constraint.[17]

The criterion had to be the individual's judicial conduct, and this often presented no clear guide. Frequently it had been a question of

15. J.O., A.C.P. Debates, December 27, 1944, pp. 604-07. The only final figures on the police purge concern only the Sûreté Nationale, in which a total of 2,019 sanctions of various kinds were taken, including 1,162 dismissals. (J.O., A.N. Debates, March 12, 1954, p. 831.)

16. The one recalcitrant magistrate – M. Paul Didier – was interned by Vichy. Of course, by the time the oath was demanded, in the summer of 1941, those most likely to refuse it on political grounds had been dismissed from the judiciary.

17. J.O., A.C.P. Debates, August 1, 1945, pp. 1723-27; A.N.C. (I) Debates, February 19, 1946, p. 369. Some sort of record for casuistry was set by the anonymous magistrate who justified the taking of the oath to the Head

passing an unjust sentence short of death lest the case – or future cases – be taken out of the judge's hands and put in those of a Vichy fanatic. The dilemma became excruciating when it extended to a choice between sentencing some innocents to death, in the name of French justice, or seeing a larger number executed by the Germans.[18] Given the Provisional Government's acceptance of the legitimacy of serving as a judge under the Vichy Regime, it was impossible to clearly define what was and what was not acceptable judicial conduct.

There had been a good deal of support in the Resistance for making participation in Vichy's special "anti-terrorist" courts automatically sanctionable, and punishable with death when the courts had ordered the execution of *résistants*.[19] The Government, however, preferred to follow the advice of the generally conservative Comité National Judiciare which opposed any condemnation *en bloc* of those who sat on the Special Courts, proposing instead dismissal for those among them who had enthusiastically carried out Vichy orders, and lesser sanctions only for those who had "complacently" carried them out.[20]

In dealing administratively with the magistrature, as in dealing with other state employees – and, indeed, in virtually all judicial proceedings as well – the search for clear guidelines had to be abandoned. The "national indignity" concept, albeit broad and imprecise, offered the only possible guide. Had the individual, within the limits of his situation, behaved as an upright citizen, a good Republican and a loyal Frenchman?

In the particular case of the judiciary, a unique dilemma was posed;

---

of State on the grounds that it mentioned neither Pétain's name nor the equivalent, "le maréchal"; thus for all who like himself believed that Vichy was illegal, they were *really* swearing allegiance to Albert Lebrun. (*Voix de Paris*, December 12, 1945.) It is legitimate, though futile, to speculate as to how often advice from London was a real factor in the decision to take the oath.

18. The question was posed in its sharpest form at the trial of the five judges who had, in a 1941 trial, sentenced three Communists to death in reprisal for the shooting of a German officer. The Germans had originally demanded ten executions; after negotiations, the victims were finally reduced to three – all of whom had been in prison at the time of the shooting. Four of the five judges were sentenced to terms ranging from life at hard labor to two years in prison; one, who had opposed the sentence, was acquitted. See Maurice Garçon, *Procès sombres* (Paris: 1950), pp. 83-136.

19. U.S., O.S.S., *Resolutions of the French National Council of Resistance* (Washington: 1944), p. 64; *Le Palais Libre*, No. 4 (November 1943).

20. Speech by P.-H. Teitgen, J.O., A.N.C. (II) Debates, August 6, 1946, p. 3011.

the more rigorous the purge of the magistracy, the fewer judges would be available to aid in the work of conducting the trials of collaborators; on the other hand, an insufficient purge in that area would risk allowing collaborators to be judged by their secret sympathizers. The situation was aggravated by two additional factors: the number of magistrates killed or taken prisoner in the campaign of 1940 or deported to Germany during the occupation, and the enormous increase in the pile-up of ordinary criminal cases, which was many times greater than the prewar average. The Government resolved to move ahead as rapidly as possible to a rigorous purge of the judiciary, at the same time taking various measures to both recruit additional judicial personnel and free judges from normal duties for work with the *cours de justice*, which soon would be employing half of the 2,000-man judicial corps.

Within two weeks of the Liberation of Paris a central purge commission for the magistrature was established which was divided into sub-sections manned by both judges and *résistants*. Almost twenty per cent of the judicial corps passed before the commission, and by January well over half of these – a total of 266 judges – had been suspended.[21] By May 1945 the "irremovability of the judiciary", temporarily suspended to deal with the unprecedented experience of the Vichy Regime, was back in force.

Purge commissions were quickly established in all departments of government. The commissions were usually made up of both ministerial employees and *résistants* nominated by the C.N.R. or some other group designated in the ministerial decree. Sometimes there were special provisions concerning their composition, such as the requirement that the commission dealing with the prison administration include two former political prisoners, or that the P.T.T. commission include either the widow of a man shot by a firing-squad during the occupation or an employee who had been imprisoned and released only at the Liberation. They often included quite subordinate personnel (a *concierge* and a supply clerk were on the commission for civilian personnel of the War Ministry), but the chairmen were frequently

---

21. Details concerning other lesser sanctions and, more important, how many of the 266 suspensions resulted in dismissals, have never been made public. What fragmentary information has been disclosed is to be found in: J.O., A.C.P. Debates, February 20, 1945, p. 122; J.O., A.N.C. (II) Debates, August 6, 1946, pp. 3007-09; J.O., C.R. Debates, January 18, 1955, pp. 58-59; *Bulletin Hebdomadaire d'Informations Judiciares*, No. 8 (June 2, 1945).

distinguished – Raymond Aron headed one purge commission. The commissions might receive complaints from any source (barring anonymous denunciations) and the commissions considered all complaints received. Their findings were, however, only recommendations; the competent minister made the final decision.[22]

How did the commissions decide the cases brought before them?[23] Some categories of activity were always a ground for sanctions. Membership in a collaborationist organization, for example, was a sufficient ground. So were such acts as informing on the anti-Vichy opinions of colleagues or subordinates, mistreatment of Jews or *résistants*, voluntary aid to Germany, or attempting to profit from the misfortunes of Jewish businessmen. The normal performance of duty was not culpable, but excessive zeal could be, particularly if its "antinational" consequences were apparent:

> An Interior Ministry official who in 1942 and 1943 made studies and recommendations to improve the training of police units employed to track down escapees from the labor draft, and who devised a faster method of checking on the issuance of identity cards, could incur a sanction, as could also a police captain who took it upon himself to correspond with officials of the Information Ministry and the premier's office in order to propose a plan for the strengthening of police and

22. Justice Minister Teitgen, defending himself in the Assembly against charges of not having sufficiently purged the magistrature, said that of 418 commission decisions submitted to him, he approved 295, imposed heavier penalties than those recommended in 103 cases, and softened the commission's recommendation in only twenty instances. (J.O., A.N.C. [II] Debates, August 6, 1946, pp. 3007-09.) Minister of the Interior Tixier maintained that with respect to commission decisions on the higher echelons of his department, he accepted all recommendations with the exception of one which he sent back for reconsideration on the grounds that the proposed sanction was not sufficiently severe. (J.O., A.C.P. Debates, December 1, 1944, p. 399.) Whether these instances are representative of the impact of ministerial review on commission verdicts it is impossible to say.

23. The following remarks on the commissions' criteria are based on Elijah Ben-Zion Kaminsky's "An Anti-Subversive Program in the French Public Service: The French Epuration Administration of 1944-53" (unpublished Ph.D. dissertation, Harvard University, 1962), pp. 132-91. Dr. Kaminsky studied Conseil d'Etat decisions on appeals from purge commission decisions. Since most of the appeals were based on alleged procedural rather than substantive flaws in the original proceedings, the Conseil reports do not, as might be supposed, give an unrepresentative selection of substantive criteria. Unfortunately there is no way of deducing from the Conseil's jurisprudence the relative frequency with which different kinds of culpable conduct became the object of a sanction. The records of the original proceedings are not available.

propaganda operations [with a view to his own promotion]. On the other hand, public health personnel and other officials who may have inadvertently and unintentionally aided Vichy or the Occupant through perfectly routine and wholly professional execution of their duties were cleared, and this even when patriots and resisters were arrested or aliens deported.[24]

As has been remarked, the definition of offenses in the ordinance on the administrative purge included "offenses of expression" and "personal attitudes". Among the kinds of opinion sanctioned were "rejoicing over the defeat of France", "remarks openly displaying a desire for Franco-German *rapprochement*", "language insulting the French Resistance" and manifestations of hatred of the Jews. Culpable opinions might have been expressed in any form – one employee was punished for having been the author of "sonnets insulting to M. Churchill" published in *Gringoire* in August 1940. Private, off-duty remarks as well as public statements or writings were punished, although an exception was made in the case of Vichyite remarks addressed to a superior when it could be demonstrated that they had been made with the intention of stilling the superior's suspicions concerning the employee's real opinions. No harmful effect of the culpable expressions had to be demonstrated, and indeed, the attempt to publish "antinational" opinions was a *malum in se*, just as much as their actual publication. However, indication of an intent to publish, as opposed to an attempt, was not punishable.

The list of possible offenses defies categorization. A schoolteacher's continued attendance at collaborationist lectures was adjudged punishable on the grounds that this "raised the risk of exerting a grievous influence". There were cases of "guilt by association", and while in general there was a presumption of innocence in the case of association with French collaborators, it was otherwise when the individual associated with Germans.

The factors which might mitigate or excuse the offense charged also varied greatly. Membership in a proscribed collaborationist group might be excused if an individual joined without realizing the nature of the organization, and then rapidly resigned. (But being delinquent in paying dues was not accepted in mitigation.) A police officer was cleared of charges of having participated in a raid against a *maquis* encampment because he had believed that he was taking part in an operation against common criminals masquerading as *résistants*. Many civil servants invoked the defense of the "double game" – that they

24. Kaminsky, p. 135.

had worked for Vichy only in order to be able to work at the same time for the Resistance. The commissions required that an organic connection between the two be shown; mere parallel activity was not acceptable as a justification. (In effect, the individual had to show that like Penelope he unravelled every night what he wove during the day.) There was a tendency to excuse simple Pétainism in the first months of the Vichy Regime, but never after November 1942. In Alsace-Lorraine, on the other hand, account was taken of the increase in German pressure with the passage of time, and even Nazi Party membership was excused if it began in late 1943 or 1944.

Although some generalizations can be made, any attempt to construct a consistent jurisprudence based on purge commission decisions must fail. It seems likely that in most cases a decision was reached "instinctively" (applying the "national indignity" concept), and then formal criteria were adjusted to impose a semblance of system on the commissions' jurisprudence. The reliance on the "national indignity" concept can be seen not only through the general impression derived from examination of commission decisions but also in the commissions' adoption of specific criteria found in the Ordinance of August 26, 1944, on National Indignity, but not in the Ordinance of June 27, 1944, which established the Administrative Purge. The commissions considered membership in organizations listed in the Ordinance of August 26 as *prima facie* evidence of "antinational behavior"; they accepted Resistance activity as a mitigating circumstance; they adopted the concept of an "offense of position" (e.g., an executive position in the Commissariat of Jewish Affairs). That the definition of the nature of offenses followed the decision on individual guilt can be demonstrated in many cases – perhaps the most striking example is that of two members of the prosecution staff at the Riom Trial, considered by the same purge commission. One of them was subjected to a sanction purely on the basis of this "offense of position"; the other was cleared.

Naturally the purge did not strike all ministries with equal rigor. It was most severe in the Ministry of Information, one that had not only been heavily infiltrated by Vichyites and collaborationists, but within which written texts could be produced to confound their authors, thus avoiding ambiguities about conduct. Of 500 employees in the central office in Paris, three-quarters were hit by a sanction of some kind, with a high proportion of dismissals. Other "political" ministries or corps, such as the Ministries of Justice and the Interior and the Conseil d'Etat had relatively many more sanctions than "technical" ministries such as Public Health.[25] The Finance Ministry and the Ministry of Foreign Affairs were also among those passed over lightly by the purge, in the latter case at least because the particularly strong *esprit de corps* within the Ministry moved officials to "protect their own".[26]

Out of a total of close to a million civil servants, 11,343 received sanctions of one kind or another under the administrative purge. Of these, somewhat more than 5,000 were removed from office.[27] In addition, an unknown number were either dismissed or demoted under the Ordinance of November 14, 1944, in which the Government gave itself two and a half months to review and revise all Vichy nominations and promotions in the administration. Another program – aimed at reducing the size of the civil service – had a tangential relation to the administrative purge. The Government listed (last) among the criteria to be applied in dismissing superfluous employees: (1) whether they were special Vichy appointees; (2) their attitude toward the Resistance; (3) whether they had received a sanction short of dismissal under the purge.[28]

The purge in the armed forces was organized on different principles from those which governed the purge in civilian branches of the

25. No systematic purge statistics by ministry have ever been made public, despite repeated requests from all sides. All generalizations must thus be constructed from fragmentary data released from time to time. See in particular the radio talk delivered on February 15, 1945, by P.-H. Teitgen, printed in *Cahiers Français d'Information*, No. 2 (February 23, 1945), 8-9. In the purge of the Conseil d'Etat, which was completed by December 20, over a third of its 152 members were called before its purge commission. Thirty-six of these received some sort of sanction, usually dismissal. (J.O., A.C.P. Debates, February 20, 1945, p. 122.)

26. *Monde*, January 12 and September 19, 1945; Raymond Brugère, *Veni, vidi, Vichy . . . et la suite: Témoignages, 1940-1945* (Paris: 1953), p. 152.

27. These figures do not include local government employees, for whom no figures are available, but among whom in any case sanctions were rare. About 5,000 employees of semi-public corporations and nationalized industries also received sanctions of various kinds. It should be reiterated that these figures do *not* include individuals automatically excluded from state employment following a judicial decision. The 11,343 sanctions have been broken down according to their nature and severity following various systems. Cf. J.O., A.N. Debates, August 3, 1948, p. 5230; J.O., A.N. Debates, January 25, 1951, p. 408; J.O., C.R. Documents, 1953, No. 276.

28. Law No. 46-195 of February 15, 1946 (J.O., February 16, pp. 1378 1379); Finance Ministry Circular No. 40 B/4 of February 28, 1946 (J.O., March 1, pp. 1783-85); Law No. 47-1680 of September 3, 1947 (J.O., September 4, pp. 8768-70); Finance Ministry Circular No. 127-36/B/4 of December 31, 1947 (J.O., January 2, 1948, pp. 42-45).

administration. A purge of sorts had been carried out in the Army of Africa while the Provisional Government was still in Algiers. There remained the so-called "Armistice Army" – the make-believe force that the Germans allowed Vichy to retain until November 1942 when it was dissolved.

On August 27, 1944, a circular was issued by Commissaire à la Guerre André Diethelm to the generals commanding the northern and southern military regions; it ordered the suspension of all officers of the Army of the Armistice who had neither participated in the Resistance nor joined the F.F.I. during the Liberation. They were to account for their activity during the occupation; if their explanations were found unsatisfactory by a jury of honor they were to be struck from the army lists.[29] Accustomed by tradition and upbringing to receiving clear directives, the officers of the Armistice Army had floundered and done nothing when no orders were forthcoming; the absence of a legitimate authority which could have commanded their return to the battle was their excuse. In effect, the Government said to them what a military court said to Marshal Bazaine who had offered the same defense seventy-five years before: "Il y avait la France".

Of course, this procedure placed an enormous premium on geographical happenstance. Army officers who chanced to be assigned to North Africa – and who were as loyally Pétainist as their colleagues in the metropole – wound up wearing the *Croix de la Libération*. Officers assigned to duty in unoccupied France – who had been no more and no less obedient to orders than those in North Africa – wound up wearing mufti.

The Army purge coincided with a broad program of reduction in the size of the armed forces. This fact, coupled with the secretiveness which surrounds all purge statistics, makes it difficult to arrive at even an approximate figure. The most common estimate is that 5,000 officers were removed from the Army of the Fourth Republic for reasons connected with their wartime behavior; the actual number is probably somewhat smaller.[30]

29. The relevant portions of the circular (No. 10,010) are quoted in Jean Montigny, "L'Epuration dans l'Armée", *Ecrits de Paris*, No. 70 (August 1950), 53-54, and in *Requête aux Nations Unies sur les violations des droits de l'homme*, submitted by the Union pour la Restauration et la Défense du Service Public (Paris: 1951), p. 154.

30. Cf. Raoul Girardet (ed.), *La Crise militaire française, 1945-1962: Aspects sociologiques et idéologiques* (Paris: 1964), pp. 20-22; Paul-Marie de la Gorce, *The French Army: A Military-Political History* (New York: 1963), p. 336; J.O., A.N. Debates, May 19, 1949 (2nd session), pp. 2704-05.

In the Navy purge, which was carried out in similar fashion, officers of flag rank were hard hit, but the purge as a whole never approached the severity of that in the Army. Despite this, internal divisions after the Liberation were deeper in the Navy. The amalgamation of the Free French forces and the (Pétainist) Army of Africa in 1943, after which the two fought shoulder to shoulder in Tunisia, Italy and on the Rhine, served to reconcile those who had originally followed different conceptions of honor and duty. The Navy, on the other hand, had no proud memories at all of the war years. They had fired on the Allies at Dakar, preferred Turkish internment to war against the Axis after the Syrian campaign; at Casablanca the Navy was the force most actively engaged against the Allies; at Bizerte thirteen French warships had been handed over to the Germans. Finally, at Toulon, the fleet had scuttled rather than flee to North Africa. While among the lower ranks the impossibility of finding technically trained replacements kept the purge within narrow limits, flag officers were removed in wholesale fashion and replaced with naval officers who had rallied to the Free French. The belief that the road to advancement was thus closed to those not within the charmed circle, combined with shame at its war-time role, exacerbated bitterness in the Navy.[31]

Despite the differences between the two services, for years after the war Army messes and Navy wardrooms were divided by the *crise de conscience* which the armed forces, more than any other section of society, had endured from 1940 to 1944. The purge, however, was the symbol and not the cause of the division and bitterness.

The total number of those removed from the French administration would doubtless have been much greater if it had not been for two factors: General de Gaulle's resolve to limit the purge as much as possible; the passive resistance to the purge of many officials within the ministries. In fact, many who were thrown out the front door quickly returned through the rear. Others, as time went by, either secured the revision of their original sanction or were reintegrated into the civil service thanks to successive amnesties.[32]

31. Cf. Rear Admiral Paul Auphan and Jacques Mordal, *The French Navy in World War II* (Annapolis [Md.]: 1959), pp. 373-80; La Gorce, *French Army*, pp. 316-17, 342-44, 350 *et passim*; J.O., A.N. Debates, May 19, 1949 (2nd session), pp. 2704-05.
32. Cf. Jacques Isorni, "L'Epuration Administrative", *Défense de l'Occident*, Nos. 39-40 (January-February 1957), 90-91; Claude Bourdet, "Pour que Revive la Collaboration", *France-Observateur*, November 6, 1952.

The administrative purge – or at least *an* administrative purge – was unquestionably necessary. In "political" ministries such as Information and Foreign Affairs the need to remove those who had been spokesmen for collaboration was obvious; equally obvious was the need for a cleanup of such key corps as the police and the magistrature. Even in "technical" ministries it was clear that an intolerable situation would have been created if *fonctionnaires résistants* remained under the authority of outspoken Vichyites and collaborationists. Resistance spokesmen complained unceasingly of the inadequacy of the purge being carried out by the Government; if the Government had been less rigorous than it was it would have risked a real explosion.

However, the practical effect of the purge in furthering the *renouvellement de la France* is doubtful – even without the reintegrations and revisions which partially nullified its effect. Aside from policy-making or "sensitive" personnel, most *fonctionnaires* perform their work well or badly according to their skills and dispositions, not their politics. In any case it appears that a good many of those whose conduct was reproved in the purge acted through sycophancy or opportunism rather than for ideological motives. No one has yet devised a satisfactory system for "purging" these qualities and replacing them with principled rectitude – certainly the *épuration administrative* did not.

To the extent that this can be accomplished the results, according to some, are not necessarily an unmixed blessing. A number of writers have maintained that De Gaulle's "dissidence" and his subsequent punishment of those who were "loyal" destroyed the tradition of obedience and respect for constituted authority in the French administration and particularly in the Army.[33] They point to the Army revolts in Algeria as the whirlwind which De Gaulle has reaped; they point to the *deuxième clandestinité* of Georges Bidault and Jacques Soustelle as an example of what comes of sanctifying "resistance". Did the administrative purge – and the purge in general – plant the seeds of discord, disobedience and disrespect in the French civil and armed services; was it, in this way, an example of what Robert Merton has called "the unanticipated consequences of purposive social action"? It does not seem likely. But neither did it do much to bring about a France *pure et dure*.

33. See Alphonse Juin, *Trois siècles d'obéissance militaire: 1650-1963* (Paris: 1964) and the citations in Girardet, pp. 158-229.

Chapter 6

A NEW POLITICS

Considérant qu'il est juste que tous les complices du régime qui a commencé par l'attentat du 2 décembre pour finir par la capitulation de Sedan, en léguant à la France la ruine et l'invasion, soient frappés momentanément de la même déchéance politique que la dynastie à jamais maudite dont ils ont été les coupables instruments;

Considérant que c'est là une sanction nécessaire de la responsabilité qu'ils ont encourue en aidant et assistant, avec connaissance de cause, l'ex-empereur dans l'accomplissement des divers actes de son Gouvernement qui ont mis la patrie en danger.

. . . Ne pourront être élus représentants du peuple à l'Assemblée nationale les individus qui, depuis le 2 décembre 1851 jusqu'au 4 septembre 1870 ont accepté les fonctions de ministre, sénateur, conseiller d'Etat ou préfet.

. . . Sont également exclus de l'éligibilité à l'Assemblée nationale les individus qui, aux élections législatives qui ont eu lieu depuis le 2 décembre 1851 jusqu'au 4 septembre 1870 ont accepté la candidature officielle . . .

Fait à Bordeaux, le 31 janvier 1871.

La délégation du Gouvernement
de la défense nationale
LÉON GAMBETTA, A. GLAIS-BIZOIN,
AD. CRÉMIEUX, L. FOURICHON[1]

IN dealing with the men of the Third Republic, the Provisional Government appeared to be following a precedent much older than that of the Government of National Defense; its program seemed to be inspired by the doctrine of original sin. The men of the old order were all damned by the sins of the regime which they had served; some, however, would be – or could be – saved. Some would be justified through the faith in the Republic which they had evidenced by not voting constituent powers to Marshal Pétain in 1940. Others, who had been tempted and had fallen, might be redeemed by works – in the Resistance. The doctrine became orthodoxy; the disciples of the new religion ousted the pagan priests of the old. If the new institutions did not truly represent the spirit of their founders, if the new religion assimilated many elements of the paganism which it replaced, if a new era in human history did not come about as quickly as the disciples had

1. Joseph Reinach (ed.), *Dépêches, circulaires, décrets, proclamations et discours de Léon Gambetta* (Paris: 1886-91), Vol. II, pp. 124-25.

anticipated – that was perhaps to be expected; it had happened that way at least once before.

The Resistance was determined that there would be no place in the political life of liberated France for the men of Vichy or those who had collaborated with Germany; but this did not mean simply turning the clock back to 1940. The hostility of De Gaulle and the Resistance to the Third Republic has been discussed in a previous chapter. This hostility was particularly marked with respect to the members of the Senate and Chamber of Deputies; their abdication on July 10, 1940, was seen as merely the latest and final instance of their unworthiness and irresponsibility. (For a number of Gaullists, contempt for the senators and deputies of the Third Republic was simply a special case of a general antiparliamentarianism; this was rarely true in the metropolitan Resistance.) With very few exceptions the Resistance was dedicated to the Republic: "When we have regained our liberty it is our democratic institutions which will be the instrument of the new republican civilization"; but these institutions were to be "rejuvenated, rededicated, purged, and operated by new men".[2]

The condemnation of the old senators and deputies was characteristically expressed in sweeping terms.

> The past is dead. The "Nationals" have betrayed France. To the Radicals who had power, to the Communists who refused to take it in 1936, we say: a sin of omission is as serious as a sin of commission. The Socialists have betrayed socialism. The men of yesterday had power in June 1940. They abdicated before the enemy and let the Republic be murdered.[3]

There was a strong current in favor of making all legislators of the Third Republic ineligible for future political office. As the Organisation Civile et Militaire put it, while there were degrees of guilt, there were no innocents. (Because the members of the O.C.M. were democrats, their impulse was to leave the retirement of these men to the electorate; because they were realists, they recognized that a legislative enactment declaring them ineligible would be necessary.)[4]

In the first year or two of the Vichy Regime, when no political figures of any consequence had joined the Resistance, and the Resistance itself was almost wholly composed of "new men", this proposal had a certain surface plausibility. But then the *ralliement* of prewar politicians to

2. *Libération* (*Nord*), August 28, 1942.
3. *Combat*, No. 45 (December 25, 1942).
4. *Cahiers* [of the O.C.M.], June 1942.

De Gaulle began, together with the formation of the Conseil National de la Résistance, including representatives of the prewar parties. Such a proposal began to look more like a self-denying ordinance than a measure to be taken against others. The problem became critical in the summer of 1943 when discussions began concerning the composition of the Provisional Consultative Assembly. Like the C.N.R., the Assembly was in large measure designed to demonstrate the breadth of De Gaulle's support; to do this effectively it had to include elected representatives of the Third Republic.

What was needed was a definition of ineligibility which, while sweeping, would still be practical. André Philip had been delegated by the C.F.L.N. to draw up plans for the Consultative Assembly. Philip proposed that four categories of men should be ineligible to sit in the projected A.C.P.: all of Marshal Pétain's ministers since June 17, 1940; collaborators of various descriptions; all those appointed to "positions of authority" or nominated as Departmental or National Councillors by Vichy; and all those 569 members of the National Assembly who had voted constituent power to the Marshal in 1940. The first·three categories were accepted as a matter of course, at least for the moment. The last also seemed both politically attractive and – almost – workable. While the Resistance had many grievances against the senators and deputies of the Third Republic, the one which was freshest and most deeply felt was the cooperation of the vast majority of them in the assassination of the Republic. Under Philip's plan all those who had participated in this "betrayal of their republican mandate" would be excluded. As a practical matter, despite the fact that well over eighty per cent of the senators and deputies at Vichy had voted "yes", this group included few leading *résistants*. On the other hand "les quatre-vingts", who had voted "no", included, beside Philip himself, such Resistance stalwarts as Vincent Auriol, Jean Biondi, Paul Giacobbi, Félix Gouin, Jules Moch and François Tanguy-Prigent. Many of those who were absent or had abstained (and thus would not be proscribed) were also prominent in the Resistance: André le Troquer, Pierre Mendès-France, Henri Queuille.

Philip's proposal, like that of the O.C.M., foundered on the rock of political necessity. The proposal would have made representation of right-wing parties virtually impossible: almost the entire Right (together with the overwhelming majority of the Radicals) had voted "yes"; of the few who had not, hardly any were available for service with the A.C.P. The same difficulty had been encountered in obtaining representatives of the Right for the C.N.R. The only parliamentary representative of the Alliance Démocratique who had voted "no" – the Marquis de Moustier – was a "Giraudist"; Joseph Laniel, who had voted "yes" but then immediately gone into opposition, represented that party on the C.N.R. A number of Resistance movements and the Socialist Party questioned the propriety of having on the Council one who had voted full powers to Pétain. A majority of the C.N.R. – which included its Communist members – decided that Laniel had "redeemed himself" through his Resistance activities.[5]

It was this consideration that determined the attitude of the "Groupe des Parlementaires Adhérant à La France Combattante" in London when it discussed the question. Adoption of Philip's criterion would mean that only a handful of left-wing deputies would be able to serve; some implied that partisan motives were involved. (Four members of the parliamentary group had themselves voted "yes": Paul Antier, Lucien Galimand, Max Hymans and André Maroselli.) The group endorsed the view of the Communist deputy Fernand Grenier when he warned against "erecting impenetrable barricades". It urged the Algiers Committee not to accept Philip's draft.[6]

In its final form the Ordinance setting up the Consultative Assembly met the objection of the parliamentary group while in principle retaining Philip's criteria. His four categories of "ineligibles" were retained; however, those in the last two categories (Vichy Councillors and "yes-voters"), could, on the basis of Resistance activity, be "relieved of ineligibility" by decision of the C.N.R.[7] Except for changes in the "relieving body", this was to be the system adopted with respect to eligibility for all elective offices in the restored Republic.

Reference has already been made to the Ordinance of April 31, 1944, "portant organisation des pouvoirs publics en France après la Libération". Besides the immediate measures called for in that enactment, it provided for the election of new municipal and departmental councils as soon as electoral lists could be reconstituted. A Provisional Representative Assembly was also envisioned. As soon as circumstances permitted, each department would elect a number of representatives proportionate to its population. When elections had been held in two-

5. Jacques Debû-Bridel, Les Partis contre Charles de Gaulle (Paris: 1948) pp. 45-46; René Hostache, Le Conseil National de la Résistance: Les Institutions de la clandestinité (Paris: 1958), p. 150; Henri Michel, Histoire de la Résistance (Paris: 1950), p. 48.

6. Lucien Galimand, Vive Pétain, vive De Gaulle (Paris: 1948), p. 68ff.; Jean Pierre-Bloch, Le Vent souffle sur l'histoire (Paris: 1956), pp. 148-56.

7. Ordinance of September 17, 1943 (J.O. [Alger], September 23, 1943, pp. 139-40).

thirds of the departments in the metropole, the A.C.P. would cease to exist and General de Gaulle's Government would hand over its authority to the Assembly, which henceforth would govern. Within a year of the total liberation of France the Representative Assembly would, in turn, hand over its power to an "Assemblée Nationale Constituante" which would decide upon the institutions which would govern the restored Republic.

(The system of piecemeal elections was predicated – as was the rest of the Ordinance – on the assumption that the Liberation would take many months, perhaps years. The rapid Allied advance in 1944 and 1945 made it seem likely that Germany's collapse was imminent, and thus that the intermediate stage of a Representative Assembly could be dispensed with. Three weeks after the German surrender in May 1945, General de Gaulle called for the election of the Constituent Assembly in the fall.)

The draft text of the Ordinance which the Government submitted to the Consultative Assembly in Algiers contained no reference to ineligibility. The C.F.L.N. accepted the Assembly's recommendation that the list of disqualifications in the Ordinance establishing the A.C.P. itself be extended to municipal and departmental councils and to the Representative Assembly. As in the Ordinance on the A.C.P., ineligibility, except in the case of Vichy ministers and collaborators, could be suspended on the grounds of Resistance activity. The "relieving authority" was changed from the C.N.R. to the prefects; Resistance activity, to be accepted as grounds for suspension of ineligibility, was to be certified by the Departmental Liberation Committees. Two hundred and sixty-three prefectoral decisions were handed down suspending ineligibility. They covered fifty-eight "yes-voters", four Vichy National Councillors, and two hundred and one Departmental Councillors named by Vichy.[8]

Several weeks after the liberation of Paris, when it became clear that the projected Representative Assembly would not in fact be summoned, measures were taken to enlarge the Consultative Assembly. The representation of the metropolitan Resistance was raised from 49 to 148; of the overseas Resistance from 21 to 26; of the Senate and Chamber of Deputies from 20 to 60; the number of representatives from the French overseas territories (12) remained the same. Suspension of ineligibility for the A.C.P. became the prerogative of the "designating authority" for each representative – e.g., an individual Resistance movement –

8. J.O., May 12, 1945, pp. 2695-96; June 26, 1945, pp. 3868-69.

instead of the C.N.R. or the prefects. The Assembly itself, however, had the power to override the decision of a "designating authority" and invalidate any selection.[9]

The designating authority for the sixty delegates from prewar Assemblies was a committee appointed by and from "les quatre-vingts" – those who had voted "no" at Vichy. The "no-voters" had hoped that all of their number would receive seats in the Consultative Assembly. At the same time, at least some of the eighty were hostile to *any* suspension of ineligibility for "yes-voters".[10] It was not the limitation of the parliamentary delegation to sixty that prevented the full representation sought by "les quatre-vingts": there were only fifty-eight members of the group available to serve. (Five did not return from deportation in Germany until later; eleven had died, including seven killed by the Germans; three held ministerial or administrative offices incompatible with membership in the A.C.P.; three were already in the Assembly representing the Resistance.) The principal difficulty was that the Ordinance enlarging the A.C.P. stipulated that the sixty parliamentary seats be distributed in accordance with the relative weight of the different parties in the Chamber of Deputies on September 3, 1939. Since this distribution had no relation to the political composition of the eighty "no-voters", only thirty-eight of that number could serve in the parliamentary delegation. The remainder was made up of Communists who had been expelled from the Assembly before July 10, 1940, abstainers, and men absent from Vichy. The "quatre-vingts" never received what they considered their due, and the ingratitude of the Republic embittered many of their number.[11]

9. This prerogative had twice been exercised by the A.C.P. in Algiers – once in the case of a North African delegate on the grounds that he was a Vichyite, once in the case of a Senator nominated by the O.C.M. on the grounds that the ineligibility to which he was subject because of his vote at Vichy had not been suspended by the C.N.R. It was to be exercised once more in the A.C.P. in France – in the case of a "yes-voter" from the Fédération Républicaine, and once in the first Constituent Assembly on the grounds that the deputy in question had been an ardent Vichyite.

10. Louis Noguerès, *Un défi à la Résistance: M. Jules Jeanneney, Ministre d'Etat* (Rodez: 1945), pp. 47-53; J.O., A.C.P. Debates, March 31, 1945, pp. 1028-40; August 3, 1945, pp. 1786-88.

11. The Constitutional Commission of the first Constituent Assembly unanimously rejected a proposal by Joseph Paul-Boncour, president of "les quatre-vingts", that seats in the "Council of the French Union" provided for in the draft constitution be reserved for those "no-voters" who failed to win election to the future National Assembly. (J.O., A.N.C. [I], *Bulletin des Commissions*, No. 17 [April 16, 1946], p. 413.) Since the war's end the survivors of "les quatre-vingts" have held annual banquets at Vichy on July 10.

While many were skeptical about what were seen as the extravagant pretension of "les quatre-vingts", the overwhelming majority of the press in liberated France was for a sweeping decree of ineligibility for the "yes-voters". Public opinion polls showed majorities of two or three to one in favor of ineligibility for the 569. One poll reported that the almost universal comment accompanying an opinion favorable to ineligibility was: "Il faut des hommes nouveaux; profitons de l'occasion".[12] The natural opponents of parliamentary ineligibility for the "yes-voters" were those who would be most damaged by the institution – the Radicals and Right-wing parties, the bulk of whose deputies and senators were in this category. But in the first postwar years these groups were too weak to make their opposition meaningful.

In early 1945, as the local and departmental elections approached, the Government slightly modified the list of activities entailing ineligibility and substantially altered the procedure for its suspension.[13] The revised list of actions which carried ineligibility included: having been a Vichy minister, having been removed from office by the administrative purge, having been fined for garnering illicit profits under the occupation, having been named a National or Departmental Councillor by Vichy, having voted full powers to Pétain on July 10, 1940, having retained a Vichy appointment to an executive position in the administration after Pierre Laval's return to office in April 1942. Collaborationist (or "unworthy") behavior in general was removed from the new list. Since the previous enactment, laws and a court system to deal with collaboration had been established, and anyone convicted of collaboration, or declared to be in a state of "national indignity" was automatically ineligible; there was thus no need to include these offenses in the new legislation on ineligibility.

As before, ineligibility might be suspended on grounds of Resistance activity. There were, however, various objections to the existing system, which gave this power to the Departmental Liberation Committees and the prefects. Members of Liberation Committees might themselves be local candidates, in which case a conflict of interest would be created. More than one prefect or C.D.L. might have jurisdiction over the case

12. *Service de Sondages et de Statistiques: Sondages*, No. 12 (April 1, 1945). Cf. *Bulletin d'Information de l'Institut Français d'Opinion Publique*, April 16, 1945. Both polls showed that while the wealthy and those on the right end of the political spectrum were about evenly divided on the question of ineligibility, those with lower incomes and those on the left favored it by margins of four or five to one.

13. Ordinance of April 6, 1945 (J.O., April 7, pp. 1914-15).

of a given individual, and return contradictory opinions. Finally, while in some departments ten or more suspensions had taken place, in seventeen there had been no prefectoral suspensions at all. It was decided to create a new, unified jurisdiction to consider the cases of all Vichy-appointed departmental and national councillors and all "yes-voting" senators and deputies whose cases had not previously been the basis of a prefectoral decision.

A "Jury d'Honneur" was created, consisting of the Vice-President of the Conseil d'Etat, the Chancellor of the Ordre de la Libération, and the President of the C.N.R.[14] It was a sovereign jurisdiction, no appeal from its decisions being permitted. The Jury made its decisions on the basis of dossiers compiled by the Ministry of the Interior, affidavits from local officials, Liberation Committees and Resistance groups, and depositions made by the individual concerned. All decisions, together with a brief indication of the reasons for the determination arrived at, were published in the Journal Officiel.

Virtually all the cases considered by the Jury were completed by the end of 1945; in 1946 a number of cases were reconsidered on the basis of new evidence; in October 1946 the Jury disbanded. Under the Ordinance of April 6, electoral ineligibility applied only to the communal and departmental elections of April and May 1945. Further ordinances and laws extended ineligibility to all subsequent local and national elections through the general elections of 1951. (In 1953 an amnesty abolished the institution of ineligibility based on wartime conduct.)

Given the brevity of the explanations offered by the *Jury d'Honneur* for its decisions, it is extremely difficult to be precise concerning its criteria. At his first hearing, Albert Rivière's presence in Pétain's cabinet from June 17 to July 11, 1940, was considered to outweigh his undisputed aid to the Resistance and to downed Allied pilots – his ineligibility was not suspended. On a rehearing, new evidence concerning his conduct while in Pétain's cabinet resulted in a reversal of this judgment.[15] Antoine Pinay – a future premier under the Fourth Republic – won a similar reversal. At his first hearing, his having accepted a post as a Vichy National Councillor was decisive and he remained

14. René Cassin, Vice-President of the Conseil d'Etat, presided over the Jury. Neither Louis Saillant, President of the C.N.R., nor Admiral Thierry d'Argenlieu, Chancellor of the Ordre de la Libération, participated in the Jury's work; their seats were filled by their deputies: Maxime Blocq-Mascart (of the O.C.M.) and A. Postel-Vinay (also of the O.C.M., later head of the Banque d'Outre-mer), respectively.

15. J.O., May 17, 1946, p. 4254; November 22, 1946, p. 9319.

ineligible; further evidence of Resistance activity (unspecified) resulted in a suspension.[16]

Behavior that was merely "correct" did not bring suspension, as in the case of a deputy who had

> behaved in an honorable and dignified fashion during the occupation, but has not established that he participated in the struggle against the enemy or the usurper in a sufficiently direct and active fashion to efface the consequences of the act which brought about his legal ineligibility.[17]

A phrase which frequently recurs in Jury decisions indicates that it set a particularly high standard for senators and deputies:

> The acts which [a certain deputy] performed in behalf of Frenchmen and the Resistance do not indicate that [degree of] participation in the struggle against the enemy which the nation had a right to expect from its elected representatives.[18]

That an individual had taken personal risks in order to aid the Resistance was generally grounds for being relieved of ineligibility, as in the case of Gabriel Debregeas, who

> took part in the struggle through rendering, from 1942, constant and valuable assistance to the *maquis*, often in perilous circumstances, which cost the life of his daughter, who was associated with his activity.[19]

But purely humanitarian activity, even if dangerous, was not enough. One deputy was not relieved of ineligibility despite the fact that he "devotedly cared for sick and wounded *résistants*, thus giving a fine example of self-sacrifice and indifference to his personal safety" since "he did not directly participate in the struggle".[20]

Almost all the full accounts accompanying a decision to suspend ineligibility stress the "active and effective participation in the struggle against the enemy and the usurper" demanded by the Ordinance; failure to satisfy this requirement, "in the strict sense", was offered as an explanation for leaving an otherwise eminently worthy individual ineligible.[21] This criterion was sometimes applied with incredible rigor, as in the unfavorable verdict returned in the case of a senator who

> showed himself hostile to the government of Vichy and favorable to the Resistance; who, being in the unoccupied zone, returned voluntarily to

16. J.O., October 7, 1945, p. 6318; October 21, 1945, p. 6762.
17. J.O., May 7, 1949, p. 4470.
18. J.O., October 14, 1945, p. 6513.
19. J.O., January 19, 1946, p. 505.
20. J.O., October 21, 1945, p. 6765.
21. J.O., January 10, 1946, p. 252.

Roubaix, knowing full well that he had been designated a hostage [by the Germans], and thereby experienced three months imprisonment. But . . . he belonged to no resistance organization and did not participate in any other way in the struggle. . . .[22]

Even heroic participation in the Resistance might not be enough if overbalanced by Pétainism which aggravated the offense of having voted full powers to the Marshal in the first place. Charles Vallin, despite his much-publicized *ralliement* to the Free French in 1942 and his subsequent military honors (five citations), could not be relieved of ineligibility because of "the very important political role that he played from 1940 to 1942 which contributed to the weakening of the nation's morale".[23]

While no hard-and-fast limiting date was adopted by the Jury, even the most active participation in the Resistance was rejected as grounds for suspension if it came very late in the day.[24] Simply "showing a hostile attitude toward the invader" was not sufficient grounds for being relieved of ineligibility;[25] however, when an individual's political opposition to Vichy, coupled with his anti-Germanism, caused him to be removed as mayor of his town and necessitated his leaving the department, it might suffice.[26] Guy La Chambre's ineligibility was suspended on the grounds that

> while the defense which he presented at the Riom Trial was restricted to technical points, it nevertheless constituted an act of resistance to the plans of the usurper, inspired by the enemy, and contributed to frustrating them.[27]

The age of an individual was taken into account: octogenarians were not expected to race about blowing up bridges. One deputy was relieved of ineligibility on the grounds that he had "participated in the struggle in so far as his advanced age permitted, demonstrating his hostility to the pseudo-government of Vichy openly and on various occasions, and aided *résistants*".[28] But something was expected of everybody – a fact discovered by the deputy who remained ineligible although he had

22. J.O., December 28, 1945, p. 8638.
23. J.O., October 21, 1945, pp. 6762-63.
24. J.O., December 15, 1945, p. 8298.
25. J.O., December 28, 1945, p. 8633.
26. J.O., October 7, 1945, pp. 6318-19.
27. J.O., October 11, 1945, p. 6410.
28. J.O., December 28, 1945, p. 8632.

"maintained a dignified attitude during the occupation [since] he did not, even taking account of his age, participate in the Resistance to the necessary extent".[29] Contrition was not a formal requirement for suspension of ineligibility, nor was the absence of it a formal bar; however, in the unfavorable judgment rendered in the case of Jean Castagnez, his having published an apologia for the vote of July 10 was, while not the primary reason for the judgment, an aggravating circumstance.[30]

Despite the rigorous standards of the *Jury d'honneur*, almost a third of those whose cases came before it received a favorable decision. Out of 416 senators and deputies whose cases were considered by the Jury, 114 (27 per cent) were relieved of ineligibility (see Table 1); out of 223 Vichy councillors, 79 (35 per cent) had their ineligibility suspended;[31] in all, out of 639 final decisions handed down by the Jury, 193 (33 per cent) were favorable. Taking into account prefectoral decisions, 172 out of 474 senators and deputies (36 per cent) and 280 out of 424 councillors (66 per cent) were relieved of ineligibility, making a grand total of 452 favorable decisions (51 per cent) out of 898 cases.[32]

29. J.O., December 19, 1945, p. 8395.

30. J.O., January 10, 1946, p. 251.

31. Of the 223, 215 were departmental councillors (75 suspensions) and 8 were national councillors (4 suspensions). The tiny number of national councillors whose cases came before the Jury as such is perhaps largely explained by the fact that many, like Pinay, were judged "à titre de député" or "à titre de conseiller départemental"; that an individual had also been a national councillor was, of course, an aggravating factor in his case.

32. It should be reiterated that tens of thousands of men (probably including some prewar senators and deputies) automatically became ineligible following sentences by *cours de justice* and *chambres civiques*. There is no practical way of determining how many senators and deputies might have become ineligible in this way. There were various attempts at defiance or avoidance of the ineligibility laws. P.-E. Flandin was among those who ran though ineligible. He was defeated, but others who ran were elected, and then had their victory annulled by the Government. (*Année Politique*, 1952, pp. 34, 36; Association des Représentants du Peuple de la IIIe République, *Lettre aux adhérents*, No. 5 [February 1948].) Sometimes relatives contested elections on behalf of men who had been rendered ineligible. After the 1951 election the veteran Communist Marcel Cachin was displaced as *doyen d'âge* of the Assembly by M. Pébellier, "a Conservative retired haberdasher from Le Puy who had never before in his eighty-five years of life been outside his native town. M. Pébellier contested the election because his son . . . was ineligible. The son wrote and the father delivered an introductory speech which, in its praise of the Marshal and condemnation of the ineligibility laws, contrasted oddly with the revolutionary discourses of the previous *doyen d'âge*." (Philip M. Williams, *Politics in Post-War France: Parties and the Constitution in the Fourth Republic* [London: 1954], p. 198.)

TABLE I.—*Suspension of the electoral ineligibility of senators and deputies* [a]

Party affiliation [b]	Jury d'Honneur Decisions				Prefectoral suspensions [c]	Totals		
	Cases heard	Ineligibility suspended	Ineligibility not suspended	% of suspensions		Cases	Suspensions	% of suspensions
Communist [d]	7	1	6	14	0	7	1	14
Socialist	80	28	52	35	7	87	35	40
Radical [e]	119	40	79	34	25	144	65	45
Right [f]	206	43	163	21	25	231	68	29
Unclassified	4	2	2	50	1	5	3	60
Totals	416	114	302	27	58	474	172	36

[a] No overall report was ever issued by the Jury d'Honneur concerning its work. I have compiled these statistics from the separate decisions recorded in the *Journal Officiel* during 1945 and 1946.

[b] Based on the last prewar official lists of groups in the Senate and Chamber of Deputies in 1939. (J.O., January 22, 1939, pp. 1178-1179; J.O., Chamber of Deputies Debates, 2nd session of June 2, 1939, pp. 1489-90.)

[c] No record exists of suspensions considered but not granted by the prefects; only affirmative decisions were recorded.

[d] Strictly speaking, ex-Communists: i.e., those who broke with the Party after the Russo-German Pact of August 1939, and thus were not expelled from the Assembly.

[e] Includes "radicalisantes".

[f] Defined as all those to the right of the Radicals, and forming part of the "Front National" in the 1936 Chamber; this designation includes those usually referred to as "Center" in prewar parlance.

105

Did political considerations – extraneous to the formal criteria of the relevant ordinance – enter into the Jury's decisions? It is sometimes held that not only the institution of the *Jury d'Honneur*, but its practice as well, was a maneuver to destroy the Right.[33] The Jury left over three times as many Rightists as Socialists subject to ineligibility (163 vs. 52); applying the more pertinent measure of the relative frequency of favorable action, the Jury's decisions were almost fifty per cent more favorable to Socialists than to Rightists (35 per cent favorable action vs. 21 per cent). If the phenomenon of Resistance had been present in equal proportions in Right and Left milieux, these figures would tend to sustain the charge of partiality. In fact, all the evidence and the opinion of every qualified observer suggests that, on the contrary, the relative incidence of active participation in the Resistance was much more disparate than the ratio of *Jury d'honneur* "relèvements" would indicate. If these figures demonstrate anything – which is questionable – it is that the Jury favored the Right.

There are other reasons – although they are only slightly less tenuous – for believing that the Jury may have been less rigorous in its standards for men of the Right than for men of the Left. While Socialists were frequently denied favorable action on the grounds that their Resistance activity had been *insufficient*, denials of favorable action to members of the Right were characteristically based on the *absence* of any record of resistance. While in more than eighty per cent of the cases in which Socialists were relieved of ineligibility the decision specified the Resistance activity which was invoked, this was only true in about half of the favorable decisions for Rightists. Finally, the impression formed from reading the summaries of the wartime conduct of many Rightists – conduct which won them suspensions – is identical with that conveyed by the descriptions of the conduct of many Socialists who received unfavorable decisions.[34]

If in fact the Jury showed the kind of partiality which is suggested by some of its decisions, there are at least three possible explanations. First, if the Right was to survive as a healthy (and above-ground) force in French politics, it needed all the charity it could get; members of

33. See, e.g., *Ecrits de Paris*, February 1947, 22-24.

34. Cf., for the Right, J.O., May 23, 1945, p. 2919; July 3, 1945, pp. 4014-4015; July 7, 1945, p. 4133; August 24, 1945, p. 5285; September 20, 1945, p. 5891; October 11, 1945, p. 6410 (two cases); October 14, 1945, p. 6512; November 6, 1947, p. 10960; for the Socialists, J.O., October 7, 1945, p. 6320 and p. 6318; October 11, 1945, p. 6411; October 14, 1945, p. 6514; October 21, 1945, p. 6766; December 15, 1945, p. 8298; December 19, 1945, pp. 8394-95.

the Jury may have feared the consequences of the submersion of its forces. Also, it is possible that – perhaps unconsciously – the Jury demanded a higher standard of conduct from Socialists in view of the behavior of so many of their comrades at the time of the July 10 vote and during the occupation. Finally, since the Socialist Party had expelled almost all of its "yes-voters" before the Jury came into existence, the Jury could refuse them favorable action without – in most cases – further practical consequences for the individual in question.

The Socialist Party carried out a more thoroughgoing purge of its own ranks than any other political party – indeed, than any other institution of any kind – in France. The groundwork for the purge of the Party after the Liberation was laid during the war: the split between the "munichois" headed by Paul Faure and the "bellicistes" under Léon Blum, which had threatened the unity of the Party before 1940, became formalized and irreparable. The former, almost to a man, voted "yes" on July 10, 1940, and subsequently often became Vichyites and even out-and-out collaborators; the latter, in the main, were *résistants*. Socialist *résistants* like André le Troquer, who had "never known that there were so many cowards and traitors in [his] party", resolved during the first year of the Vichy Regime to be rid of them.[35] In May 1941 the Comité d'Action Socialiste, the Party's underground executive committee, decided that not only those of the Party's senators and deputies who had voted full powers to Pétain would be expelled, but those who abstained as well. Procedures were instituted for the total reorganization of the Party; even members of long standing would be readmitted to the "purified" Party only on the presentation of Resistance credentials.[36]

After the Liberation, the Socialist Party demonstrated that its underground pronouncements had been seriously intended. Every departmental federation carried out a root-and-branch purge, carefully examining old members and new applicants alike. At the Party's special National Congress in November 1944, 96 of the 151 surviving members of the Party's prewar parliamentary delegation were either expelled or suspended. Of the 85 (living) "yes-voters" in the Party, 74 were permanently excluded, 9 (on the basis of Resistance activity) were suspended

35. Le Troquer's remark (following the vote of July 10, 1940) is quoted in Tony Revillon's *Carnets: Juin-Octobre 1940* (Paris: 1945), p. 120.
36. Jean Pierre-Bloch, *Mes jours heureux* (Paris: 1946), p. 102; Daniel Ligou, *Histoire du socialisme en France: 1871-1961* (Paris: 1962), pp. 487-91, 500-11; *Populaire (Nord)*, No. 24 (September 15, 1943); *Populaire (Sud)*, No. 19 (December 1943).

temporarily, 1 deputy, for "exceptional service to the Resistance", was fully reinstated, 1 case was postponed for later determination. Out of 5 who abstained at Vichy, 4 were excluded, 1 suspended; of the 20 members of the Socialist delegation absent from Vichy, 7 were excluded, 1 suspended.[37] No other party carried out a purge which even approached that of the Socialists in scope and rigor. The new Secretary-General, Daniel Mayer, in his report to the Party's 1945 Congress, announced that the Party had been "purified, reinvigorated, rejuvenated, renovated and transformed" by the removal of unworthy comrades.[38] Certainly they had tried. One measure of their success – albeit a partial one – is provided by Philip Williams, who observed that despite the Socialist purge,

> many more than half the Socialist candidates in the election of October 1945 had already held elective office in the Third Republic – much the highest proportion of any political group. At the beginning of the 1946 legislature the Socialists had fewer young deputies (aged 35 or less) than any of their rivals.[39]

The Radicals' purge was considerably milder than that of the Socialists, although it was not inconsiderable. In Algiers, in June 1944, a Congress of the Radical-Socialist Party expelled 5 Radicals who had held positions in Pétain's cabinets: Georges Bonnet, Camille Chautemps, Albert Chichery, Lucien Lamoureux and Jean Mistler. The Congress unanimously resolved that the Party would exclude "all those who . . . by their approbation, collaboration, or acceptance of titles, responsibilities or honors, have compromised with the enemies of the Nation or of the Republic".[40] At their "Petit Congrès" in December 1944, the Radicals expelled 34 of their prewar senators and deputies, and suspended 2 for four years. Of the 34 men expelled, 27 were "yes-voters", as was 1 of those suspended; the rest had been absent from

37. *Les Décisions du Congrès national extraordinaire* [1944] (Paris: n.d.), pp. 9, 16; Jules Moch, *Le Parti socialiste au peuple de France* (Paris: 1945), pp. 67-69. At the 1945 Congress a handful of those suspended were reintegrated; in later years some of those who had been excluded were readmitted, while the applications of others were refused. (*38ᵉ Congrès national: Rapports* [Paris: 1946], p. 9; *Bulletin Intérieur du Parti Socialiste*, No. 37 [November-December 1948], 30; *Monde*, February 26/27, 1950; Ligou, p. 517.)
38. *37ᵉ Congrès national: Rapports* (Paris: 1945), p. 3.
39. *Op. cit.*, p. 69.
40. Marc Rucart, "Quoi, le Parti Radical-Socialiste", *La République Française*, I, 9 (October 1944), 4.

Vichy at the time of the vote. (Four of the expelled "yes-voters" were later relieved of ineligibility by the *Jury d'honneur*; the remainder stayed ineligible.) The Party kept in its ranks 50 of the surviving 77 Radicals who had voted "yes" at Vichy, most of whom, in law, remained ineligible.[41] Had the Radical Congress not come on the heels of the Socialist purge, it is likely that the Radical housecleaning would have been even milder. As it was, the "radicaux de gauche" – a group which included Albert Bayet, Pierre Cot, Jacques Kayser, Pierre le Brun, Jammy Schmidt and Madeleine Zay (the widow of Jean) – complained bitterly of the inadequacy of the purge in their Party, which allowed the "munichois" to return to power.[42]

The procedure followed by the Communists in their "purge" was closer to that of their ideological homeland than to that of the other parties. For the French Communist Party, "traitor" meant not one who had betrayed France–or only incidentally that–but rather one who had betrayed the Party. In almost every case, the betrayal consisted in having opposed the Russo-German Pact of August 1939. Many of these "renegades" were summarily executed both before and after the Liberation. René Nicod, who had quit the Party at the time of the Pact, voted "no" on July 10, and been imprisoned for almost four years by Vichy, was the object of a furious Communist assault in the A.C.P., of which he was a member; the failure of the majority to accede to the Communist demand that Nicod be excluded from the Assembly was characterized as "an act of anti-Communist aggression".[43] Nicod could not be ignored, but where possible, dissident Communists who had been neither Vichyites nor collaborators became "unpersons": when Marcel Cachin, as *doyen d'âge* of the Assembly, read out the list of deputies "morts pour la France" he omitted the name of Roger Benenson who had left the Party in 1939 and died in a German concentration camp; the Communist press omitted another Communist "renegade" from a list of the hostages shot at Châteaubriant.[44]

None of the other parties carried out purges of any kind. The Mouvement Républicain Populaire (M.R.P.), as a new party, had no past to disavow. The parties of the Right were of no mind to further limit their

41. Parti Radical-Socialiste, *Petit Congrès des 19, 20 et 21 décembre 1944: Rapport moral* (Paris: 1944), pp. 18-20; *Combat*, December 22, 1944; *Monde*, December 23, 1944; *Patrie et Liberté: Le Parti Radical-Socialiste pendant la Résistance* (n.p.: n.d.), pp. 16, 27-29, 36.
42. *Voix de Paris*, March 29, 1946.
43. J.O., A.C.P. Debates, March 16, 1945, pp. 531-39.
44. Angelo Tasca ["Rossi"], *La Physiologie du Parti communiste français* (Paris: 1948), pp. 444-45.

already depleted parliamentary resources; they carried out regroupments and realignments, but no purge.

Liberated France presented a political picture which in almost every aspect showed a radical break with the past. For the first fourteen months after the Liberation the Provisional Government ruled extraconstitutionally, but it was assumed on all sides that when normal processes were restored, there would be no going back to the Third Republic. All sections of opinion, with the sole exception of the Radicals, favored the creation of a new, "Fourth Republic". In the referendum of October 1945, over 96 per cent of the voters opted for scrapping the Constitution of 1875 and starting fresh.

There was a revolution in the relative weight of political tendencies as well. The communal elections in the spring of 1945 foreshadowed the dramatic changes of the fall. "Modérés" and Radicals lost their majority in a third of the communes which they had controlled before the war (the drop was much more dramatic in good-sized towns); the Socialists more than tripled, and the Communists more than quadrupled, the number of municipalities they controlled. Since conservative "notables" generally do much better on the local level than their confrères on the national level, the handwriting on the wall was plain.

The election of the Constituent Assembly, which accompanied the referendum, demonstrated the extent of the revolution which had been wrought. In the last prewar election (1936), the Right had received over 42 per cent of the votes cast; in 1945, its share was under 16 per cent. The Radicals and their allies dropped from over 22 per cent to under 9 per cent. The Socialists, on the other hand, climbed from under 20 per cent to over 25 per cent, while the Communists jumped from under 16 per cent to over 26 per cent. The M.R.P. – born in the Resistance – astonished political observers by gaining 24 per cent of the popular vote in its first appearance. In the popular vote – and in the new Constituent Assembly as well – there was a "Marxist majority".

There was an even more radical change in the men who represented the parties. At the first postwar general election, 93 per cent of the candidates were making their political début. Of those elected to the First Constituent Assembly, 85 per cent had never sat in a prewar legislature.[45] Their "newness' was not the only thing that characterized the men of the new Assembly – and those that were to follow. Eighty per cent of the First Constituent Assembly (and of the two Assemblies

45. Raoul Husson, *Elections et referendums des 21 octobre 1945, 5 mai et 2 juin 1946* (Paris: 1946), pp. xiv-xxii, xxxi.

TABLE 2.—*Selection of legislators in the Fourth Republic from the ranks of the Resistance*[a]

	Communists	Socialists	Radicals	M.R.P.	Moderates	Gaullists	Poujadists	Unclassified	Total
1. Deportees, condemned to death, arrested by Gestapo, interned, anti-Pétain deputies in 1940	24	27	13	10	14	11	—	2	101
2. Resistance from abroad – London, Algiers, etc.; followers of General de Gaulle	7	5	17	11	7	16	3	8	74
3. Founders and heads of the Resistance; leaders of Free French, of secret unions, of political organizations	42	27	5	21	5	13	1	6	120
4. Cadre and actives in the Resistance and in other secret groups	161	87	14	65	6	13	1	8	355
5. "Compagnons de la Libération" and holders of the "Médaille de la Résistance," not classified under the preceding rubrics	—	24	7	15	3	7	—	3	59
6. Holders of *Croix de Guerre* or other military honors (1939-45)	—	4	16	8	10	10	4	1	53
7. Prisoners of war not otherwise classified	—	2	3	2	3	3	5	1	19
Not Active in the Resistance:									
Under 21 in 1943	12	—	1	2	3	—	3	—	21
Over 21 in 1943	—	15	32	43	69	7	19	5	190
No accurate information	—	7	13	39	22	11	5	6	103
Collaborators and retainers of official posts during the Vichy regime	—	—	3	—	10	—	3	1	17
Total deputies elected in Metropolitan France	246	198	124	216	152	91	44	41	1,112

[a] This table is additive, but certain deputies could have been classed under several rubrics. Those classified under a given rubric are *not* here classified under other rubrics. Some classifications are necessarily arbitrary, and it is probable that lacunae exist in the documentation available. It is estimated, however, that most deputies classed under the heading "No accurate information" were *not* active participants in the Resistance.

Reproduced by permission of M. Mattei Dogan, from his article "Political Ascent in a Class Society: French Deputies 1870–1958" in Dwaine Marvick (ed.), *Political Decision Makers* (Glencoe [Ill.]: 1961), p. 86.

111

elected in 1946) had been active *résistants*.[46] Most estimates place the percentage of active *résistants* in the adult population at one or two per cent; this tiny élite completely dominated the political scene in 1945 and 1946. While its relative influence subsequently waned somewhat, throughout the Fourth Republic deputies, senators and ministers were largely drawn from the ranks of the Resistance. (See Table 2.) The list of *Présidents du Conseil* who had been in the first rank of the Resistance includes Bidault, Faure, Gouin, Laniel, Marie, Mayer, Mendès-France, Mollet, Pleven, and Queuille. In the first years of the Fifth Republic, men who first came to prominence in the Resistance led the Government (De Gaulle, Michel Debré, Jacques Chaban-Delmas), the Right-opposition (Georges Bidault, Jacques Soustelle), and the Left-opposition (Claude Bourdet, André Philip).

The parliamentary purge, which aimed at "renewing" French political life, had retired hundreds of prewar politicians; in relative terms it was more severe than the purge in any other area. And the French parliament *was* renewed; the overwhelming majority of postwar legislators were "new men". *Post hoc ergo propter hoc?* Probably – or at least largely – not. There were undoubtedly men who would have been returned to the legislature if the *Jury d'Honneur*, or their party, had not excluded them. But the radical shift in political strength in the new Assemblies, and the dramatic success of Resistance candidates, indicated that more fundamental causes were at work.

France in the postwar period was "résistantialiste" in spirit. (Most observers attribute the dramatic postwar gains of the Communist Party largely to its success in presenting itself as the most *résistant* of all the parties.) New men, with Resistance credentials, had an immense advantage over veterans of the Third Republic, who shared in the opprobrium attached to that regime. Frenchmen said, as they entered the voting booths, what they had said about the Ordinance on ineligibility: "Il faut des hommes nouveaux; profitons de l'occasion".

46. Mattei Dogan, "Political Ascent in a Class Society: French Deputies, 1870-1958", in Dwaine Marvick (ed.), *Political Decision Makers* (Glencoe [Ill.]: 1961), pp. 85-87.

Chapter 7

A NEW SOCIETY

At this very moment – in the *maquis*, on the Italian front – men are dying in order that France may once more be free and great – to sweep away forever the forces which have delivered our country to the fifth column. In the first rank of these forces stands that rotten press which has never stopped serving the interests of profit in preference to those of France; which has shamefully enlisted itself under the banner of the enemy. There can be no question of negotiating with it, of allowing it to practice legal maneuvers, thanks to which it would be enabled to resume its abominable role. IT MUST BE SUPPRESSED AND ANNIHILATED.

> Underground manifesto of
> the Fédération Nationale de
> la Presse Clandestine.[1]

THERE were few areas of French life that had not been affected by the Vichy Regime and the German occupation; few in which Pétainists and collaborationists had not risen to the top; and consequently few in which the Resistance did not wish to see retribution and reform. The Resistance determination to build a new France, "pure et dure", implied sweeping measures of renewal in all areas of French life, not just the public sector.

Much of Resistance thought concerned itself with "réformes de structure" in the economy: a large measure of state control of industry, widespread nationalizations, and the installation of a new economic "ruling class". To include all attempts at economic reform under the rubric of the purge would be unwarranted. In some respects nationalizations were a part of the purge, in so far as confiscatory measures were justified on the grounds of the owners' collaboration. This was the case with the Renault automobile company, the Société Gnôme et Rhône (airplane engines), the Berliet automobile works, the Société Francolor (chemicals), and some others. (In the event, the only important case in which compensation was denied the owners of nationalized property was that related to the holdings of Louis Renault, who died in prison in 1944 before he could be tried.) But the principal rationale for nationalizations was economic: the debates concerning them, the procedures adopted, and the results obtained lie outside the scope of the present work.

---

1. *Pour une presse patriote, honnête et libre* (n.p.: n.d. [early 1944]).

Another economic program – that which made provision for the confiscation of "illicit profits" garnered during the occupation – does fall within the scope of this study. Consideration of this program has been omitted because of the almost total absence of information concernings its operation.[2]

Aside from the economy, a number of other institutions in French society were the objects of attempts at "renewal". The success of these attempts was uneven. The press experienced – temporarily – an almost complete *renouvellement*, and there was an attempt to purge the world of letters. The Académie Française and the Catholic Church were "purged" only to a very limited extent; on the other hand there was a thorough housecleaning in the trade union establishment. There were minor purges in various other areas.

The German occupation was a time of testing for all French institutions, and not least for the newspapers of France. Newspapers published in the North faced three alternatives in June 1940. They could flee from the advancing German armies and reestablish themselves in the "Free Zone": in practice, this option was exercised only by newspapers published in Paris, whose national clientele made such a step worthwhile (e.g., *L'Action Française, Le Figaro, Le Temps*). They could simply cease publication: in Paris this course was chosen by *L'Aube, L'Epoque, L'Intransigeant, L'Ordre,* and *Le Populaire*. Or – and this was the option chosen by the great majority of newspapers outside of Paris – they could continue publication under the German occupation. *Le Matin, L'Œuvre,* and *Le Petit Parisien* were the only important Paris dailies which chose this course.[3]

Those papers which chose to continue publication did so for a variety of reasons, ranging from collaborationist principles, through

2. French officialdom is close-mouthed concerning all aspects of the purge; with respect to the functioning of the departmental confiscation committees a complete silence has been observed. Inquiries at the Ministry of Finance, under which the committees operated, were fruitless; so was examination of annual state budgets, in an attempt to find receipts from confiscations. Dorothy Pickles estimates that twelve billion francs were confiscated in 1945-46. She compares this figure with the 800 billion francs spent by the German occupying forces from 1940 to 1944 and concludes that the program was a fiasco. (*France Between the Republics* [London: 1946], p. 188.) This opinion was shared by French officials with whom I discussed the question.

3. *Paris-Soir* was a special case. The staff fled to the South and published the paper there. In Paris the Germans, without the consent of the owner, set up a puppet *Paris-Soir* which appeared under the old name throughout the occupation.

opportunism and indifference, to a misguided sense of obligation. Pierre-Henri Teitgen, Minister of Information in the Provisional Government, described the following evolution in the wartime experience of those who continued publishing their newspapers "in good faith":

> One begins by saying: "We aren't committing treason by making a concession to the occupier – it is in the national interest; we are safeguarding innocents, preventing executions, limiting deportation; it's only a small concession, if we make it we can stop there." And then the next day, following her technique of taking small bites, Germany demands another concession, and since one has agreed to the first, one dares not refuse the second, which is no more serious than the one which came before; the second leads you to the third, to the fourth, to the fifth, and the entire series leads you to complete abasement.[4]

In November 1942, newspapers in the South – whether indigenous publications or "refugees" – had to decide whether to collaborate or "se saborder": the consequences of continued publication under German occupation were clear from the experience of northern newspapers during the preceding two years, and there was no longer a "Free Zone" to which one could flee. Of the Paris dailies which had fled in 1940, *Le Figaro* and *Le Temps* "scuttled" in November 1942, *Paris-Soir* continued publication through 1943, and *L'Action Française* kept going until the Liberation. A relatively small number of indigenous southern papers chose voluntary suspension.

In addition to prewar newspapers which continued publication, the journalistic establishment of occupied France included many new ventures, especially in Paris. The new papers, frequently the recipients of German subsidies, represented a variety of collaborationist viewpoints, and were designed to appeal to various clienteles. Among the most important in Paris were *L'Atelier* (collaborationist trade unionist), *Aujourd'hui* (edited by Georges Suarez), *Le Cri du Peuple* (P.P.F.), *La France Socialiste* (collaborationist socialist), *La Gerbe* (literary), *Les Nouveaux Temps* (an imitation *Temps*), *Le Pilori* ("hebdomadaire de combat contre la judéo-maçonnerie"), and *La Révolution Nationale* ("cagoularde").

The Resistance assumed as a matter of course that the "presse allemande de langue française" – whether of prewar or wartime origin – would be suppressed at the Liberation. And they were equally unanimous that this must not mean a return to the status quo ante bellum. The "presse pourrie" of the Third Republic would give way to a new

4. *Combat*, October 28, 1944.

journalistic establishment – honest and independent – based largely on the press of the Resistance. The new press would

> no longer be enslaved by the moneyed groups, who . . . controlled opinion by means of their papers as it suited their interests, which were neither those of truth nor of the country. . . . The press must never again be prey to advertisers . . . who took over supervision of editorial policy . . . transforming a supposedly free press into a propaganda service. . . . There shall be no more secret payments of funds from hidden sources which place a newspaper under foreign control and transform it – as we have seen all too often in recent years – into an underhanded medium of treason.[5]

Resistance opinion on the purge of the press was not simply the sum total of scattered remarks in underground newspapers. Special groups were formed with the specific intention of making recommendations to the Algiers Committee concerning the press. *Ad hoc* groups began discussions in the spring of 1943; a special commission of the Comité Général d'Etudes considered the question; so did commissions of the Comité National des Journalistes and the Fédération Nationale de la Presse Clandestine.

There was broad agreement on fundamentals: that collaborationist newspapers should disappear; that at least provisionally the Resistance papers should use their facilities when, "au grand jour", they appeared openly. However, a number of questions remained unresolved. Should sanctions be applied only to papers which were zealously collaborationist, or to all those which appeared legally under German censorship? Should newspapers which appeared in the "Free Zone" before the German invasion be forbidden to appear, or only those which had appeared under the Germans? If the latter, what should be the limiting date for each zone? If newspapers which appeared under Vichy were not in principle condemned, should they be allowed to reappear under their old titles? What disposition should be made of the assets of requisitioned newspapers? These and many other questions remained the subject of disagreement in the underground discussions; indeed, a final decision concerning some of them was not reached until almost two years after the Liberation.

The C.F.L.N.'s original press legislation provided only for the immediate Liberation period. All newspapers still appearing legally at the

5. Manifesto of the Comité National des Journalistes, *Les Cahiers Français*, May 1944.

time of the Liberation were to be suspended and their property sequestered. Regional press committees consisting of representatives of the prewar press unions, the C.D.L.'s, and the Ministry of Information would be charged with authorizing new papers to appear, using, if necessary, the premises of suspended publications. Preference would be given to Resistance newspapers, but some prewar publications might be authorized to reappear (under their old titles). Two key questions were left for future determination: what criteria would be adopted in deciding which papers would be allowed to reopen (with or without their old titles); what would be the final disposition of the assets of sequestered papers?[6]

The actual takeover of the premises of the old newspapers at the Liberation was disorderly, but rarely violent. The Government ratified, rather than directed, the occupation of newspaper buildings, which were divided among Resistance papers on the basis of informal agreements they had made themselves. In the midst of the Liberation of Paris, days before the entry of Leclerc's troops, the underground press emerged into the light of day. *Le Populaire* took over the premises of *Le Matin*; *L'Humanité* and *Le Parisien Libéré* began publishing on the presses of *Le Petit Parisien*; *Combat*, *Défense de la France* and *Franc-Tireur* used the facilities of *L'Intransigeant*, where the Germans had been publishing their own *Pariser Zeitung*. The first issues of the new Paris press were sold on the street-corners amid the gunfire of the insurrection. In the provinces, too, Resistance newspapers took over the plants of suspended publications. However, in many departments there were no underground newspapers capable of transforming themselves into regular dailies. In those localities entirely new ventures frequently sprang up, sponsored by Resistance organizations or Departmental Liberation Committees.

In no area of French life had the purge been as swift and as radical. Francisque Gay of the Underground Press Federation confessed that during the occupation he had been skeptical of their chances of carrying out their "audacious plans for a total *renouvellement*"; but six weeks after the Liberation of Paris it was clear to Gay that "on the essential points, our most ambitious objectives have been accomplished in one stroke".[7]

The new press was strikingly different from the old – most obviously in its format, which was drastically reduced as a result of the severe paper shortage. Striking too was the sense of excitement it generated,

6. Ordinance of June 22, 1944 (J.O. [Alger], July 8, p. 550).
7. *L'Aube*, October 7, 1944.

an impression heightened by the amateurism of many of the new ventures. But most important of all was the political revolution which had taken place in the French press. It was a complete *renversement*. In 1939 the Radicals and parties of the Right controlled newspapers with 46·2 per cent of the total newspaper circulation (and in addition enjoyed the tacit support of most formally non-partisan publications);

TABLE 3. – *Evolution of the French press: 1939-49[a]*

Tendency[b]	1939	1944	1947	1949
Independent and non-political[c]	10 (41·6%)	14 (14·9%)	17 (20·0%)	14 (20·4%)
Communist	3 (5·2%)	31 (26·8%)	25 (22·2%)	20 (17·3%)
Socialist	10 (6·2%)	25 (21·0%)	26 (14·8%)	21 (12·0%)
Radical	20 (16·9%)	9 (5·4%)	19 (13·6%)	14 (17·4%)
M.R.P.	—	15 (13·6%)	22 (16·3%)	11 (9·3%)
Right	61 (29·3%)	13 (7·3%)	22 (10·9%)	20 (15·1%)

[a] Based on statistics in Jean Mottin, *Histoire politique de la presse: 1944-1949* (Paris: 1949), p. 143. The first number in each group refers to the total number of newspapers of that tendency printing at least 20,000 copies. The number in parentheses refers to the share of those newspapers in the total circulation of newspapers of that size. (Papers of over 20,000 circulation accounted for about 90 per cent of total newspaper circulation throughout.)

[b] Political tendencies are here defined somewhat broadly; i.e., "Radical" includes "radicalisante", etc.

[c] Newspapers in this category were generally more conservative in 1939 than in 1944; subsequently they drifted part of the way back.

the Socialist and Communist press combined accounted for 11·4 per cent of the total readership. In late 1944 the share of the Radicals and the Right had dropped to 12·7 per cent; the Socialists' and Communists' share had risen to 47·8 per cent. and now it was they who had the support of much of the "non-partisan" press. (See Table 3.)

Once the political revolution in the French press was accomplished – and it was accomplished immediately after the Liberation – political positions on press questions hardened according to the principle of *cui bono*. The Socialists, the Communists, and the Resistance newspapers installed in the sequestered printing plants had a vested interest in making permanent the existing situation. The Radicals, the Right, and the owners of sequestered newspapers attempted to "normalize" the press situation – which for them meant returning in so far as possible to the status quo ante bellum. The M.R.P. – which as a new party, gained from the *renouvellement* of the press, and as the inheritor of much of the Right, lost – was divided. For over a year after the Liberation, however, party positions could not be directly translated into legislation, since the Provisional Government ruled by fiat. After the Constituent Assembly was elected in the fall of 1945, a press law was enacted which – temporarily – satisfied the Assembly's left-wing majority. Until that law was passed, in the spring of 1946, the Left, and the new press, experienced months of frustration and anxiety.

During the summer of 1944, in a Ministry of Information circular advising local authorities on the policy to be followed toward the press, limiting dates were established after which continued publication carried a presumption of culpability: fifteen days after June 25, 1940, for the Northern Zone; fifteen days after November 11, 1942, for the Southern.[8] In an Ordinance dated September 30, 1944, the Government ratified the suspension of papers published between those dates and the Liberation (as well as papers which commenced publication after June 25, 1940). Suspensions would be lifted (1) if the proprietors or administrators of a newspaper were acquitted of charges of collaboration; (2) if the Government decided not to prosecute them; (3) if no action had been taken within six months of the date of the Ordinance. (In the event, the automatic expiration of suspension was extended several times by subsequent ordinances.)

The Ordinance was silent on the question of what would happen to the sequestered establishments of newspapers whose proprietors were convicted. More ominous from the point of view of the new press was the implication that newspaper owners who were acquitted would have their establishments returned to them. What, then, would happen to

8. The circular is printed in Jean Pierre-Bloch, *Le Vent souffle sur l'histoire* (Paris: 1956), pp. 287-92. The choice of November 26, 1942, has been alleged to have been aimed particularly at *Le Temps*, which, since it had not ceased publication until November 29, would thus be beyond the pale. It is certainly true that there was great hostility toward *Le Temps*, which before the war had been the organ of the Comité des Forges, and had been ardently *munichois*. There are reasons to believe that the allegation may be well founded. Cf. Hubert Beuve-Méry, *Du "Temps" au "Monde"* (Paris: 1956), pp. 13ff.; Abel Chatelain, *Le Monde et ses lecteurs sous la IVe République* (Paris: 1962), pp. 37-42; Claude Hisard, *Histoire de la spoliation de la presse française* (Paris: 1955), pp. 69-70; Raymond Millet in *Le Monde*, April 4, 1947.

the Resistance newspapers currently installed in their premises? The mood of the new press became one of embattled self-defense.

In February 1945 the new press received reassurance on one – relatively minor – point. The Government decreed that the use of titles which had appeared under the occupation would be permanently banned, even if the newspapers which had borne them were permitted to reopen.[9] In the words of Minister of Information P.-H. Teitgen, these "drapeaux de Vichy" were "à jamais enfouis dans la fosse commune de nos déshonneurs nationaux".[10]

The next major enactment concerning the press was the Ordinance of May 5, 1945. This decree, in order to expedite the determination of the guilt or innocence of papers which appeared under the occupation, introduced a new concept into French law: that of the criminal responsibility of corporations. Trials of individual newspaper proprietors were, it was found, inconclusive in determining the behavior of the newspaper itself, particularly in cases of multiple ownership. Henceforth the newspapers themselves would be tried. If found guilty, press corporations were to be dissolved and their property confiscated;[11] if a

9. Ordinance of February 17, 1945.

10. *Combat*, October 28, 1944. Some, however, rose from the grave. General de Gaulle gave the semi-official Catholic newspaper *La Croix* permission to reappear with its old title, despite the fact that its appearance was "quelque peu prolongée" in the Southern Zone after the arrival of the Germans. (*Mémoires de guerre* [Paris: 1954-59], III, 114.) In fact, *La Croix* had ceased publication only on June 21, 1944, when the interruption of rail traffic by sabotage and Allied bombing made it impossible for the paper to reach its subscribers. The prohibition of the use of old titles was sometimes flouted, or, more often, evaded, both by prewar establishments whose suspension was lifted, and new papers wishing to cash in on the reputation of their predecessor. Sometimes a word was added to the old title (e.g., *La Dépêche du Midi* instead of *La Dépêche*); sometimes a word was subtracted (e.g., *Le Provençal* instead of *Le Petit Provençal*). Sometimes there were minor changes (e.g., *Le Petit Bleu de l'Agenais* replacing *Le Petit Bleu du Lot-et-Garonne*); sometimes a verbal maneuver was employed (*Aspects de la France*, which replaced *L'Action Française* as the organ of French monarchism, unofficially called itself "A.F."); sometimes a complete change in title was consistent with a stress on continuity (*Le Monde*, which occupied the premises of *Le Temps*, and employed many of its staff members, printed its title in the distinctive typeface identified with *Le Temps*). There were, so far as I have been able to discover, no prosecutions for evasions of the Ordinance of February 17, 1945.

11. If there were mitigating circumstances the court might decree partial instead of total confiscation. Even in cases of total confiscation, some stockholders might be indemnified if they had tried to prevent the newspaper's criminal activity or if they had been prevented by the circumstances from doing so.

newspaper was found innocent, or if the Government dropped proceedings against it, it would have its rights and property restored.

The provision in the Ordinance for the restoration of the property of acquitted newspapers made explicit the threat to the new press which had only been implied in the Ordinance of the previous September. At first the Resistance press was satisfied with the assurances of the Minister of Information, who announced that the trials were being held largely for the sake of form.[12] Reassuring too was the language of the Ordinance itself, which spoke of a presumption of guilt on the part of the newspapers in question, and listed culpable acts in such a fashion as to make it seem that the role of the courts would consist of little more than certifying the fact of publication during the occupation.

The confidence of the new press that it would be confirmed in its occupancy of the premises of the sequestered papers quickly disappeared; of fifty-five newspapers whose cases were decided during 1945, less than half were found guilty.[13] The Fédération Nationale de la Presse Française (F.N.P.F.), spokesman for the new press, was convinced that only drastic action could prevent their displacement by the "presse de la trahison". The new papers were convinced that only legislation which provided for confiscation by decree, rather than by the vagaries of judicial action, would suffice to protect their interests.[14] The newly elected Constituent Assembly – with its Socialist-Communist majority–provided the natural instrument for enacting such legislation.

Early in 1946 Gaston Defferre, Socialist Minister of Information in the new Government, introduced a bill which at last satisfied the demands of the Resistance press. All newspapers which had appeared under the occupation, with the exception of the handful already authorized to appear (e.g., *La Croix*) were to be expropriated. Their assets would be handed over to a state holding company, the Société Nationale des Entreprises de Presse (S.N.E.P.), which would sell or lease them to the new press. Newspapers found guilty of collaboration would receive no compensation; those found innocent (or not prosecuted) would be compensated on the basis of an assessment of the worth of their holdings as of June 25, 1940, minus the expenses of the S.N.E.P.

12. J.O., A.C.P. Debates, December 1, 1944, pp. 402-03.
13. J.O., A.N.C. (I) Debates, April 14, 1946, p. 1802.
14. The subsequent handling of press cases by the Ministry of Justice and the courts demonstrated the wisdom of the F.N.P.F.'s attitude. By the end of 1948, when all but 35 cases had been settled, there had been 115 guilty verdicts, 30 acquittals, and 393 decisions not to prosecute – which under the law had the same effect as acquittals. (Jean Mottin, *Histoire politique de la presse: 1944-1949* [Paris: 1949], pp. 31-32.)

Although the political configuration of the new Assembly made passage of the "Loi Defferre" certain, the debate was long and bitter. The Radicals and the Right condemned the proposal as not only unjust, but as a brazen political maneuver. Even before the 1945 elections the Radicals had claimed "foul" – asserting that since their Party was deprived of the means of expression which they had had in 1939, the results of the election were falsified in advance; they had demanded the restoration of the prewar proportions.[15] In the 1946 Assembly debates, Edouard Herriot, the grand old man of the Radical Party, explained the Radicals' poor electoral showing by pointing to the press revolution: they had been "fighting machine guns with wooden sabers".[16] Worst of all, from the standpoint of those disadvantaged by the press revolution, was that the process was self-sustaining. An Assembly based on the "falsified" election was about to freeze the new political status quo by making the *renversement* in the press permanent.

The Left disputed the contention that the redistribution of the press had significantly affected the outcome of the election. Defferre pointed out that the Right had received over 40 per cent of the vote in four departments in which it had no daily newspaper, and under 10 per cent in three departments where they had one or two. The Radicals had received 36 per cent of the vote in Savoie, where they had no newspaper; under 10 per cent in fourteen departments where they had papers.[17] The appeals to the principles of equity, liberalism, and freedom of the press seemed to the Left merely rhetorical devices on the part of defenders of collaborating newspaper owners.[18] The final vote on the bill was, with minor exceptions, along straight party lines. The Socialists, the Communists, and those allied to them, voted "yes"; the Radicals and the Right voted "no"; the M.R.P., except for a few defectors to the two other camps, abstained. The Socialist and Communist votes alone, even if all others had been opposed, were sufficient to carry the bill, which became the Law of May 11, 1946.

15. Parti Républicain Radical, *36ᵉ Congrès* [August 1945]: *Résolutions* (Paris: 1945), p. 16. Cf. Parti Républicain de la Liberté, *Le Programme du P.R.L.* (Paris: 1946), p. 6.
16. J.O., A.N.C. (I) Debates, March 13, 1946, p. 712.
17. *Ibid.*, p. 732. These figures of course, prove nothing except that there is not a one-to-one relationship between press circulation and electoral success – which nobody had claimed. Undoubtedly the press revolution had an effect on the 1945 (and subsequent) elections, but it is difficult to say how much.
18. See, e.g., J.O., A.N.C. (I) Debates, April 14, 1946, p. 1788; Mouvement de Libération Nationale, *Premier Congrès National: Janvier 1945* (Paris 1945), pp. 79-80.

A NEW SOCIETY

Political partisanship in the treatment of press questions did not end
with the passage of the Law of May 11, 1946. The Law merely authorized transfers to the S.N.E.P. – the actual process of transfer was in the
hands of politicians who sat in the cabinet. Their use of this power
strikingly illustrates the split between the parties on the press. Philip
Williams has summed up the differences in the way Ministers of Information from different parties applied the Law.

> The two Socialist ministers transferred an average of over twenty a
> month, compared with less than four a month while ministers of other
> parties were in office. The contrast was still more startling in respect of
> papers which had not been condemned. Sixty of these were transferred
> during the period [1946-48], more than two-thirds of them (including
> most of the biggest) by the two Socialists. Under them the rate of transfer
> of such papers was nearly one a day, under M.R.P. ministers one a
> month, and under R.G.R. ministers one in four months.[19]

The Resistance newspapers, the parties of the Left, and the F.N.P.F.
protested ministerial sabotage of the law, but to no avail. Because of the
power of the Minister of Information to apply (or block application of)
the press law, that post became a crucial bargaining point in the construction of coalition cabinets. A tangled jurisprudence was created, as
local courts "interpreted" the press law in a sense completely opposed
to both its language and the clear legislative intent. Private agreements
between old and new papers, arranged with the blessing of the
S.N.E.P., became more and more common, as both sides sought to
regularize their situation. The tangle was not, however, completely
unsnarled until 1954, when a revised press law was adopted which
satisfied all but the irreconcilables on both sides.

The press purge brought about a temporary *renversement* in the relation between each party's share of the press and its share of the vote.
Before the war the Socialists and Communists had less than 60 per cent
of their "fair share" of the press, in terms of circulation, while the
Radicals and the Right had a third and a fifth more than "their share"
respectively. In 1944-45 it was the latter groups that were relatively
disadvantaged, and the Socialists and Communists who were overrepresented in the press. By 1946-47 both the Socialists' and the Communists' share of the press was almost exactly proportionate to their

19. *Politics in Post-War France: Parties and the Constitution in the Fourth
Republic* (London: 1954), pp. 390-91. The R.G.R. – "Rassemblement des
Gauches Républicaines" – was a coalition organized around the Radical
Party.

share of the electorate; the Radicals' share of the press, though in absolute terms much lower than before the war, was higher relative to their vote; the press of the Right was still below parity, but was climbing fast. (See Table 4.) After 1947 the balance was redressed (or "over-redressed") still further.[20]

The press purge gave the Resistance newspapers a running head start at the Liberation. The access to the sequestered printing plants which they received was an enormous financial advantage. The system of prior government authorization for publication, which lasted until 1947, had been occasioned at least as much by the paper shortage as by a desire to purify the press; nevertheless, the effect was to give the new press a protected quasi-monopoly for almost three years. In addition, the press which emerged from the underground enjoyed an enormous moral authority in the "résistantialiste" France of the immediate postwar years.

Despite these advantages, within a few years the new press – with very few exceptions – either disappeared or was completely transformed. By early 1947 thirty-six new newspapers had closed their doors; five years later the casualty list included 185 dailies and 453 weeklies.[21] Half of the Paris newspapers which appeared (or reappeared) during the insurrection have disappeared, including *L'Aube*, *Ce Soir*, *La France Libre*, *Front National*, *L'Homme Libre*, and *Libération*. Most of those which survive have changed beyond recognition. *Défense de la France* became *France-Soir* at the end of 1944, although until 1946 its masthead carried the legend: "Défense de la France, fondé sous l'occupation, 14 juillet 1941". Then, on the same day that banner headlines in *France-Soir* announced "Les quadruplés sont nés hier en 1 h 9 mn", it abandoned the formula which recalled its origins and substituted: "Le plus fort tirage et le plus forte vente de tous les journaux français".[22] *Combat*, edited by Albert Camus in the first postwar years, was sold to a North African entrepeneur when bankruptcy threatened. (*Combat* is one of a tiny handful of newspapers in France which retains any reference to its Resistance origins on its masthead; the phrase "De la Résistance à la Révolution", though appearing in characters of ever-decreasing size, has never quite disappeared.) *Le Parisien Libéré* and *Franc-Tireur* (rebaptized *Paris-Jour*) have become completely commercial ventures.

Ironically, the one newspaper which conspicuously retains the élan,

20. See Table 3, p. 118.
21. Mottin, p. 42; J.O., A.N. Debates, May 9, 1952, p. 2306.
22. Jacques Kayser, *Le Quotidien français* (Paris: 1963), p. 46 n. 13.

TABLE 4. – *Changing relationship between parties' share of vote and share of press*

Political parties (including allies and affiliates)	1936-39[b]			1944-45[c]			1946-47[d]		
	% of vote	% of political press	Share of press relative to share of vote	% of vote	% of political press	Share of press relative to share of vote	% of vote	% of political press	Share of press relative to share of vote
Communist	15·6	9·0	57·7%	26·5	36·2	136·6%	28·3	28·5	100·7%
Socialist	19·9	10·8	54·3%	25·0	28·3	113·2%	17·9	19·0	106·1%
Radical	22·1	29·3	132·6%	8·9	7·3	82·0%	11·1	17·5	157·7%
M.R.P.	—	—	—	23·9	18·4	77·0%	26·0	21·0	80·8%
Right	42·4	50·9	120·0%	15·7	9·9	63·1%	16·0	14·0	87·5%

[a] Election statistics from *Encyclopédie politique de la France et du monde*, 2nd ed. (Paris: 1950), I, 358; press statistics from Jean Mottin, *Histoire politique de la presse: 1944-1949* (Paris: 1949), p. 143.

[b] Voting statistics from the elections of April 22, 1936; press statistics as of August 1939.

[c] Voting statistics from the elections of October 21, 1945; press statistics as of December 31, 1944.

[d] Voting statistics from the elections of November 10, 1946; press statistics as of March 1, 1947.

the sense of dedication, and the spirit of cooperative endeavor which characterized the Resistance press of 1944, is a newspaper with no Resistance antecedents, one which did not appear until some months after the Liberation – indeed, one whose appearance was attacked and resented by many "vrais résistants". The creation of Le Monde as the successor to Le Temps is the one permanent and substantial contribution of the press purge to French journalism. This by itself is perhaps sufficient justification – if justification is needed – for the entire operation.

At the time of the Liberation the Comité National des Ecrivains included virtually all Resistance writers (and those anxious to establish themselves as such). Among its members were Louis Aragon, Simone de Beauvoir, Julian Benda, Albert Camus, Georges Duhamel, André Malraux, François Mauriac, Jean Paulhan, Jean-Paul Sartre, and Vercors. In September 1944 the C.N.E. called on the Government to take rigorous judicial action against collaborationist writers.[23] This was done, and authors figured prominently in the early trials. Henri Béraud, Robert Brasillach, Charles Maurras, George Suarez, and other well-known writers were among the first to appear before the new cours de justice. For this reason, professionally sponsored sanctions against writers were not very widespread. A writers' purge commission was established in the spring of 1945, composed of representatives of various literary associations, but since the cases of leading collaborationist and vichyssois writers had been preempted by the courts, they generally had to content themselves with relatively minor figures. The only writers of note who received sanctions were André Castelot, André Thérive, and Henry de Montherlant. They were forbidden to publish their writings for terms ranging from one to two years (the maximum penalty allowed).[24]

23. Lettres Françaises, September 9, 1944.
24. J.O., June 26, 1946, p. 5746; January 26, 1947, p. 1040. Among artists, the purge was a much less serious business than among writers. The purge commission for "artists, painters, cartoonists, sculptors and engravers," like that for writers, included representatives of the leading professional associations. Lest the Commission's work become the occasion for the airing of irrelevant feuds, the artist-members were reminded in the decree establishing the commission that they sat as representatives of all artists, "of all esthetic tendencies". With the exception of political cartoonists, it is difficult for artistic creation to be intrinsically "antinational"; not surprisingly, most of the sanctions taken by the artists' purge commission were directed against this group. Vlaminck was the only artist of note who received a sanction, and

While purge commission sanctions against writers were generally rare and slow in coming, official action was taken to ban the distribution of a certain number of their books. Early in 1945 collaborationist, anti-Semitic, and Vichyite works were ordered removed from bookstores and returned to the publishers. Among the authors whose books appeared on the lists circulated by the Contrôle Militaire des Informations were Louis-Ferdinand Céline, Drieu La Rochelle, Charles Maurras, Jean Luchaire, Georges Suarez, and Abel Bonnard.[25]

There was an unofficial as well as an official writers' purge. In September 1944 the C.N.E. published a "blacklist" of tainted writers. The preface to the list stressed that those whose names appeared on it were not equally guilty. The purpose of publishing it was to announce the vow of the members of the C.N.E. not to have any "professional contact" with those listed (i.e., they would not themselves write for periodicals which published works by those blacklisted). The list included René Benjamin, Jacques Benoist-Méchin, Henri Béraud, Georges Blond, Abel Bonnard, Robert Brasillach, André Castelot, L.-F. Céline, Alphonse de Châteaubriant, Drieu La Rochelle, Alfred Fabre-Luce, Bernard Faÿ, Sacha Guitry, Abel Hermant, Maurice Martin du Gard, Charles Maurras, Henry de Montherlant, and George Suarez.[26]

In the fall of 1944, when all the press was "résistantialiste", this kind of boycott seemed an effective sanction. Even without the threat of boycott, Resistance-oriented journals were not likely to publish the works of *vichyssois*, nor would such writers submit their works to them. As the character of the press changed – which it did rapidly – the function of the blacklist became purely moral. And even the moral force of the blacklist, and of the unofficial literary purge in general, was dissipated by the crudely partisan use made of it by the Communists.

André Gide, it was alleged, had not only "objectively served the enemy" by the anti-Communism of his prewar *Retour de l'U.R.S.S.*, but had raised serious doubts about his patriotism by his "sudden zeal at the end of 1940 to study the German language". Another charge was his "slander" of the French peasantry by asking, in his 1940 *Journal*, how many of them "would not willingly accept Descartes and Watteau

---

it was purely symbolic, since its term had expired by the time it was pronounced: the decision, dated June 24, 1946, forbade him to exhibit or sell his works for one year as of September 1944. (J.O., June 26, 1946, p. 5745.)

25. *Bibliographie de la France: Chroniques*, CXXXIV, 4th series, Nos. 1-2 (January 5-12, 1945), 8-9 (February 23-March 2, 1945), 14-15 (April 6-13, 1945), 22-24 (June 1-15, 1945).

26. *Lettres Françaises*, September 16 and October 9, 1944.

as Germans if that would make them sell their wheat for a few cents more"?[27] (This at a time when the Communists were denouncing General de Gaulle as an agent of British imperialism.) Paul Nizan had been one of the leading literary lights of the Communist Party before the war. He broke with the Party over the Hitler-Stalin Pact, then was killed in action in the campaign of 1940 (at the same time that Maurice Thorez was deserting his unit and fleeing to Moscow). After the war the Communists saw to the removal of "the traitor Nizan's" works from an exhibition of writings of *résistants* and veterans; the false rumor was spread that Nizan had cooperated with the police in the 1939 suppression of the P.C.F. (The slander was protested by a group of writers which included not only Raymond Aron, Albert Camus, and François Mauriac, but also many who were close to the Communists: Julian Benda, Jean-Paul Sartre, Simone de Beauvoir.[28])

In the months following the Liberation the C.N.E. came more and more under the influence of Communist cultural commissars. Some, like Camus, had seen this coming from the beginning, and resigned in the fall of 1944. Father Bruckberger reports the following conversation between Camus and Mauriac at that time:

M: Why did you resign?
C: For the sake of honesty. I can't allow my name and my signature to be used by a [Communist] majority . . . whose standards and tactics we both know. . . . It is for me to ask you why you *don't* resign.
M: Because of solidarity.
C: No, M. Mauriac, it is on account of fear. You fear them and that's why you let them lead you where they will.
M: Perhaps you are right.[29]

By 1946 most prominent non-Communist writers had left the C.N.E.: formally over the issue of the continued indiscriminate use of the blacklist; actually because of Communist domination. Georges Duhamel, Jean Paulhan, François Mauriac, and Jean Schlumberger were among those who resigned in 1946. Their resignations were the occasion of a lively polemical exchange on the blacklist and the writer's "right to error".[30]

27. Louis Aragon in *Lettres Françaises*, November 25, 1944; J.O., A.C.P. Debates, July 7, 1944, pp. 141-42.
28. *Combat*, April 4, 1947.
29. *Nous n'irons plus au bois* (Paris: 1948), pp. 32-34.
30. *Lettres Françaises*, March 8 and December 27, 1946; January 10, 1947; *Nouvelles Epîtres*, Nos. 14, 20, 45 and 47; Georges Duhamel, *Tribulations de l'espérance* (Paris: 1947), pp. 412-18; Jean Paulhan, *De la paille et du grain* (Paris: 1948), p. 57.

Despite the partial discrediting of the literary purge, there was a *renouvellement* in French letters. It was due, however, less to the purge than to general political and demographic factors. After the First World War, the old had dominated French literary life while "the young remained at Verdun, on the Marne, and on the Yser". After the Liberation the situation was reversed. The old men had either died (Romains Rolland, Jean Giraudoux) or been discredited by their association with Vichy (Béraud, Céline, Maurras, De Montherlant). Jean-Paul Sartre noted that when Jacques Maritain was asked his impressions of the Fourth Republic, he said "France lacks men". He meant, said Sartre, "it lacks men of my generation". The young writers of the Resistance – Camus, Vercors, Sartre himself – took their place. And it was difficult for them to prevent Resistance camaraderie from influencing their literary behavior, and thus the entire literary climate.

> How could a *résistant* critic say to a *résistant* author that he finds his novel on the Resistance no good at all? He does say it, because he is an honest man, but he lets it be understood that the book, while it fails, has a quality rarer and more valuable than if it had succeeded – a sort of "virtuous aroma."[31]

The literary *renouvellement* was, of course, far from complete, and it never succeeded in breaching the walls of that monument to French intellectual life, the Académie Française.

Few institutions in French society were more "vichyssois" and "collabo" than the Académie Française. Many of the immortals who for years had been fighting a defensive action on behalf of Bishop Bossuet against the Enlightenment became rhapsodic Pétainists when the Marshal lent the authority of the State to their camp; other academicians cooperated enthusiastically with German propaganda efforts. Georges Duhamel and others did what they could to limit the extent to which their Pétainist and Germanophile colleagues compromised the assembly itself, but the only immortal who was actually a *résistant*, in the sense that he engaged in illegal underground activity, was François Mauriac.

Not unnaturally, the Academy was the subject of bitter remarks from the Resistance after the Liberation; there was even talk of dissolving the 300-year-old assembly. General de Gaulle evidenced his willingness to fulfill the chief of state's role as "protector" of the Academy, but suggested that it would be in the Academy's interest to

31. All quotations in this paragraph are from Sartre's "La Nationalisation de La Littérature", *Temps Modernes*, I, 2 (November 1, 1945), 204-07.

restore its tarnished image by inviting *résistant* writers to fill the existing vacancies. The General reported that "my comforting remarks had been favorably received, but my suggested reforms less so".[32] At the annual meeting of the five Academies of the Institute in October 1944 Jérôme Tharaud, representing the Académie Française, devoted most of his "discours sur la libération" to the theme of "forgive and forget".[33]

Government ordinances beyond the Academy's control automatically excluded four of its members when they were sentenced to national degradation: Abel Bonnard, Abel Hermant, Charles Maurras, and Marshal Pétain. The chairs of the first two were filled in 1946, but the Academy pointedly refrained from filling those of Pétain and Maurras until after their deaths in 1951 and 1952.[34]

Other prominent Pétainists and collaborators remained in the Academy; more were later elected, although sometimes candidates who were "trop compromis" were defeated. Paul Bourget once described the Academy as one of the four great European fortresses of defense against the Revolution, the others being the House of Lords, the Papacy, and the Prussian General Staff. Nothing that happened after the Liberation changed the accuracy of that sobriquet.

The Catholic Church, like the French Academy, was a monument of conservatism which had embraced Pétain's "National Revolution". (As with the Academy, the attitude of the Church was not monolithic, but the proportion of *résistants* – even in spirit – was as small.) During the occupation, non-Catholic *résistants* generally refrained from attacking the Pétainism of the clergy; they had no moral or political investment in the reputation of the clergy (rather the reverse) and did not want to risk a breach with their Catholic comrades. Catholic *résistants*, however, were not only personally disturbed at the line taken by a number of bishops, but feared for the future reputation of the Church.[35]

32. De Gaulle, *Mémoires*, Vol. III, p. 116.
33. J.O., November 9, 1944, pp. 1249-50.
34. Pétain was also a member of the Académie des Sciences Morales et Politiques, one of the other four Academies which, with the Académie Française, make up the Institut de France. This section of the Institut also refused to fill the Marshal's vacant chair until after his death, when Albert Schweitzer became Pétain's successor. However, the Académie des Sciences expelled Georges Claude long before his conviction for collaboration automatically excluded him from state-connected bodies such as the Institut.
35. See *Véritas*, No. 2 (August 25, 1941); *Défense de la France*, No. 9 December 1941); *Cahiers Politiques*, No. 5 (January 1944); and the "Open Letter from the Priests and Chaplains of the Maquis to the Cardinals and Bishops of France" (May 14, 1944) in the B.D.I.C. collection "France/Occupée/Résistance/Maquis".

Specific proposals for a purge of the Church were rare; however, one enthusiastic priest of the Resistance proposed that

> patriotic priests establish Ecclesiastical Liberation Committees in each region, and that all cases [of collaboration] concerning the clergy be submitted to them. [This] purge is necessary if the clergy is not to lose its influence in the nation. The measures taken [by the Committees] will be submitted to the Minister of Justice via the Papal Nuncio.[36]

Needless to say, this recommendation was not adopted.

While very little public action was taken with respect to clerical collaboration, the Government was not completely indifferent to the activity of the hierarchy under Vichy. At the Liberation of Paris Cardinal Suhard, an ardent supporter of Pétain, received a chilly reception when he met with General de Gaulle's representatives, and he was refused permission to officiate at the mass of celebration at Notre-Dame. The arch-collaborationist Cardinal Baudrillart had conveniently died before the Liberation, sparing the Church the embarrassment of seeing one of its princes in the dock, or, alternatively, sparing the Government the embarrassment of exempting from prosecution one of the most vocal and violent collaborationists in France. The Papal Nuncio, Mgr Valeri, was "disaccredited" along with all other diplomatic representatives at Vichy, and his successor, Mgr Roncalli (the future John XXIII) had to deal with the Government's demand for the removal of compromised bishops. The exact number of dismissals sought by the Government is uncertain – it may have been as many as thirty or thirty-five. In the spring of 1945 agreement was reached on the removal of seven bishops, the whole matter being managed with a minimum of publicity.[37]

The trade-union purge was important not so much for what it accomplished, as for what it symbolized – a major realignment of forces within the French trade-union movement. The conflicts which found expression in the purge were rooted as much in prewar as in wartime conflicts, and its meaning can only be understood in terms of those conflicts.

36. Cited in Henri Michel, *Les Courants de pensée de la Résistance* (Paris: 1962), p. 345.

37. André Latreille, "Les Débuts de Mgr. Roncalli à la Nonciature de Paris: Souvenirs d'un Témoin, Décembre 1944-Août 1945", *Revue de Paris*, August 1963, 66-74.

Founded in 1895, the Confédération Générale du Travail (C.G.T.) split into Communist and non-Communist wings in 1921. The Communist minority took the name "C.G.T. Unitaire" (and were subsequently referred to as "unitaires" as opposed to the Socialist-oriented "confédérés"). As part of the Popular Front *rassemblement* of the French Left, the C.G.T. and the C.G.T.U. were reunited under the former name in 1936. At the moment of unity the Communists had about a quarter of the total strength of the movement, a proportion that increased steadily up to the war. By that time, the non-Communists in the C.G.T. were themselves split – principally, or at least manifestly, over questions of foreign policy. Roughly half of the "confédérés", under the leadership of René Belin, were sympathetic to the magazine *Syndicats*, which was strongly anti-Communist and anti-Soviet, and equally strongly pro-Munich; the other half, followers of Léon Jouhaux, were for resistance to Nazi Germany as the keystone of French foreign policy and were unequivocally opposed to appeasement. Thus in the late 1930's the C.G.T. was divided between a Communist (anti-Munich) left, an anti-Communist (pro-Munich) right, and a non-Communist, anti-Munich center.

It is impossible to overestimate the depth and bitterness of the split within the "unified" C.G.T. The Communists and a section of the Socialists were deeply (and to all appearances irrevocably) committed to resistance to Nazi Germany. Their traditional struggle with French capitalism was seen as inextricably tied to the struggle against appeasement of Hitler – the policy of "the trusts". For the right wing of the trade-union movement – as for the French Right in general – the most dangerous enemies were the Communists at home, the Soviet Union abroad. Some favored appeasement because of a traditional pacifist commitment, others because of sympathy with fascism, others because Hitler was a "bulwark against bolshevism". There could be no permanent reconciliation of the two points of view; the only question was whether the Left or the Right would retain control of the organizational apparatus in the inevitable split.

A temporary victory was won by the Left in November 1938 when the C.G.T. Congress at Nantes condemned the Munich agreement, urged firm resistance to Germany, and denounced the alliance of the *Syndicats* group with Marcel Déat and Jacques Doriot. But no organizational schism resulted, and the followers of the *Syndicats* line continued to denounce the "warmongers" in ever more violent language. Ludovick Zoretti of the Teachers' Federation accused Léon Blum of being concerned only with saving the Jews in the Sudetenland; Raymond Froideval endorsed Déat's plea that no Frenchmen should "die for Danzig".[38]

When the split came it took very different lines than those which had been anticipated. The Russo-German Pact of August 22, 1939, opened the eyes of the Communists in the C.G.T. to the fact that the struggle between Hitler and the West was an imperialist conflict. When, a week later, war was declared, the *Syndicats* group became formal if unenthusiastic anti-Nazis. Some trade-union federations (miners, seamen, P.T.T.) began to expel their Communist members immediately following the declaration of war. The decision to exclude Communists from the C.G.T. as a whole was taken on September 18, the day after the Russian invasion of Poland. While formally only those who "would not or could not" condemn the Russian invasion of Poland were to be expelled, the criterion adopted in practice was an individual's attitude toward the Pact; those who refused to make a statement were considered to approve it and were expelled. Communist-dominated unions were dissolved by government decree, and parallel non-Communist organizations created by the C.G.T. From time to time the C.G.T. executive committee entered mild protests at the repressive policy of the Government, which arbitrarily arrested and interned thousands of Communist trade-unionists; for the most part, however, the C.G.T. preserved an attitude of official "neutrality", while the *Syndicats* group cheered on the repression.

The establishment of the Vichy Regime brought new splits – and new reconciliations – to the French trade-union movement. Most of the leaders of the *Syndicats* group became Pétainists. Belin, spokesman for the group on the prewar executive committee of the C.G.T., became Pétain's Minister of Labor. Many of Belin's associates joined him at the Ministry; others founded and published Vichyite and collaborationist trade-union newspapers, such as *L'Atelier* and *Au Travail*. In the fall of 1940 the C.G.T., together with the Confédération Française des Travailleurs Chrétiens (C.F.T.C.), was dissolved by a decree issued over Belin's signature. Local trade-unions, which were not dissolved, were integrated into a new corporate structure based on the "Charte du Travail" drafted by Belin and his colleagues.

38. Henry W. Ehrmann, *French Labor from Popular Front to Liberation* (New York: 1947), pp. 106-10. While Professor Ehrmann does not believe that this campaign was the result of "wilful treachery, personal ambition, or outright corruption", he has no doubt that it was financed by outside funds, and he hints strongly that it was, at least in part, paid for by Foreign Office secret funds dispensed by Georges Bonnet.

Those trade-unionists who were hostile to Belin's corporate conceptions lost no time in manifesting their opposition to Vichy policy. Less than a week after the dissolution of the C.G.T. and C.F.T.C., representatives of the two federations issued a "Manifeste des Syndicalistes Françaises" which reaffirmed the signers' faith in a free trade-union movement. The C.G.T. and C.F.T.C. were reconstituted as underground organizations. In September 1942 conversations began between Léon Jouhaux (for the "confédérés") and the Communist C.G.T. leaders who, although they had been "underground" since September 1939, had only been reminded that they were French patriots in June 1941, when Hitler invaded the Soviet Union. The discussions continued after Jouhaux's arrest and deportation to Germany. In April 1943 agreement was reached on the reunification of the two wings of the C.G.T. The new (underground) executive committee was organized on the basis of the September 1939 proportions: five "confédérés", three "unitaires". Both the C.F.T.C. and the reunified C.G.T. were represented in the Conseil National de la Résistance and the Consultative Assembly in Algiers. *Résistant* trade-unionists denounced the Labor Charter as "not a treaty of social peace, but an instrument of police repression – a hypocritical comedy".[39] Underground trade-union newspapers were published; illegal strikes were organized; workers on the railroads and in key industries organized sabotage. Resistance trade-unions were in the forefront of the struggle against Vichy and the Germans. The former members of the *Syndicats* group were citizens of one of "les deux Frances" from 1940 to 1944; *résistant* trade-unionists were citizens of the other.

The Provisional Government left the task of purging the trade-union movement to the unions themselves; government enactments simply provided the framework of the procedure, criteria, and sanctions to be applied. The Ordinance of July 27, 1944, annulled all Vichy labor legislation, and annulled as well the exclusion of Communist trade-unionists from the C.G.T. in September 1939. (The underground reunification of the C.G.T. had already annulled the Communists' exclusion in fact, but the bracketing of the 1939 C.G.T. action with Vichy anti-union legislation had the advantage, from the Communist point of view, of seeming to underwrite their thesis that the 1939 exclusion was part of the same Belinist policy of "anti-communist aggression" followed by Vichy.)

A national "commission de reconstitution des organisations syndicales" was to be established, as well as analogous commissions on the

39. Quoted in Michel, *Courants*, p. 180.

departmental level. On both levels the commissions were to consist of five representatives of the C.G.T. and two from the C.F.T.C. Until unions were reconstituted and could act on their own, the commissions were to provisionally bar from union office anyone who was known to have

> furthered enemy designs either directly, or indirectly, by his voluntary cooperation with the actions of [the Vichy Government], in particular by voluntarily cooperating in production for the benefit of the enemy, in the deportation of workers, or in the destruction of trade union liberties.[40]

The "commissions de reconstitution" carried out their work on the basis of a joint C.G.T.-C.F.T.C. directive which outlined both the criteria to be employed and the sanctions to be taken. Purge measures were to be taken as a matter of course in the case of those who participated in the publication of *L'Atelier*, *Au Travail*, or similar newspapers, and those who were members of Vichyite and collaborationist trade-union committees. Participation in organizations established under the "Charte du Travail" posed a more delicate problem. The Resistance had advised workers to remain in their unions; some *résistant* unionists considered that their duty to the Resistance included membership in Vichy coordinating committees. (The instructions were not clearly worded, and could legitimately be interpreted in various ways.) On the other hand, some had zealously cooperated in the new committees' assault on traditional unionism. Since Resistance instructions had urged continued union activity in order to combat the influence of "Chartiste" conceptions, those in this latter category could hardly invoke Resistance orders as an excuse. The joint directive could only advise that Resistance instructions be taken into account in reaching decisions on an individual basis.

With respect to criteria for sanctions, the joint directive was well within the limits of the Ordinance of July 27, 1944. These limits were transcended, however, in the directive's list of applicable sanctions. In the first place, the Ordinance restricted the commissions' power to excluding individuals from trade union office; the directive allowed – and the commissions exercised this prerogative – exclusion from union membership as well.[41] Secondly, the Ordinance had assigned only pro-

40. C.G.T., *Compte rendu des travaux de la Commission Nationale de Reconstitution des Organisations Syndicales et Travailleurs* (Paris: 1946), pp. 4-6.

41. A few cases of total exclusion were appealed to the Conseil d'Etat on the grounds that commissions had exceeded their legal authority. The Conseil accepted the appeals and reversed the judgments, but the number of cases involved was small, and the effect of the reversals minimal.

visional powers to the commissions; their decrees were to have force only until unions were reorganized and could decide cases for themselves. The joint directive's list of sanctions included temporary suspension, but only as the lowest on a scale of five possible penalties, the most serious being exclusion from a trade-union for life.[42] Further, the commissions continued to meet and decide cases many months after the unions were reconstituted. (The Government subsequently modified the Ordinance, retroactively legitimatizing definitive and post-reconstitution sanctions; commission decisions were also made binding on the individual unions.[43])

The National Commission was responsible for the cases of officers of both national trade-union organizations and departmental inter-union federations. Between October 1944 and December 1945 it handed down 316 sanctions; three-quarters of the cases – including those of the most prominent trade-unionists, and those in which individuals received the heaviest sentences – were decided within the first six months of its work. The Commission's decisions included 133 exclusions from trade-union organizations for life, 36 for a term of from two to fifteen years; 30 individuals were barred from holding trade-union office for life; 119 for periods of from two to fifteen years.[44] All but a handful of the National Commission's sanctions were directed against C.G.T. (as opposed to C.F.T.C.) officials.

The number of cases which came before departmental commissions (whose jurisdiction extended only to purely local officials), as well as those heard by internal union committees, is not known; it does not seem to have been large. Most local committees, like the National Committee, had a non-Communist majority.[45] It is nevertheless frequently asserted that Communists made use of the trade-union purge to remove their enemies from the C.G.T. and pave the way for their takeover of that organization. A number of cases are cited in which non-collaborators and non-"Chartistes" were expelled, intimidated, or even murdered; others are cited in which collaborationist trade-unionists received a clean bill of health because they were willing to play the Communist game.[46] While it is impossible to make any definitive evaluation

42. In practice, of 316 National Commission decisions, all but one applied definitive sanctions.

43. Law of February 25, 1946.

44. Totals based on reports of individual decisions in C.G.T., *Compte rendu, passim.*

45. *Ibid.*, pp. 4-6.

46. Cf. C.G.T., *26e Congrès National* [1946] (Paris: 1946), pp. 84, 88, 125-26, 339-43; Elijah Ben-Zion Kaminsky, "An Anti-Subversive Program

of these charges, it is probable that many are well-founded. The Communists, in the trade-union arena as elsewhere, were quick to apply the epithet "collaborationist"; they were particularly prone to equating prewar membership in the *Syndicats* group, or support of Munich, with collaboration. In September 1943 the (Communist) Union des Syndicats Ouvriers de la Région Parisienne noted that in addition to removing wartime traitors from the C.G.T., it was necessary to eliminate

> the *munichois*, who were among those most anxious to hand everything over to Hitler on a silver platter. They were the men who embraced the abominable phrase: "plutôt la servitude que la guerre" . . . these men were responsible for the defeat of France: . . . we will not let this fifth column reorganize, we will not let it again poison the trade union movement. . . . Their presence would be the opening wedge of another split; in the last twenty years we have had two, and they have cost the working class dearly. The workers would be astonished, and confidence in the trade union movement would be undermined, if "repentant" *munichois* were again placed at the head of the movement.[47]

It is not improbable that in some instances Socialist trade-unionists cooperated in the application of sanctions against men whose only "crimes" dated from the last days of the Third Republic. The bulk of the trade-union purge was carried out in late 1944 and early 1945 – during the Communist-Socialist "honeymoon". In so far as Socialist trade-unionists were aware of competing with the Communists for the allegiance of the working class, their greatest fear was being thought less implacable, less "résistantialiste" than the latter.

Despite whatever efforts that may have been made to use the trade-union purge for partisan purposes, it is unlikely that they were more than a very subordinate factor in the takeover of the C.G.T. by the Communists. So far as the purge itself was a factor, it was the congruence between Belinism and Vichyism that was decisive, not tendentious

in the French Public Service: The French Epuration Administration of 1944-1953" (unpublished Ph.D. dissertation, Harvard University, 1962), pp. 310-313; Georges Lefranc, *Les Expériences syndicales en France de 1939 à 1950* (Paris: 1950), pp. 119 n. 11, 154, *et passim; La Révolution Prolétarienne*, July 1947, 25-27; August-September 1947, 10-14; March 1949, 22/86; April 1949, 18/114; May 1949, 24/152; June 1949, 4/164; February 1950, 9/41-12/44; March 1950, 20/84; May 1950, 20/148; July 1950, 30/222-31/223; June 1951, 24/216; *La Revue Syndicaliste*, January 1949, 2; February 1949, 1-4; May 1950, 21; Alfred J. Rieber, *Stalin and the French Communist Party: 1941-1947* (New York: 1962), pp. 179-83.

47. *Bulletin*, No. 5.

use of the purge machinery. By the dynamism that they had shown in the 1936 sit-down strikes, the Communists had gained wide – perhaps decisive – support among industrial workers. Whatever losses in support the Communists suffered in 1939-41 were more than overbalanced by the gains which accrued to them through their Resistance militancy. Communist gains over the Socialists in postwar elections – gains which were particularly marked in working-class districts – were the reflection on the political level of the same developments which brought them ascendancy in the C.G.T.[48]

There were other purges – most of them neither of great extent nor of great significance. There had been occasional demands by the underground press for a purge of the theater; charges were, however, more often directed against the "social collaboration" of performers than against culpable professional activity. A theatrical purge commission was set up, but it handed down few interdictions and none against leading performers. The head of the State Broadcasting Company described that organization's criteria as follows:

> A certain number of artists and specialists of all kinds used to broadcast from Radio Paris. Now Radio Paris was a German station. Does that mean that these artists collaborated with the enemy? It is certain that all were wrong not to refuse the offers made to them – offers which were often both insistent and menacing. All men are not heroes, however, and actors can rarely afford to wait for better days. What we did was to agree to employ people who had worked for Radio Paris only to earn their bread and butter, and on condition that they had undertaken only literary or artistic work. This leniency will not be extended to those who had any part in propaganda broadcasts.[49]

A few prominent performers were arrested at the Liberation, Maurice Chevalier and Sacha Guitry being the best known. Chevalier had been falsely reported by the German press to have made a tour of German cities during the war; in fact, he had performed for French prisoners of war at the camp where he himself had been a prisoner in 1918. He quickly secured his release. (However, because of the wide

48. After the 1947 split in the C.G.T. which gave birth to the non-Communist C.G.T.-Force Ouvrière, a few *épuré* trade unionists were admitted to the new federation. Others joined the C.F.T.C.; a few, together with some ex-Communists (class of '39) and Gaullists, formed the Confédération du Travail Indépendente, which never attained much importance; most entered other fields.

49. Quoted in Pickles, *France*, pp. 180-81.

circulation of the German reports, he was under an unofficial cloud for some time.) Guitry – who became something of a symbol of the "social collaborator" – was interned for a time, but the case against him was eventually dropped. A few other performers came before the *chambres civiques*: Cécile Sorel was declared *indignée* for having solicited the gift of a confiscated Jewish apartment; so was the film actress Corinne Luchaire (Jean's daughter) who had an illegitimate child by a German officer. The world of the theatre was hardly the fulcrum of French society, and apart from a certain bitterness at Guitry's impunity, not the subject of much popular attention.

In the case of lawyers and doctors, responsibility for a purge was delegated to their respective professional associations. In neither case were an appreciable number of sanctions taken. Practitioners of "the oldest profession" did not get off so lightly; one of the principal arguments advanced in favor of the "Loi Marthe Richard" which closed French brothels was the extent to which they had been centers of "collaboration".

The effectiveness of the purge varied enormously. In those cases in which the purge corresponded to independent secular changes it was "successful" (parliament, the trade-union movement). The most decisive state action could not effect a permanent change unless the foundation of the institution was itself fundamentally altered. The press purge was effective for a time because the Provisional Government "seized the means of production" and administered them for the benefit of the new press; when state control ceased, when free market mechanisms began to operate again, the results of the press purge began to melt away. When state action was half-hearted, and when the institution concerned resisted *renouvellement*, little was accomplished (the Catholic Church, the Académie Française). As a result of all the various purges French society was not, as had been hoped, transformed. But it was not quite the same either.

Chapter 8

NULLUM CRIMEN SINE LEGE

For the law brings wrath, but where there is no law there is no transgression.

Romans 4: 15

The law, like art, is always vainly racing to catch up with experience. At every turn of history it presents the citizen with new obligations, and renders dangerous the exercise of his liberty in some sphere by suddenly rendering that exercise an affront to the liberty of others. It is the task of judges and legislators to alter the law that it may cope with these capers of time. By a gross inappropriateness judges and legislators are described always as sitting, the one on the bench, the other in the House of Commons or the House of Lords; for in fact they run, they run fast as the hands of the clock, reaching out to the present with one hand, that they may knot it to the past which they carry in their other hand.

REBECCA WEST[1]

I N previous chapters I have attempted to show how the purge was largely the product of a desire for *renouvellement*, rather than a simple lust for vengeance – although the latter, to be sure, was always present. This primacy of "renouvellisme" is least true with respect to the most publicized and most dramatic part of the purge – the judicial punishment of collaborators. Resistance determination to see collaborators in the dock had more to do with a desire for *renversement* than with a desire for *renouvellement*; it responded to the thirst for retribution on the part of men who for years had been hunted down, imprisoned, and tortured by the followers of Pétain and the agents of Germany.

But side by side with this passionate longing was the attachment of *résistants* to those principles of justice and equity which distinguished them from the rulers of Nazi Germany and Vichy France.

If we heeded the appeal of our heart and our indignation, all of us would go as far as some of our colleagues desire, and shoot the guilty out of hand. How understandable that would be, when we think of the torture which our comrades in France are undergoing. How legitimate and excusable it would be for us to use the same procedure as our enemies. But we aren't Vichy, we aren't the Germans. We stand for liberty, respect for the law,

1. *The Meaning of Treason* (New York: 1947), p. 64.

140

and belief in human dignity; it was to affirm these beliefs that we have struggled and resisted. . . . Our true grandeur will lie in maintaining and respecting our national traditions . . . in our unshakable devotion to justice and respect for individual rights, even those of the most despicable criminals.[2]

The decrees of the Provisional Government concerning judicial action against collaborators had to reconcile the appeals of the heart with respect for the traditions of French justice.

The principle of *nullum crimen sine lege, nulla poena sine lege*, that laws enacted after the crime which they set out to punish are worse than no laws at all, is one common to all systems of jurisprudence. It would be hard to find a principle more fundamental not only to traditional conceptions of law, but to the layman's instincts of equity. The French Revolutionary Constitution of 1793 noted that the enactment of retroactive laws was the hallmark of tyranny; Benjamin Constant considered retroaction "the most evil assault which the law can commit" and added that a retroactive law was "no law at all"; article four of the French Penal Code stated (and states) that no offense, no misdemeanor, no crime can be punished by penalties that were enacted after the act was committed.

The widespread abhorrence of retroactive legislation is rooted in the proposition that if a man knows in advance the consequences of his acts – or at least whether or not they are legal –he may legitimately be held accountable for them; if not, not. In France, the overwhelming majority of the population believed Vichy to be the legal and legitimate government of France. They might support or oppose its policies (as they supported or opposed the policies of the Third Republic), they might hold various opinions on its degree of subservience to Nazi Germany, they might even, as a matter of conscience, disobey its laws and enter into an illegal existence. But if they followed this last course there was no doubt in their minds that what they were doing *was* illegal; conversely, those who obeyed that Government's commands had no doubt that they were following the only legal road. The degree of political support enjoyed by the Vichy Regime declined drastically during the four years of its existence; its recognition by Frenchmen as *the* French government, while it also declined somewhat, remained to the end.

But the Provisional Government could not accept this picture of

2. André Philip in the Consultative Assembly, J.O., A.C.P. Debates, January 15, 1944, pp. 11-12.

reality; to do so would be to renounce any punishment of the men of Vichy. Instead, the G.P.R.F. denied what had been apparent fact to tens of millions of Frenchmen in favor of an artificial set of juridical postulates. Vichy was not the legal government; it was, in the language of hundreds of ordinances, "the *de facto* authority, calling itself 'Government of the French State' '', or alternatively, "the usurper". Its orders, unlike those of a legal state, did not absolve the executant of responsibility; they were to be considered only as a form of *force majeure* – a mitigating circumstance if they could not be evaded or circumvented, no excuse at all if they could.

Not only was the Vichy Regime properly speaking (from July 11, 1940, on) declared illegal by the Provisional Government in Algiers, but this illegality was extended back to the formation of the Pétain cabinet under the Third Republic (June 17). The Armistice itself was thus illegal; not only had France continued to be at war with Germany in law (an armistice, in international law, merely suspends hostilities), but in fact as well.

General de Gaulle had taken Vichy's juridical nullity for granted from the beginning; it was in any case clear that the adoption of this doctrine was a practical necessity. As early as June 1942 the O.C.M., in its *Cahiers*, had noted the necessity of declaring Vichy illegitimate whatever the obvious merits of the arguments on the other side; the unthinkable alternative would be to "renounce the punishment of practically all the acts committed in favor of the occupying power". As a result, there was virtually no public discussion of the question in the Consultative Assembly in Algiers. Even given this, however, questions remained. Clearly the prewar treason legislation had not been intended to deal with a situation such as France faced in 1944; would it then suffice?

There were various difficulties with the prewar texts. First of all, they "had not foreseen the unprecedented situation of a French government, unquestionably illegitimate, but nevertheless a *de facto* government, making itself an accomplice of an enemy occupying power".[3] Some form of legislative action was called for "to fill the gaps in [France's] existing arsenal of laws which disarm it before 'the anti-France' ''.[4]

3. François de Menthon in the Consultative Assembly, July 10, 1944, J.O., A.C.P. Debates, July 27, pp. 147-54.

4. *Au service de la renaissance française: Propositions du Parti communiste relatives aux premières mesures à prendre lors de la libération par les différents départements ministériels* (Paris: n.d. [early 1944]), p. 27.

Could this be done within the context of the prewar Penal Code; without introducing frankly retroactive penal legislation? The unanimous answer of the Resistance was "yes". The conservative Organisation Civile et Militaire, the Comité Général d'Etudes, the judges and lawyers meeting secretly in Paris to advise the C.F.L.N., the Communists (whose respect for legal niceties was minimal when their enemies were in the dock) – all answered "yes".[5]

In principle, this advice was followed by the Committee. In so doing they were not narrowly limiting themselves, for shortly before the war the articles of the French Penal Code had been considerably broadened, and most collaborationist activity could be dealt with under these provisions. Propaganda in favor of enemy activities, furnishing men or materials to the enemy, enrollment in enemy-organized or subsidized groups, acts harmful to the security of the French state or the liberty of its citizens, acts which tend to demoralize the population, and that final catch-all under Article 75, "intelligence with the enemy with a view to favoring his endeavors" – all these and more were included within the broad scope of the prewar legislation within which the Committee pledged itself to work.

Despite the breadth of the existing statutes, and the desire to avoid retroactivity, there was general agreement concerning the need to "interpret" some of the provisions of the prewar Code. Accordingly, legislation was enacted by the C.F.L.N. "to facilitate the Court's interpretation of [the prewar] texts".[6]

There were three principal interpretive modifications. The first, enacted several months before the main Ordinance on the prosecution of collaborators, was intended to plug any possible loophole through which informers might escape. Two ordinances provided that handing over or informing on *résistants* or others sought by the Germans and Vichy was to be "interpreted" as an act "harmful to the national defense" under Article 83 of the Penal Code.[7]

---

5. For the O.C.M. see the June 1942 issue of their *Cahiers*; for the C.G.E. see their *Questionnaire*, cited by Henri Michel, *Les Courants de pensée de la Résistance* (Paris: 1962), pp. 347-48. The composition, functioning and opinions of the underground legal groups are discussed in René Hostache, *Le Conseil National de la Résistance: Les Institutions de la clandestinité* (Paris: 1958), pp. 344-46; Jacques Charpentier, *Au service de la liberté* (Paris: 1949), p. 210; *Bulletin Hebdomadaire d'Informations Judiciaires*, No. 6 (May 19, 1945). For the Communist position see *Au service de la renaissance française*, pp. 27-28.

6. J.O., A.C.P. Debates, July 27, 1944, pp. 147-54.

7. Ordinances of January 17 and 31, 1944.

THE RESISTANCE VERSUS VICHY

The second followed directly from the doctrine of Vichy's nullity. Since Vichy had no legal existence, it could not offer its servants that immunity which French law traditionally offered those executing superior orders. The C.F.L.N. did not, however, carry the doctrine of Vichy's non-existence to the point of absurdity, but rather made important distinctions:

> Neither a crime nor a misdemeanor shall be charged against the authors or accomplices of the acts in question when the acts have been performed *in the strict execution of orders or instructions, entirely without personal initiative, and without exceeding those orders or instructions*, or when the act consists simply of the fulfillment of professional obligations *without willful participation in anti-national activity*.
>
> Nevertheless, no laws, decrees, rules, orders or authorizations of the *de facto* authority called "Government of the French State" shall constitute justification within the meaning of Article 327 of the Penal Code, nor authorization or approval as provided in the definition of certain infractions, *when the accused was personally able to evade their execution, and when his responsibility or moral authority was such that his refusal would have served the nation.*
>
> Nor shall the provisions of paragraph 1 of this Article apply to the denunciation or handing over of persons, nor to individual acts of violence, nor to willful delivery of material, documents, or information to the enemy. [Italics added.][8]

The last of the three principal modifications of prewar legislation was based not directly on Vichy's nullity, but on its corollary – that the C.F.L.N. had continued to carry on the war in the name of France. The 1939 changes in the Penal Code laid down that the Government could assimilate France's allies to France herself so far as wartime acts were concerned. That is, actions against an ally of France could be defined as juridically indistinguishable from (and punished as) acts against France. On September 26, 1939, a decree of the Daladier Government so defined the then allies of France.

Given the doctrine of the illegitimacy of the Armistice and the continuation of the war, this decree clearly included Great Britain. The Ordinance of June 26, 1944, went further and declared that the troops

8. The original Ordinance, dated June 26, 1944, used a slightly different formulation. Instead of referring to the "responsibility or moral authority" of the individual, it was restricted to those "holding a position of administration or command" and able to evade execution. The wording given in the text above was substituted by the Ordinance of September 14, 1944, and was incorporated in the final version of the text on the prosecution of collaborators, the Ordinance of November 28, 1944. The effect of the change was to give considerably more latitude to the courts in interpreting this rule.

of "any Allied nation at war with the Axis powers", as well as *résistants* and escaped prisoners of war, were to be considered, for the purposes of the Penal Code, as French troops. Thus the United States and the Soviet Union were "assimilated" under the Penal Code, and those who had fought the former in the Phalange Africaine, or the latter in the Légion des Volontaires Français, were brought within the scope of the Code.

Even with these "interpretations", however, the Penal Code was not a completely satisfactory instrument for performing the work which had to be accomplished. Its use would at the same time punish too few and too harshly. Minor collaborators might slip through the coarse mesh of the existing laws and thus continue to play a nefarious role in French public life; also, the penalties prescribed by the Penal Code were too rigidly severe to be appropriate or practical for dealing with "les petits".

Résistants were principally interested in punishing "les grands coupables". But they also wished to see sanctions taken against "indirect collaborators" – men whose offenses were not covered by the prewar Penal Code. There were those who participated in anti-Semitic agitation; there were the *déatistes* and *doriotistes*; those who failed to act as well as those who acted criminally, like the doctors who certified forced laborers as healthy – "not only those who actively served the enemy, but also those who were servile".[9]

It would be possible to deal with these categories of "unworthy Frenchmen" only if the criterion adopted was not legalistic but moral. "The fundamental principle behind the task of purification must be 'patriotism'. . . . We must appeal to the '*sense of honor*' . . . the idea of crime against the nation must be introduced" [italics in original].[10]

The problem, in any case, was not how to swell the prison population, or exhaust the ammunition of the firing squads, but how to build a France *pure et dure*. And to do this, penal sanctions were not necessarily required; rather

> all those who by their action or propaganda either indirectly aided the enemy or worked for the establishment in France of a political order inspired by Hitlerite doctrines . . . [had to be] temporarily or permanently disqualified from exercising any public function in the largest sense, from participating, in any form, in political or public life.[11]

9. *Cahiers* [of the O.C.M.], I (June 1942).
10. *Ibid.*
11. C.G.E. *Questionnaire*, Michel, *Courants*, *loc. cit.*

There was virtually unanimous agreement, from the right to the left of the Resistance spectrum, on the need to introduce a new measure which would at the same time be both an instrument of *renouvellement* and a *lex mitior* – substituting a lighter penalty for the harsh sanctions of the Penal Code.

In response to demands from the metropolitan Resistance and from the Consultative Assembly the Government, on June 26, 1944, submitted to the Assembly a "Proposed Ordinance Instituting National Indignity".[12] In language almost identical with that suggested by an underground group, the draft defined "national indignity" as the "state entered into" by one who "directly or indirectly, voluntarily aided Germany or her allies, or harmed the unity of the nation or the liberty and equality of Frenchmen".[13]

The Government did its best to avoid frankly labelling the measure as retroactive. National indignity was called not a crime, but a "state" into which one entered by the performance of listed acts; one's presence in that "state" was to be "declared" – not by a frankly judicial body, but by a "jury d'honneur". In presenting the measure to the Assembly, Justice Commissioner François de Menthon maintained that if it had been a choice between presenting a retroactive law or no law at all he would have chosen the former course, but it had not been necessary.[14]

This conception did not survive the Assembly session at which the bill was discussed. Dumesnil de Gramont, *rapporteur* of the proposal, expressed the majority sentiment:

> Unless we distort the laws and make them say what was never in the minds of their authors, it is clear that there are a great many kinds of collaboration that aren't covered at all by the laws in force on June 16, 1940. . . . The government, in drawing up the law instituting national indignity has tried to escape this difficulty by . . . a purely verbal artifice. For [the Government], national indignity is neither a crime nor a penalty, but a state involving certain disqualifications. . . . This solution lacks both clarity and frankness.
>
> We believe, together with the Committee of Jurists of the Resistance, that it would be better to admit unambiguously that national indignity is

12. J.O., A.C.P. Documents, No. 108.

13. Cf. "Rapport reçu de France", *Cahiers Français*, No. 51 (December 1943). Albert Colombini points out that the language of the Ordinance is very close to that employed in the Law of October 29, 1793, defining the competence of the Revolutionary Tribunal. ("Le Crime d'Indignité Nationale", *Les Lois Nouvelles*, 1946, p. 3 n. 1.)

14. J.O., A.C.P. Debates, July 27, pp. 147-64.

a new offense, born of the extraordinary circumstances brought about by the defeat; and therefore we believe that there should be no hesitation in giving the penalty retroactive effect.[15]

With minor modifications resulting from the Assembly's deliberations, the Ordinance instituting national indignity was promulgated on August 26. The *exposé de motifs* is frank, clear and enlightening concerning the inspiration of the enactment.

> The criminal conduct of those who collaborated with the enemy did not always take the form of a specific act for which there could be provided a specific penalty . . . under a strict interpretation of the law. Frequently it has been a question of antinational activity reprehensible in itself. Moreover, the disciplinary measures by which unworthy officials could be removed from the administration are not applicable to other sections of society. And it is as necessary to bar certain individuals from various elective, economic, and professional positions which give their incumbents political influence, as it is to eliminate others from the ranks of the administration.
>
> Any Frenchman who, even without having violated an existing penal law, has been guilty of activity defined as antinational, has degraded himself; he is an unworthy citizen whose rights must be restricted in so far as he has failed in his duties. Such a legal discrimination between citizens may appear serious, for all discriminatory measures are repugnant to democracy. But it is not contrary to the principle of equality before the law for the nation to distinguish between good and bad citizens in order to bar from positions of leadership and influence those among the French who have rejected the ideals and the interests of France during the most grievous trial in her history.

The definition of the acts constituting unworthy conduct was both broad and specific. It included any voluntary aid to the Axis after June 16, 1940, or any wilful act of what might be termed "lèse-liberté-égalité-fraternité". Among the enumerated specific acts, performance of which would carry a presumption of guilt, were:

1. having been a member of any of Pétain's cabinets;
2. having held an executive position in either Vichy's propaganda services or in the Commissariat for Jewish Affairs;

15. *Ibid.* The Government advanced various other arguments by way of denial that it was introducing retroactive legislation. The most cogent was the contention of René Cassin and others that the introduction of national indignity represented the retroactive substitution of a lighter for a heavier penalty (*lex mitior*) – a practice specifically permitted under the French Codes.

3. having been a member, even without active participation, of collaborationist organizations;[16]
4. having helped organize meetings or demonstrations in favor of collaboration;
5. having published writings or given lectures in favor of the enemy, collaboration with the enemy, racism, or totalitarian doctrines.

Performance of any of the enumerated acts did not automatically entail national degradation for life. The court was to take into account not only the importance and frequency of the acts, but also any pressure that might have been exerted on the individual.[17] If extenuating circumstances were found, the penalty might be inflicted for a minimum of five years. Further, the court might suspend the penalty in the case of those who, subsequent to the acts charged against them, "rehabilitated" themselves, either by military action in the war against the Axis or by participation in the Resistance.[18] Finally, the courts could (and frequently did) simply acquit an individual despite the fact that technically he came within the scope of the Ordinance (for example, by membership in a proscribed organization).

The list of disqualifications in the original Ordinance was consistent with the aim in view: barring the unworthy from positions of leadership and political influence. Among the disqualifications were: exclusion from the franchise and from eligibility to elective office; a ban on public

16. This provision underwent several modifications before the definitive version was established (in the Ordinance of December 26, 1944). At all times, the list of collaborationist organizations in the Ordinance was not regarded as limiting. In the original Ordinance, membership in some listed organizations was to be considered culpable at any time after June 16, 1940; in others, only if the membership continued past January 1, 1942. In its final form, the Ordinance set January 1, 1941 (the morrow of Montoire), as the limiting date. The final list (which had undergone minor additions and subtractions since August) consisted of: Service d'Ordre Légionnaire, Milice Nationale, Légion des Volontaires Français, Amis des L.V.F., Parti Populaire Français, Légion Tricolore, Parti Franciste, Service d'Ordre Prisonnier, Groupe Collaboration, Phalange Africaine, Parti National Collectiviste, Mouvement Social Révolutionnaire, Rassemblement National Populaire, Comité Ouvrier de Secours Immédiat.

17. This last was not contained in the original Government proposal, but was added on the recommendation of the A.C.P.: one of the rare cases in these years when the Assembly proposed the softening of a Government proposal.

18. The original provision called for "active participation"; this was altered in the Ordinance of December 26 to "sustained and effective active participation"; a measure of self-defense against the *septembristes*.

employment; loss of rank in the armed forces (and of the right to wear decorations); exclusion from directing functions in semi-public corporations, banks, other financial institutions, as well as the press and radio industries; exclusion from office in trade-unions and professional associations; exclusion from the legal, teaching and (the regular exercise of the) journalistic professions; exclusion from such state-connected bodies as the Institut de France; a ban on keeping or bearing arms. None of these penalties could be parcelled out, but had to be applied *en bloc*. (Violating, or aiding and abetting the violation of any of these measures, was punishable by up to five years in prison.)

There were, in addition, two discretionary measures which could be added to this list. The first, contained in the original Ordinance, was a temporary ban on residence in a given area. The second was added by a modifying ordinance of September 30: confiscation of all or a part of the property of the *indigné*. A derivative consequence of national degradation, probably unintended by those who drafted the legislation, was the loss of pension rights, since a 1924 law had stipulated that pension payments are suspended during the term of sanctions involving the loss of civic rights. For a variety of reasons, complete and permanent loss of pension rights turned out to be the exception, not the rule.[19]

These, then, the laws: an "interpreted" Penal Code for the principal offenders; national indignity for the less guilty. But the large problem remained of how these laws were to be applied: what courts and what procedures would be best?

Some favored the most summary of proceedings (or no proceedings at all), at least when it came to the leading collaborators:

> When the treason has been public and avowed, the forms of justice should be reduced to the strict minimum. Verification of identity followed by the death sentence is the only possible form of justice for those who have publicly made themselves the agents and the recruiting sergeants of the enemy.[20]

Others favored strict adherence to form and the utilization of regular

19. First, under the 1924 Law, if the individual deprived of civic rights had a wife or minor children, they received that portion of the pension which they would have received in the event of his death. Second, while the *cours* and *chambres* could not remove individual consequences of national degradation, but had to apply or suspend the penalty *en bloc*, presidential pardons (which were numerous) could be selective, and were frequently used to reinstate pension rights. Finally, amnesties with retroactive effect intervened.

20. *Résistance*, No. 6 (January 25, 1943).

military tribunals, while still others would use the basic form of military tribunals, but with various changes in their composition and procedure.

In the Algiers Consultative Assembly, particularly at the height of the discontent over the slow pace of the purge in North Africa, there were many – by no means all of them on the extreme left – who favored popular tribunals with minimal procedural guarantees. All of the Government's critics insisted on the need for juries made up of *résistants*, and the Assembly unanimously resolved that at least "special procedures" be employed.[21]

At first the C.F.L.N. seemed determined to stand by normal procedures, although making some procedural concessions in the interests of speed. This was the position defended by François de Menthon and André Philip in the January 1944 debate.[22] But during the spring a series of suggestions and opinions arrived from underground study groups which altered the Committee's opinion. The Resistance jurists, meeting secretly at the Palais de Justice in Paris were convinced that it would be impossible to find sufficient personnel to man military tribunals, and pronounced for special courts with juries consisting of patriotic citizens.[23] The Comité Général d'Etudes supported this line of thought. They proposed departmental courts, consisting of a presiding judge, two war veterans, and two *résistants* named by the Government. This court of five would be in charge of the pre-trial examination of all cases, and would in addition try the less serious ones. The more serious cases they would send to a higher court, presided over by the President of the *Cour de Cassation*, and containing, in addition, two *résistants* named by the government.[24]

The Government's Ordinance was in many respects strikingly similar to the C.G.E.'s proposal. In explaining the measure to the Consultative Assembly (it had not been consulted before its promulgation), De Menthon said that it had

aimed at reconciling two preoccupations: on the one hand, respect for legal forms and the traditional guarantees of republican justice; on the other hand, the desire to judge rapidly and allow the Resistance to play its role in the judicial punishment of collaboration.[25]

21. J.O., A.C.P. Debates, January 15, 1944, *passim*.
22. *Ibid.*, pp. 6-8, 11-12.
23. Hostache, pp. 345-46; *Bulletin Hebdomadaire d'Informations Judiciaires*, No. 6 (May 19, 1945).
24. *Questionnaire du C.G.E.*, cited by Michel, *Courants*, pp. 348-49.
25. J.O., A.C.P. Debates, July 27, 1944, pp. 147-54.

The provisions of the Ordinance of June 26 responded to that two-fold aim. The "cours de justice", set up by the Provisional Government as France was liberated, were miniature versions of the *cours d'assises*, the traditional French tribunals for felonies. There were principal courts in each of the twenty-seven districts of the *Cour d'Appel*, sub-sidiary courts in each *département* – and these in turn might be divided into sub-sections as the need arose (the Paris Court had seventeen sub-sections). Despite their basic resemblance to the Assize Courts, there were several significant modifications in the organization and proced-ures of the new jurisdictions.

The *cours de justice* retained the traditional French institution of the examining magistrate (*juge d'instruction*) who conducts a personal interrogation of the accused with a view to determining whether the Government should bring him to trial or drop the case. In the new courts, however, while the examining magistrate could recommend one course of action or the other, the final decision was taken out of his hands and put in those of the state prosecutor.[26] There were at least two reasons for this change in procedure.

It was (correctly) anticipated that the mutually reinforcing factors of a purge of the magistrature and the creation of over a hundred new jurisdictions would put a serious strain on the personnel resources of the French judiciary. All sections of opinion were extremely anxious that the collaboration trials be completed as quickly as possible. (The Ordinance provided for a cut-off date [unspecified] after which no new cases could be opened.) Any step which could speed up the procedure without doing substantive violence to equity was clearly desirable.

At the same time, the Government was constantly aware that cases before the courts of justice could be politically explosive. Leaving the decision on prosecution to a judiciary which many suspected of being lukewarm toward the purge would risk outbursts of popular indigna-tion if prominent collaborators were not indicted. Placing the decision in the hands of an official of the Ministry of Justice gave the Govern-ment a valuable instrument of control. (Of course, this power cut both ways: the Government could choose to quash an indictment rather than send a marginally guilty individual before what appeared to be a "hanging jury".)

The *cours d'assises* had been composed of three judges and twelve lay

26. The grand jury function of the *chambre des mises en accusation* was likewise dispensed with, and the only appeal from the local prosecutor's decision was to his superior, the *Procureur de la République*.

jurors. The new *cours* divided the *cours d'assises* by three: they were made up of a single judge (again, the question of availability of judicial personnel was determining) and four lay jurors. They met together to determine both verdict and sentence by majority decision. The most significant change was not, however, in the size of the jury, but in the method of its selection.

The normal method was for panels to be drawn up by a commission consisting of a superior court judge and representatives of the *conseils généraux*. There were two reasons which made the use of this procedure impossible. The first reason was practical and unanswerable: most of the *conseils généraux* had ceased to exist. Their personnel had been drastically altered by Vichy so that they might serve as an instrument of the "National Revolution"; dozens of *conseils* were dissolved at the Liberation, and could not be replaced by new elections for many months. The second reason was political: the Resistance urgently demanded that it be allowed to play a role in the trials of collaborators.

The solution adopted was to substitute for the defunct *conseils généraux* the Departmental Liberation Committees, which in any case were exercising those advisory functions normally the prerogative of the *conseils*. The jury panels for the Courts of Justice were to be drawn up by a Commission consisting of a superior court magistrate and two delegates from the Liberation Committee in the area. The list was to include only those men and women (this last was an innovation) "who had never ceased to demonstrate their patriotic sentiments".[27]

No feature of the new court system came in for more sustained or more bitter criticism. The more moderate critics observed that

> the jurors thus designated were *résistants*, called to judge adversaries of the resistance. They were usually persons of good faith. But what impartiality could the accused expect from a deportee who had returned from Buchenwald or from a mother whose son had been shot by the *milice*?[28]

27. This of course clearly implied that they should be, if not *résistants*, at least Resistance sympathizers. However, in addition to the traditional exclusion from juries of those whose personal relations with the accused might carry the presumption of partiality either way, the Ordinances provided that no one could be a judge or juror in a given case who had previously dealt with the case as a participant in a "Resistance Tribunal".

28. Charpentier, *Au service*, p. 259.

Many, however, went further. "Because of the manner of their composition, the juries ceased to be a guarantee of impartiality in favor of
the accused, and became an infallible instrument of partisan vengeance."[29]

The polemics on this question were *dialogues des sourds*, because
behind the attack lay a complete misconception of the juridical philo-
sophy underlying the purge. The opponents of the purge, when they
were not unreconstructed Pétainists and collaborators who damned
De Gaulle and all his works, were for the most part upholders of the
"sword and shield" theory of recent history. France in 1940-44 had
needed both De Gaulle and Pétain; there were many legitimate ways
to have served France, and honorable, courageous men could have
chosen either. It was regrettable that men on each side were blind to
the services performed for the country by those on the other; surely
no one thus blinded could judge "impartially".

Whatever the merits of the "sword and shield" theory as a descrip-
tion of reality, and it is not totally devoid of merit, it was in the climate
of 1944 totally unacceptable to the Provisional Government. A good
citizen could no more be "impartial" vis-à-vis the crime of Vichy's
existence and policies than he could be impartial with respect to the
crimes of robbery or murder. The juror's oath to "judge without hate"
meant without hatred of the accused, not hatred of the crime, which
must, indeed, be assumed.

Finally, both supporters and attackers of the *Cour de Justice* system
contrasted an idealized picture of the "*sang froid* and the serenity of the
judge in dealing with common law crimes" with cases of collaboration
in which "serenity is more difficult to retain [because] this crime leaves
none of us indifferent".[30] It is perhaps permissible to question the
"serenity" of the mother empanelled to judge a kidnapper, or, to take
a more banal example, the *bourgeois* called upon to judge a crime against
property.

In any event, these were the juries that deliberated on, these were
the courts which judged, the cases of well over 100,000 Frenchmen.
(The Courts which heard accusations of national indignity – called

---

29. Louis Rougier, "La France est-elle un Etat de Droit?" *Ecrits de Paris*,
February 1950, 87. A number of C.D.L.'s had Communist majorities, and in
some departments they may have empanelled a disproportionate number of
Party members or sympathizers. In the event, however, according to state
prosecutors with whom I discussed the question, Communist jurors behaved
as unpredictably and inconsistently as non-Communists.
30. P.-H. Teitgen, *Les Cours de justice* (Paris: 1946), p. 30.

"chambres civiques" – were attached to them, and shared their organization and procedures in virtually every respect.[31])

The Ordinance of June 26, 1944, had established the jurisdictions
competent to deal with collaboration, but had made no special provision
for the trials of Pétain and his ministers. The Government was committed to trying them, but for a long time was uncertain concerning the
means to be employed. The only Vichy minister tried in Algiers,
Pucheu, had gone before an Army Tribunal. The Provisional Government, after its establishment in France, continued for a time to favor
the use of military courts for top Vichy personnel. On September 13,
1944, the Military Tribunal of Paris was ordered to begin preparing
the prosecution of Pétain and his ministers.[32] But the trials of these
men were intended to be the symbol of their rejection by the nation,
and thus it was finally decided that a "High Court", which would
symbolically represent the nation, would be preferable.

> France's internal order and the world situation demanded that the 1940
> capitulation, the breaking of alliances, and deliberate collaboration with
> the enemy be judged without delay in the persons of the leaders who had
> made themselves responsible [for these policies]. Otherwise ... how, and
> in whose name, could France claim the status of a major belligerent and
> victorious power? . . . Since the persons concerned . . . had played a
> political role, the courts which judged them had to be politically qualified
> to do so.[33]

31. The name of the *chambres civiques*, but not their attributes, underwent
two modifications during 1944. Called "jurys d'honneur" in the original
Government bill submitted to the Assembly, they were changed to "sections
speciales" (of the *cours de justice*) in the Ordinance of August 26, 1944. A
month later, because of the unfortunate connotations of this phrase (it had
been the name given by Vichy to extraordinary repressive tribunals), the
name was changed to "chambres civiques", which they retained throughout
their life. One minor difference between their procedure and that of the *cours
de justice* was that they could receive cases not only from the government
prosecutor, but also directly from the C.D.L.'s. The *chambres civiques* were
not the only bodies which could sentence an individual to national degradation. While the *cours de justice* and the *Haute Cour* only heard cases in which
the defendant was charged with a penal offense, national degradation was
always automatically added to whatever penal sanctions they handed down.
Even if a man appearing before one of these jurisdictions was found innocent
of the penal offenses with which he was charged, he might be found guilty of
national indignity and sentenced to national degradation.
32. Guy Raïssac, *Un soldat dans la tourmente* (Paris: 1963), pp. 350-51.
See also the cabinet communiqué in *Combat*, October 11, 1944.
33. Charles de Gaulle, *Mémoires de guerre* (Paris: 1954-59), III, 109-10.

Such a body was in fact in existence: the Senate of the Third Republic, which under the Constitution was the body charged with trying ministers for crimes against the state. There were, however, compelling reasons why the Senate would not do. First, its political composition had not accurately reflected the sentiment of the country before the war – certainly it did not do so in 1944. Secondly, to use the Senate of the Third Republic would imply the continued legitimacy of that regime. While the Provisional Government held – on a highly abstract level – that the Third Republic had never ceased to exist, it was resolved to replace it with a Fourth, and had no desire to extend the *de facto* life of its institutions. Finally, since the overwhelming majority of Third Republic senators had "automatically resigned" on July 10, 1940, by voting full powers to Pétain, only a tiny rump of the Senate was still in existence. For all of these reasons, and also in order to give the Resistance a voice in the decisions of the High Court, it was decided to create a new body.

This new jurisdiction, the "Haute Cour de Justice", was established by the Ordinance of November 18, 1944. It had jurisdiction over the *chef d'Etat* (Pétain), the *chef du Gouvernement* (Laval), plus all cabinet and sub-cabinet officers and colonial governors who had participated in the "governments or pseudo-governments" sitting in France between June 17, 1940, and the Liberation. It would consider acts before or after this period if they were related to acts committed during it. Thus Pétain could be charged with a long-standing plot against the Republic which bore fruit between June 17 and July 11, 1940. Similarly, Marcel Déat, Joseph Darnand, Jacques Doriot, and Fernand de Brinon could be charged with acts committed during their term of office in the "Government-in-Exile" at Sigmaringen. Accomplices of the designated individuals could also be dealt with by the High Court (although in fact none were).[34]

The court was to be composed of twenty-seven members: three jurists who would preside, and twenty-four jurors chosen by the Consultative Assembly. The Assembly was to draw up two lists: one of fifty senators and deputies holding office on September 1, 1939; the other of fifty men who had not been legislators at that time. Twelve names were to be chosen by lot from each list in order to make up a jury. The court's *commission d'instruction* was similarly mixed: five pro-

34. The idea was considered, however – Charles Maurras being one individual whose trial before the High Court was under consideration even though he had never held an official position. (J.O., A.C.P. Debates, December 5, 1944, p. 423.)

fessional judges and six men chosen by the Assembly. The court thus constituted was to be completely sovereign. It could assign whatever penalty it wished – from death to national degradation – to any crime. There was no provision for appeal. (Presidential pardons were, however, applicable to High Court verdicts.) And, breaking with normal French procedure, verdicts pronounced *in absentia* were to be executed without a retrial.

The overall system adopted by the Provisional Government for the judicial punishment of Vichyites and collaborators was far from ideal: the laws employed were in fact, if not in name, retroactive; the courts were "juridictions d'exception". Given the problems confronting the Government, it is hard to see how these lapses from legal norms could have been avoided. How the system worked in practice will be considered in the next chapter.

Chapter 9

PRISONERS AT THE BAR

The engineers, masons and contractors who built the Atlantic Wall walk among us undisturbed. They are even building new walls . . . the walls of new prisons where they are locking up the journalists who made the mistake of saying that the Atlantic Wall was a good thing.

JEAN PAULHAN[1]

The Liberation of France was accompanied by surprising revelations. From all sides there sprang up *maquisards doublement clandestins*, whose existence was as unknown to the leaders of the Resistance as it was to the Germans. At the same time we learned that an enormous number of men had solicited – even begged for – positions in the Vichy government only to better deceive the enemy and work for his defeat. Even the employees of the *Commissariat aux Affaires Juives* took up this work only in order to be of assistance to the poor persecuted Jews. . . . For years the whole world was mistaken concerning the real personnel of the Resistance.

THE MARQUIS D'ARGENSON[2]

T HE long-anticipated trials of Vichyites and collaborators were the most publicized part of the purge. They were also the most disappointing part, and their failure became, for many *résistants*, symbolic of the death of all their dreams of "les lendemains qui chantaient". There was a potential seed of discontent in the different conception of the task of justice held by the metropolitan Resistance and by General de Gaulle. The Resistance wanted a sweeping, root-and-branch purge that would renew and renovate the country. All of De Gaulle's pronouncements, on the other hand, stressed the need to forgive and forget. "A tiny number of *malheureux*", "a handful of *misérables*": these were the phrases which the General used to describe those who should be tried. While the Resistance desired a surgical operation which would cut off diseased members lest they continue to infect the body politic, De Gaulle's leitmotif was "France needs all her sons".[3]

This difference in the "quantitative" desires of De Gaulle and the Resistance was, however, much less important than what united them

1. *De la paille et du grain* (Paris: 1948), p. 98.
2. *Pétain et le pétinisme: Essai de psychologie* (Paris: 1953), p. 117.
3. *Mémoires de guerre* (Paris: 1954-59), III, 405, 421. A. J. Liebling commented on the difference in outlook which separated De Gaulle from the Resistance as follows: "Every Frenchman feels in some degree guilty for the debacle of 1940 – if only because he let himself be bamboozled into a sense of

157

on this question. Both were agreed that the task of justice should be accomplished quickly, so that the positive work of reconstruction and renovation could be begun. Both were dedicated to the idea that justice should be proportionate: "Nous frappons d'autant plus fort que les coupables seront plus haut". For reasons largely beyond the control of the Provisional Government, these hopes were unfulfilled. The trials dragged on for years; disproportionate verdicts caused widespread disgust. The purge ended not with satisfaction at a job, albeit an unpleasant job, well done; not with reconciliation and the restoration of national unity – but with a universal sense of frustration and bitter disappointment. Barely a year after the liberation of Paris, Albert Camus wrote:

> It is clear that henceforth the purge in France is not only lost, but discredited. The word "purge" was painful enough in itself; the thing has now become odious. The failure is complete. . . . Too many have shouted for death as if prison at hard labor was inconsequential . . . too many have claimed that it was a return to The Terror when dishonor and denunciation were rewarded with a few years in prison. . . . In any case, we see ourselves impotent. . . . Today we can only attempt to prevent the most flagrant injustices from further poisoning an atmosphere which Frenchmen already find difficult to breathe.[4]

The enormity of the task confronting the judicial authorities was clear – no one expected that it could be completed overnight. Less apparent were the many practical obstacles that had to be overcome. Transportation and communication had broken down. The police and the judiciary could not be an effective tool of repression until they themselves had been purged. Finally, there was the monumental task of establishing, amid this chaos, over two hundred new courts, each with an investigative and prosecuting staff. (At the height of their activity the *cours de justice* and *chambres civiques* employed almost half of the judicial personnel of the country.)

In the Paris area there were almost 4,000 arrests in the week following the Liberation; a week later the total had risen to between 6,000 and 7,000; by early October 10,000 persons were interned – most of them

---

security before it happened. But the traitors personify the guilt of all, which makes the honest men all the more bitter against them. In punishing the traitors, Frenchmen were punishing a part of themselves. Only he who feels himself without guilt is reluctant to cast a stone; he lacks the requisite imagination. General de Gaulle, the most self-righteous of Frenchmen, was one of the least vindictive against the erring brothers." (*The Republic of Silence* [New York: 1947], p. 368.)

4. *Combat*, August 30, 1945.

in the Vélodrome d'Hiver and the former Jewish concentration camp at Drancy. A total of 80,000 people were arrested throughout France in the wake of the Liberation.[5] Those arrested were held in "administrative internment", a security measure enacted by the Daladier Government shortly after the beginning of the war in 1939 and renewed by the Provisional Government. "Sifting commissions" were immediately established – five were at work in Paris within a week of the Liberation. The three-man commissions were made up of representatives of the Departmental Liberation Committees, the Ministry of Justice, and the police. They worked night and day; by the end of 1944 the number of those detained without having had a preliminary examination had been reduced to 5,000.[6]

Parisians knew that thousands had been arrested, but wondered when the trials were going to begin. Reports reaching Paris from the

5. Henri Denis, *Le Comité Parisien de la Libération* (Paris: 1963), pp. 137, 239; *Figaro*, September 1, 1944; *New York Times*, September 17, 1944; *Combat*, October 23, 1944; *Carrefour*, January 6, 1945. The number of arrests in France was the lowest, relative to population, of all the occupied countries of Western Europe. In Denmark about 22,000 persons were arrested in the two days following the Liberation. (C. C. Givskov, "Danish 'Purge Laws'", *Journal of Criminal Law*, XXXIX [1948], 448.) In Norway there were 24,000 arrests. (Johs Andenoes, "La Répression de la Collaboration avec l'Ennemi en Norvège", *Revue de Droit Pénal et de Criminologie* [Brussels], XXVII, 7 [April 1947], 604.) In Belgium between 50,000 and 70,000 suspects were arrested in September 1944. The number detained declined to just under 40,000 by May 1, 1945, but after V-E Day, as a result of indignation at the first verified accounts of concentration camps from returning survivors, another 20,000 were arrested. (Henry L. Mason, *The Purge of Dutch Quislings: Emergency Justice in the Netherlands* [The Hague: 1952], p. 173 n. 12.) In Holland there were not only relatively more arrests than in France, but, incredibly, more in absolute terms. Between 120,000 and 150,000 persons were arrested, 96,000 being the highest number detained at any given time (October 1945). By September 1946 there were still 62,000 detainees, exclusive of these already sentenced to prison terms. (Mason, p. 40; W. J. Ganshof van der Meersch, *Réflexions sur la répression des crimes contre la sûreté extérieure de l'Etat belge* [Brussels: 1946], pp. 76-77.)

6. J.O., A.C.P. Debates, December 27, 1944, pp. 604-07; Denis, pp. 138-39, 239-40; *Carrefour*, January 6, 1945. Many tragic errors had been made, however. When the wife of Georges Albertini, Marcel Déat's right-hand man, was interned (for no good reason), their child was handed over to the public welfare authorities. By the time she was released the child had died. (*Franc-Tireur*, January 21/22, 1945.) A more widespread problem was excessively long internments without real hearings. In one case a man was held in custody for more than two years before he was able to convince the authorities that they had confused him with another person of a similar name. (*Cahiers des Droits de l'Homme*, N.S., Nos. 44-48 [May 1948], 361-62.)

provinces indicated that, there at least, justice was taking its course: collaborators were paying for their treason, the *milice* for its outrages. But in the capital, in the weeks following the Liberation, not one trial took place. September passed, and most of October, and still the courts were inactive. In other parts of the country military tribunals were functioning until the *cours de justice* could be established; in Paris there was none. The Resistance press was not slow to voice its impatience.

The reason for the delay was a judicial log jam of unprecedented dimensions. In Paris there were 700 dossiers on the desks of the examining magistrates at the beginning of October; a month later this number had tripled; during November it doubled: by the beginning of December the *juges d'instruction* of the Paris court alone faced a backlog of over 4,200 cases. This experience was repeated all over France: by February 1945 the corps of examining magistrates had disposed of over 25,000 of the 60,000 dossiers that had been opened. But it was a labor of Sisyphus. In the following months over 60,000 new cases had to be opened, and it was well into 1946 before the backlog of cases *à l'instruction* fell below the 20,000 mark. Hopes for an early end to the work of the *cours de justice* died beneath an avalanche of paper.[7]

Frustration at the delays in beginning the trials established a mood of disillusionment with the purge – and even, to an extent, with the fruits of the Liberation in general – which later was to deepen. The purge did not rate as high as the fuel shortage as a source of discontent, but as Dorothy Pickles, who was in Paris at the time, has observed:

As months went by, and the food situation not only showed no sign of improvement, but even deteriorated, people were disappointed or dismayed but, on the whole patient. They understood why the Allies had

7. The French Government has neither published nor made available systematic statistics concerning the progressive activity of the *cours de justice*. My calculations are based on information drawn from the following sources: J.O., A.C.P. Debates, December 5, 1944, p. 423; February 20, 1945, pp. 120-21; J.O., A.N.C. (I) Debates, August 6, 1946, p. 3012; A.N.C. (I), *Bulletin des Commissions*, No. 8 (February 12, 1946), p. 160; J.O., A.N. Debates, December 12, 1951, p. 9100; July 11, 1952, p. 3939; March 23, 1954, p. 1213; *Cahiers Français d'Information*, No. 1 (February 16, 1945); No. 6 (March 23, 1945); No. 16 (June 1, 1945); No. 58 (April 21, 1946); *Bulletin Hebdomadaire d'Informations Judiciaires*, No. 1 (April 14, 1945); No. 5 (May 12, 1945); No. 6 (May 19, 1945); No. 8 (June 2, 1945); *Notes Documentaires et Etudes*, S.F., LXXX, No. 245 (February 26, 1946); *Bulletin de l'Association Nationale des Avocats*, XXVI, 83 (March 1946), 19-20; Pierre-Henry Teitgen, *Les Cours de justice* (Paris: 1946), pp. 32-33; *Monde*, June 19, September 1 and December 19, 1945; February 8, 1946; May 30, 1947; December 22, 1949; *Aube*, May 30, 1947.

not been able to deliver the promised supplies, that it would take time to overcome the transport breakdown and the black market, and that the acute shortage of labour and coal complicated everything. They were exasperated but not disillusioned. . . . The technical obstacles in the way [of the purge] were less apparent to the general public than were the obstacles to improvement in the food supply. It was not a task in which France needed the help of her Allies. . . . The purge . . . was regarded as a symbol, as a test of whether something had really changed in France since the Third Republic had foundered in defeat and occupation. As it became clear that it was not going to be carried out with either the speed or the thoroughness that public opinion demanded, the result was, inevitably, disillusionment.[8]

Once the trials began – and in Paris they began in late October – dissatisfaction centered not on delays, but on "incoherence". Some categories of collaborators, it was alleged, were punished too severely, while others were punished too lightly – or escaped altogether. The trend of verdicts was said to differ widely from one region to another. Even when the same court considered apparently identical cases, verdicts seemed almost capricious.

At the outset, what rankled most deeply was that those whose trials had been most ardently desired were not available for judgment. Marshal Pétain, Pierre Laval, Joseph Darnand, Marcel Déat, Jacques Doriot – all were in Sigmaringen, out of reach, for the moment, of French justice. Others had found asylum abroad, or in "internal immigration".[8a] Logic and passion both demanded that "les chefs de file de la trahison" be the first in the dock – but this was impossible. Delay-

8. *France Between the Republics* (London: 1946), pp. 177-78.

8a. Thousands of collaborators, including a number of cabinet ministers (e.g., Abel Bonnard) found refuge in Spain. Others fled to Switzerland (e.g., Henri du Moulin de Labarthète, Pétain's *chef du cabinet*, and Horace Carbuccia, publisher of *Gringoire*). Some lived (and died) in obscurity in the Italian Tyrol (Marcel Déat, Alphonse de Châteaubriant). Still others (e.g., Charles Lesca, publisher of *Je Suis Partout*) went to South America. Religious establishments inside France sometimes sheltered collaborators fleeing justice. The most dramatic case of "internal immigration" was that of the Radical deputy Jacques Ducreux. When in 1952 Ducreux was killed in an automobile accident, two identity cards were found on his body: one bore the name under which he was elected, the other that under which he was wanted for collaboration (Jacques Tacnet). The Assembly subsequently imposed stricter rules concerning credentials. (See Maurice-Yvan Sicard ["St.-Paulien"], *Histoire de la collaboration* [Mayenne: 1964], p. 522; Michèle Cotta, *La Collaboration* [Paris: 1964], p. 287; *Etudes de Presse*, N.S., No. 4 [April 15, 1952], 237; *Parisien Libéré*, November 19, 1946; *Combat*, March 21 and 22, 1947; *Monde*, March 22 and 25, 1947; *Année Politique*, 1952, p. 29.)

ing the start of the trials until the prime defendants were available was out of the question, so the Government had to look elsewhere for the first to answer for their own activity and – symbolically – for the policy of collaboration.

Practical considerations dictated that the first to be tried be those whose dossiers could be constituted most rapidly. Political considerations demanded that the first cases be those of the best known and most hated of the available collaborators. As a result, at least in Paris, journalists and propagandists formed a large proportion of "la première charrette". These men were not only well known, but their written and spoken words were clearly recorded and irrefutable.

The first case before the Paris *cour de justice* was that of Georges Suarez, who had been lavishly paid by *Aujourd'hui* for promoting collaboration, affirming that informing on *résistants* was a sacred duty, and repeatedly calling for the stepping up of executions of Jews and Communists. Suarez was sentenced to death and shot. Other journalists whom the Paris court sentenced to death or long terms of imprisonment during its first weeks of operation were Henri Béraud of *Gringoire*, Robert Brasillach of *Je Suis Partout*, Captain Paul Chack of *Aujourd'hui*, Lucien Combelle of *La Révolution Nationale*, Stephane Lauzanne of *Le Matin*, Robert Macot of Radio-Paris, Charles Tardieu of *L'Echo du Nord*, and Guy Zucarelli of *Les Nouveaux Temps*.

While journalists and propagandists were tried early, public officials, whose activity was characteristically both ambiguous and obscure, were generally only tried after a delay of several months. Only much later were "economic collaborators", whose cases required long and patient examination, brought to trial. When "les économiques" were tried, it was often found that juries – even juries made up of "durs" – were reluctant to convict. It was difficult to draw the line between legitimate and illegitimate commercial dealings with the Germans; jurors generally felt that the accused "had to make a living".[9]

The impression became widespread that journalists were being made the scapegoats, while others, particularly economic collaborators, went free or received only token penalties. Jean Paulhan's quip – which forms one of the epigraphs to this chapter – sums up popular feeling. (There was, in fact, a solid kernel of truth behind Paulhan's sally: often the only construction firms which were equipped to undertake emergency reconstruction projects were those which, because they had

9. This is the explanation given me by ex-prosecutors with whom I discussed the failure of the Government to deal promptly and severely with economic collaborators.

collaborated, had kept their equipment and personnel intact.) There were suggestions of corruption – that wealthy men could "buy" the dismissal of their case, or, at a minimum, its postponement until a time when tempers had cooled. The "thèse de complot" was a favorite of the Communist press, but they were far from having a monopoly on it; there is nothing that a French newspaper loves as much as the hint of corruption and collusion in high places.

It is undoubtedly true that journalists were treated with relatively greater severity than others, although the extent to which this was true was exaggerated in the popular mind. The cases of prominent journalists were virtually the only ones reported in the skimpy press of 1944 and 1945. News had to be drastically edited to fit into the restricted two- and four-page formats of the newspapers, and the more numerous trials of *miliciens*, informers and others went unreported, or were simply listed statistically in a half-inch note at the bottom of the last page. Furthermore, the experience of the Paris court – from which the press of the capital drew its conclusions – was not typical: as the headquarters of the collaborationist press, that jurisdiction had a disproportionate number of journalists amongs its "clientele". But even in Paris, of the ninety-five persons executed after sentencing by the *cour de justice*, only a handful were journalists; fifty had been torturers in the employ of the Germans or the *milice*, thirty had been informers.[10] Charges of corruption and collusion are all unproven and, at this point, probably unprovable; there is, in any case, no reason to believe that such practices were widespread.[11] The related charge – that it was advantageous to have one's case delayed, since the courts were less severe later on – is likewise not demonstrable, although it is inherently plausible and probably true. However, as in the case of the belief that journalists were being made the scapegoats, appearances exaggerated reality. The cases of prominent collaborators – whose offenses called for more severe penalties – were deliberately scheduled before those of lesser offenders; men whose guilt was patent were tried before men whose activity was

10. These figures are taken from a memorandum, dated October 15, 1957, which Procureur-Général André Boissarie sent to General de Gaulle, at the latter's request, to provide information for De Gaulle's *Mémoires*. Procureur-Général Boissarie kindly lent me a copy of the memorandum. Cf. the (incomplete) list of *cour de justice* cases in *Défense de l'Occident*, Nos. 39-40 (January-February 1957), 64-70.

11. Former officials of the Ministry of Justice recounted stories to me of ministerial intervention on behalf of economic collaborators; the accounts seem credible. These same informants, however, stressed that such cases were extremely rare.

ambiguous. Finally, trials and executions received relatively more attention in 1944-45 than later on.[12]

A much more serious and telling charge with relation to "incoherence" is that the severity of the courts varied from department to department. This is unquestionably true, and the differences are staggering.[13] The total number of cases per 10,000 population varied from 12 in Limoges to 44 in Orléans (the median was 27). The number of *cour de justice* cases (excluding those heard before *chambres civiques*) ranged from 5 per 10,000 population in Rennes to 26 per 10,000 in Aix (median 13). Differences of the same magnitude appear when one examines the disposition of those cases which came before the courts. In Montpellier the *cour de justice* acquitted 7 per cent of those who came before it; in Caen 25 per cent were acquitted (median 14 per cent). Death sentences pronounced in the presence of the accused were 2 per cent of all penalties in Douai; 19 per cent in Dijon (median 6 per cent).[14]

12. As with so many other questions concerning the purge, the unavailability of detailed statistical material makes it impossible to arrive at any firm conclusion regarding changes in jurisprudence with time. My attempts to test the assertion of progressive leniency on the basis of fragmentary data have revealed no clear pattern. It is perhaps of some interest to note the pattern of executions following death sentences handed down by the Paris *cour de justice*: 1944 – 11; 1945 – 21; 1946 – 19; 1947 – 13; 1948 – 15; 1949 and 1950 – 16. (Boissarie memorandum, *op. cit.*) Cf. the summary of High Court verdicts in Chapter 10 and Appendix F. Henry L. Mason asserts that in Holland sentences for collaboration were "invariably" more severe immediately after the Liberation than after 1947, but offers no statistical evidence. (*Op. cit.*, p. 187 n. 36.)

13. The following remarks are based on calculations I have made using statistics on the work of the *cours* and *chambres*, by district, through the end of 1948, which were published in *Cahiers Français d'Information*, March 15, 1949. My statistical findings are presented in detail in Appendix E, together with a map showing the districts. I have omitted from the present discussion (but not from the tables in the Appendix) figures for the districts of Bastia (Corsica) and Colmar (Alsace-Lorraine). In the former district, the tiny number of cases makes any statistical treatment meaningless and misleading. In the latter, the special circumstances of incorporation into the Reich produced a unique situation, statistically and otherwise: even with the highest percentage of quashed indictments of any district, there were more cases brought to trial, and more guilty verdicts as a percentage of the population, than anywhere else. At the same time, because of the same special circumstances, death sentences were rarer in Alsace-Lorraine than anywhere else.

14. Many more death sentences were pronounced *in absentia* than in the presence of the accused. Since these sentences had no practical effect (if the accused turned up he was retried), they were often pronounced to let off steam, or to give the impression of stern implacability, and are not a reliable index of severity.

These figures, striking as they are, do not reflect the extent of the differences. Each court district included between three and seven departmental courts – and some of these were in turn divided into sections. The spread between the incidence of cases in a given department, and the degree of severity with which they were treated, is thus probably appreciably greater than that indicated by the district totals; the fact that a given district is, on a particular scale, close to the median may disguise the fact that it contained within it courts with both the highest and lowest percentages with respect to the phenomenon being measured.

No clear geographical pattern emerges from the available statistics. Only with respect to the frequency with which the death penalty was pronounced does anything resembling a pattern emerge. Those districts in which it was pronounced with the greatest frequency – Dijon, Grenoble, Limoges, Montpellier, Poitiers, Riom, Toulouse – are all further south than those in which it was applied least often – Amiens, Angers, Caen, Douai, Paris, Rouen. But there were a number of districts in the South – Chambéry, Nîmes, Pau – in which it was employed relatively less often than in some northern districts – Bourges, Orléans, Rennes.

What are we to make of these discrepancies, and how are we to account for them? We can, at present, do little more than note them. The fact that district figures are themselves only averages has been mentioned. Figures concerning the frequency and severity of judicial action are meaningful only when compared to crime statistics – of which we have none. Indices of severity, to be comparable, must include data concerning the specific variety of criminal behavior being dealt with; of this too, we are ignorant.

Even if we knew much more than we do at present about the real and significant differences in the jurisprudence of the *cours de justice*, we still would not know how to explain it. It has been suggested that it is common knowledge among French lawyers that even in normal times, and with respect to ordinary criminal offenses, jurisprudence varies greatly from region to region.[15] This phenomenon does not seem sufficient to account for the differences in severity among the *cours de justice*. Other variables which might have influenced the courts include the extent of German and *milice* exactions – and of Resistance activity – in

15. See André Boissarie, "Vérité sur la Répression", *Monde*, June 5, 1948. I have attempted to test this assertion by comparing cases before the *cours d'assises* of various districts, but the number of serious cases is too small to make statistical verification of Boissarie's contention possible.

each department; the political complexion of each area and of the Departmental Liberation Committees, which played an important role in choosing the jurors; local pressures of various kinds; and finally, the personal inclinations of local judicial personnel – both judges and prosecutors.[16] All things considered, it seems likely that satisfactory explanations of regional variations will probably continue to elude the historian.

But "incoherence" was not just a question of regional variations; even within the same court, there seemed to be no relationship between the seriousness of the crime and the severity of the sentence. In Paris, for example, General Pinsard, a responsible military leader, was sentenced to life imprisonment for swearing an oath of loyalty to Hitler and conducting a campaign to recruit Frenchmen to fight with the Germans on the Russian front; two young *miliciens* who had been present at Georges Mandel's assassination, but had not actually participated in the deed, were executed. The Count de Puységur, "an obscure scribbler whose writings will never influence anyone", was sentenced to death[17]; Stephane Lauzanne, editor of the influential, German-subsidized *Le Matin*, was sentenced to twenty years' imprisonment. Captain Paul Chack, chairman of the "Committee for Anti-Bolshevik Action", was executed; Georges Albertini, secretary-general of the equally Germanophile (and much more important) Rassemblement National Populaire, was sentenced to five years' imprisonment. Two weeks after the Albertini verdict Simone Delb, a typist in the office of Jean Hérold-Paquis, a pro-German propagandist, was sentenced to life at hard labor.

Throughout the fall and winter of 1944-45, Albert Camus, then editor of *Combat*, had been carrying on a running debate with François Mauriac (who wrote regularly for *Le Figaro*) on the subject of the purge.[18] Camus, whose daily editorials movingly portrayed the Wordsworthian atmosphere of liberated Paris, rejected both hatred and forgiveness: the former because it was foreign and repugnant to him; the latter because it would be an insult to dead comrades and destroy

16. This last may or may not account for the disparity in the percentage of cases which reached trial. Of all *informations* opened, twice as many went to trial in Agen-Bordeaux-Toulouse (74-78 per cent) as in Limoges-Paris-Rouen (37-42 per cent). The median was 66 per cent.

17. *France* (London), November 24, 1944.

18. The principal articles on each side appeared in *Combat*, October 20 and 25, 1944; January 5 and 11, 1945; *Figaro*, September 8, October 13, 19 and 22/23, December 12, 1944; January 2, 7/8 and 12, 1945.

all chances of building the new society for which the Resistance had fought. Mauriac – "St François des Assises" – was the apostle of reconciliation and pardon; "let he who is without sin among you cast the first stone" was the text of his weekly sermon.

On January 5, 1945, after two and a half months of experience with the *cour de justice* of Paris, Camus wrote resignedly:

> Now it is too late. Journalists who have not deserved it will still be condemned to death. Recruiting agents who have proved eloquent will still be partially acquitted, and weary of so lame a justice, the people will continue to intervene from time to time in affairs that should no longer be their concern. A certain natural common sense will save us from the worst excesses; weariness and indifference will do the rest. One can get accustomed to anything, even to shame and to stupidity. . . . But we do not write this without bitterness and without sadness. A country which fails in its purge is ready to fail in its restoration. Nations bear the mark of their justice. Our country should be able to show the world something other than these disordered features. But clear thinking and human integrity cannot be learned. Lacking these, we shall have need of petty consolation. We can see that M. Mauriac is right; we shall have need of charity.[19]

Camus' disgust with shockingly disproportionate verdicts was shared by his colleagues. *Franc-Tireur* wrote of "the grave risk that justice will become the object of the most dangerous kind of ridicule"[20]; this view found many echoes in the press, the Resistance movements, and the Consultative Assembly.[21] Dissatisfaction with the trials was not confined to the ardent and articulate editors of the Resistance and its representatives in the Assembly. Public opinion polls during the winter of 1944-45 showed broadly-based impatience and frustration with the course of justice. Verdicts were generally regarded as too slow in coming, often too lenient, and, above all, disproportionate.

19. Camus' capitulation to Mauriac was, for the moment at least, partially rhetorical. On January 11 he wrote of Mauriac's charity as constituting admirable morality but deplorable citizenship. Three years later, however, in a talk at a Dominican monastery, he announced that "regarding the fundamentals, and on the precise point of our controversy, François Mauriac, and not I, was right". (*Actuelles* [Paris: 1950], pp. 212-13.)

20. January 3, 1945.

21. All sections of the non-Communist Resistance – even the most *enragé* – opposed particular sentences as being too harsh. The Communists, while they frequently drew invidious comparisons between severe sentences for the "lampistes" and over-indulgent ones for "les grands responsables", never, to my knowledge, directly protested that a particular sentence was too harsh.

Sometimes disproportionate verdicts were attributed to the influence of an insufficiently purged corps of judges and state prosecutors; some, it was said, secretly braked judicial action, while others sought to efface the memory of their Vichyite past by becoming "durs des durs". (Commenting on the prosecutor who demanded life imprisonment for Hérold-Paquis' typist, *Aurore* expressed the hope "that if ever a Jew appears before him now he will forget the hatred for 'that accursed race' which he expressed so often during the occupation".[22]) Procedural reasons were invoked: the use of smaller juries, hurried pre-trial examinations. The principal explanation for "incoherence" was not, however, to be found in procedural flaws or human frailty among those carrying out the trials; this explanation lay in the very nature of the task of the courts.

Normally, society is able to categorize criminal offenses and assign appropriate penalties – or ranges of penalties – to each. There are different "grades" of burglary, depending on whether it is committed during the day or at night, armed or unarmed, in occupied or unoccupied premises; the penalties are scaled according to the category. Offenses of collaboration resisted such categorization. They could be roughly divided into those to be judged by the *chambres civiques* and those sent before the *cours de justice*, but the categories were broad, the dividing line hazy, and the range of penalties in the latter jurisdiction reached from death to suspended national degradation.

One of the most persistent problems – and one that was never really solved – was the question of the relative severity to be exercised toward the supervisors and executors of policy. The slogan of striking harder the higher up the administrative ladder one went was workable as long as it was a question of purely administrative responsibility. It was not much help when the courts had to apportion blame and punishment between an obedient underling, whose hands were red with the blood of *résistants*, and his hierarchical superior, who had ordered his action while simultaneously rendering services to the Resistance. (Those in more responsible positions not only had greater possibilities of "playing a double game", but frequently had done so – perhaps as a result of greater foresight and a corresponding recognition of the path of enlightened self-interest. Subordinate officials typically lacked the imagination, the habit of initiative, and the opportunity to do so.)

An outraged mother would demand the heaviest penalty for the man who tracked down and dragged off her son to deportation and death. At his trial, the policeman involved would claim – truthfully – that he

22. April 6, 1945.

was simply obeying the orders of his chief. And at *his* trial, the latter would call witness after witness to attest – also truthfully – to the multiple services he had performed for the Resistance, and the extent to which he had braked German and Vichy terror.

One of the most striking illustrations of this dilemma was furnished by the respective trials of René Cussonac, a police official, and his superior, the regional prefect, Alexandre Angeli. Cussonac, who had conducted a savage campaign against *résistants*, *réfractaires* and Jews, pleaded that he had only been carrying out orders. A stream of witnesses testified to his blind obedience; Angeli himself, called as a defense witness, said that Cussonac "wouldn't know how to begin to question an order". Cussonac was sentenced to death and executed. At the trial of Angeli, under whom Cussonac had worked, numerous witnesses testified to his contact with the Resistance and his sabotage of repressive measures. After an earlier death sentence was annulled, he was sentenced to four years' imprisonment.[23]

The "double game" was the most popular defense among officials, and there was frequently some truth to the claim. In the case of those with responsibilities for the conduct of foreign affairs, the "double game" usually consisted of the maintenance of contacts with the Allies. Many others invoked it on the basis of contacts with the Resistance.

When, during the occupation, the Resistance made contact with administration officials, it realized that it was "offering a future alibi" to the men concerned, but accepted this as the necessary price for effective infiltration of Vichy's state machinery. After the Liberation, many "Resistance hermits" claimed that they had been "infiltrating" even when they had had no organizational ties and no evidence to substantiate their claimed activity. Claude Bourdet, who until his arrest by the Germans was head of "Noyautage des Administrations Publiques", noted that

the idea of "noyautage" on one's own rarely holds water. Since 1943 there were numerous opportunities for contact with the Resistance. If internal Resistance contacts seemed too dangerous, there was the more tightly organized France Combattante network – less revolutionary and less "political". If even De Gaulle seemed too closely allied to "judéo-maçonnerie" for the prudent patriot, there were the many British Intelligence networks. If even Churchill's orders seemed a bit tainted with a

23. Cf. Paul Garcin, *La Haine: Reportage clandestin, 1940-1944* (Paris: 1964), pp. 153-96; "Cour de justice [de Lyon]. Audiences du 29 novembre 1944ff. Ministère public. C/Angeli. Débats complets" (Paris: 1945) [unpublished typescript in the B.D.I.C.], *passim*.

subversive spirit, in 1943 and 1944 the American services developed in both zones and could furnish guarantees, even to the most reactionary, based on Leahy's flirtation with Vichy and Eisenhower's with Giraud and Darlan. . . . When someone claims isolated patriotic activity to counterbalance his service to the enemy or to Vichy, the obvious explanation is that he worked neither with the Resistance nor with the Allies, either because he considered the cause of Vichy and the enemy the only legitimate one, or because he considered it the only profitable one.[24]

Sometimes the claim was ludicrous, as when Jean Luchaire asserted that after the end of 1942 he became disenchanted with collaboration and became a "résistant" by listening to the B.B.C. He continued preaching collaboration, however, since, as he explained to the court, if he let his readers in on his "double game" the Germans would know too. The Court was not impressed with his "resistance" and sentenced him to death.[25] Luchaire's case was an exception; usually there was at least some real substance to the alleged double game.

Even more widespread than the "double game defense" – and almost always at least partially true – was the defense that the actions under examination had been performed with the good of France as their goal. Collaboration had been undertaken to make the best of a bad situation. From Pétain and Laval down to petty officials, industrialists and journalists, the claim was that by their action they had prevented greater German exactions. It might be a question of substituting Gallic anti-Semitic measures for the *Endlössung*, keeping factories going to prevent the deportation of their workers, carrying out bloodless expeditions against the Resistance instead of leaving it to the tender mercies of the Germans, or simply establishing good relations with the Germans so that they would be amenable to suggestion.

The nature of the offenses charged, the extent to which collaboration was paralleled by resistance, the motives of the defendants – all these varied enormously. We have become resigned to the fact that perfect proportionality between crime and punishment is an ideal which must

24. *Combat*, February 10, 1949.
25. Maurice Garcon (ed.), *Les Procès de collaboration: Fernand de Brinon, Joseph Darnand, Jean Luchaire* (Paris: 1948). The fabulous salary which Luchaire had received was a factor which weighed heavily against him. "Wherever the secret funds were to be found, there he found the interests of his country," the prosecutor observed. In general, propagandists who made a good thing financially out of supporting collaboration, particularly when (as in Luchaire's case) the money was of German origin, were treated more harshly by the courts.

be perpetually beyond our reach; we make do with the best approxima-
tion available. In the case of the purge trials, even such an approxima-
tion was virtually impossible.

Customarily, courts try not men, but offenses. The character of the
defendant may be introduced as a mitigating or aggravating circumstance, but it is – ordinarily – not central to the proceedings, or at least
not acknowledged to be. It is the criminal act which is at the center of
the court's attention. What was the crime? Did the defendant do it?
What were its consequences? These are the crucial questions. Only
secondarily is the defendant himself – the whole man, his conduct "in
the round" – on trial. This has usually been the case even in those trials
which have become political *causes célèbres*: Dreyfus, Sacco and Van-
zetti, the Reichstag Fire Trial, the Moscow Trials. Of course, these
trials raised larger issues than those of factual guilt or innocence, but
that question remained the crux of the controversies which surrounded
the cases.

In many of the cases before the *cours de justice* concentration on the
offense was possible. The trials of murderers and torturers, like the
members of the Bony-Lafont "French Gestapo", could be conducted
in the same way as those of common criminals – which indeed they
were. The trials of informers could also center on the offense and its
consequences, which were often tragic: deportation, torture, death.
The cases of informers frequently revealed the most sordid of private
motives. Not untypical is the case of a wife who, while her husband was
a prisoner of war in Germany, installed her lover in her apartment.
When the husband escaped and returned home the two lovers sent an
anonymous note to the German military police; the husband was captured and returned to Germany. (The *cour de justice* of Versailles
sentenced the man to ten years imprisonment, the wife to five.)[26]

But in a great many cases, and in almost all of the most celebrated
ones, it was not an act, or even a series of acts, that was in question.
The specific acts listed in an indictment were usually tacitly stipulated
by the defense; what was in dispute was whether these particular acts,
taken out of the context of the defendant's total behavior, accurately
reflected either his intentions or the main thrust of his activity. The
juries were, in effect, asked to judge *the man*, not the specific acts
alleged, nor the position he had held. And as there were as many different kinds of men in the dock (and in the jury box) as there are pebbles
on the beach, a clear and consistent jurisprudence was out of the

26. Yves-Frédéric Jaffre, *Les Tribunaux d'exception: 1940-1962* (Paris:
1962), p. 204.

question. Two sections of the Paris *cour de justice*, hearing identical charges, attested by the same witnesses, against two members of the same police brigade, could acquit one and sentence the other to twenty years at hard labor.[27] Angeli, who received a death sentence in Lyons, could be retried in Paris on the same evidence and receive a four-year prison sentence. By early 1945 disillusionment with the work of the *cours de justice* was not only general, but virtually complete.

The most publicized and most important of the trials were, however, still to come: those of the chiefs of Vichy, who were to appear before the High Court. Logically, Pétain should have been the first to be tried before the High Court. There was no reason why he could not have been swiftly tried *in absentia*, since later in the spring of 1945 plans were made to do just that. However, for reasons that remain obscure, the Government decided that two elderly military leaders should be the first to answer for the policy of Vichy: Admiral Estéva, who as Resident-General of Tunisia had cooperated with the Axis at the time of the Allied landings in North Africa; and General Dentz, who had gone much further along the road of military collaboration in Syria in 1941. The decision to try these two first was justified on the grounds that their cases laid the foundation for the trial of the Marshal, by "demonstrating the disastrous military effects of the policy of collaboration followed by Marshal Pétain".[28]

Estéva, who had been blindly obedient rather than pro-Axis, and who had in his favor the fact that he had released political prisoners at the time of the German entry into Tunis, was sentenced to life imprisonment in March. Dentz, who had actually fought against the Free French, and requested German air attacks against the British, was sentenced to death in the following month. (The sentence was commuted to life imprisonment by General de Gaulle.)

Glad as the Resistance was to see the policy of Vichy symbolically condemned in the persons of Estéva and Dentz, these two were distinctly of the second rank, and agitation continued for the swift trial of Pétain *in absentia*. Immediately after Dentz' trial in April the Government announced that Pétain's would be held on May 17. The *instruction* was begun, but within a few days of the announcement, word was received in Paris that the Marshal had crossed the German-Swiss border and was headed for France. De Gaulle, although publicly

27. J.O., A.N.C. (I) Debates, February 26, 1946, p. 470.
28. *Bulletin Hebdomadaire d'Informations Judiciaires*, No. 6 (May 19, 1945).

committed to trying Pétain, indicated privately that he had no desire to see the Marshal punished.

> I considered it necessary both from an international and a national point of view that French justice give a formal verdict, but I also hoped that some accident would spare the soil of France an accused man of eighty-nine, a leader once distinguished by the most exceptional powers, an old soldier in whom, at the time of the catastrophe, many Frenchmen had put their trust, and for whom, in spite of everything, many still felt respect or pity. General de Lattre asked me what action he should take if his troops, which were approaching Sigmaringen, happened to find Pétain or his former ministers. I replied that all must be arrested, but that so far as the Marshal himself was concerned, I hoped that no such encounter would take place. . . . When [the Swiss ambassador] came to announce to me Pétain's presence in Switzerland, I told him that the French Government [*sic*] was not at all eager to have Pétain extradited.[29]

But Pétain wished to return, and on April 25 he crossed the Franco-Swiss border, where he was arrested by General Koenig, and thence transported to imprisonment at the Fort of Montrouge.

Pétain's return meant a longer *instruction*, and the May 17 target date had to be abandoned. The Resistance, which desired to have Vichy's symbolic condemnation take place in as public a manner as possible, pressed for holding the trial in a large hall – preferably the Palais Bourbon or the Palais du Luxembourg. The Government, anxious to avoid demonstrations, chose to hold it in the Palais de Justice, which could be effectively blockaded.

The Resistance had long been dedicated to the punishment of the Marshal, but the population at large had been, at the time of the Liberation, disposed to treat him with indulgence. By the time his trial opened, on July 23, public opinion had dramatically switched, and his condemnation was demanded by the overwhelming majority of Frenchmen. (See Table 5.)

The condemnation was, of course, forthcoming, after a trial which lasted three weeks. It could not have been otherwise, for as *Combat* noted (and everyone realized), "if Pétain is innocent, all those who fought the occupant are guilty".[30] The events which transpired in the Palais de Justice between July 23 and August 15 were not a trial, but an elaborate ceremonial aimed at symbolically condemning a policy.

29. *Mémoires*, III, 111-12. Cf. Georges Duhamel's account of a talk with De Gaulle shortly after the Liberation, in which the General said of Pétain: "Let him go and live on the Riviera." (*France-Illustration*, July 28, 1951.)
30. April 25, 1945.

TABLE 5. – *Evolution of public opinion on Marshal Pétain's fate*[a]

	September 1944	January 1945	April 1945	May 1945	July 1945[b]	August 1945[c]
Death penalty	3% } 35%	21% } 61%	31% } 76%	44% } 84%	— } 84%	40·5% } 81%
Penalties short of death	32%	40%	45%	40%	—	40·5%
No penalty	64%	39%	24%	16%	16%	19%

[a] The first question asked was "Faut-il infliger une peine au maréchal Pétain?" Those who replied affirmatively were asked "Laquelle?" The percentages given are for those with an opinion on the subject; the "don't knows" amounted to nine or ten per cent. The data on which this table is based are taken from the *Bulletin d'Information de l'Institut Français d'Opinion Publique*, No. 2 (October 16, 1944); No. 10 (February 16, 1945); No. 16 (May 16, 1945); No. 18 (June 16, 1945); No. 21 (September 1-16, 1945). Cf. the very similar results obtained by the Service de Sondages et de Statistiques (*Sondages*, No. 14 [May 15, 1945]).
[b] On the eve of Pétain's trial. In this poll respondents were not asked which penalty they thought appropriate.
[c] During the trial.

174

Considered as a demonstration of justice it was, as Georges Bernanos remarked, "on a par with the scuttling of the French fleet at Toulon in 1942, which was held up as a demonstration of military heroism".[31]

Judged by dramatic standards, the trial was not much better. The audience was fidgety, not least because of the incredibly crowded conditions in the relatively small courtroom, which resulted in journalists literally sitting in each others' laps. The star, Pétain, was ·mute, allegedly because of his refusal to recognize the competence of the court – in fact, equally as much because of his senility.[32] Finally, the script was radically rewritten half-way through the second act.

The major portion of the original indictment dealt with the period prior to the establishment of the Vichy Regime on July 11, 1940. Pétain's alleged relations with "the Cagoule" before the war, his alleged intrigues with Laval and Weygand aiming at power, the negotiation of the Armistice, and the "complot" of July 10 – these were the dominant themes in Prosecutor Mornet's opening statement. The concentration of the indictment on events surrounding the Armistice may have reflected De Gaulle's influence. Though he claimed that he was "particularly careful not to influence the prosecution", he expressed irritation at the fact that, in the event, Pétain's trial did not center on the Armistice, since all subsequent actions had, in his view, "flowed inevitably from this poisoned spring".[33]

Virtually every available luminary of the Third Republic passed through the witness box: Blum, Daladier, Herriot, Jeanneney, Lebrun, Marin, Reynaud, Weygand, and many more. Their appearance was not without interest, nor was it lacking in drama. There was Léon Blum, sobbing as he spoke of his imprisonment at Pétain's order, Daladier's tub-thumping oration, and the vindictive confrontation between Reynaud and Weygand over responsibility for the Armistice. But it all had very little to do with the charges against Pétain – most of the eminent witnesses (with the exception of Blum) were principally concerned with defending their own role.

Half-way through the trial there was a *coup de théâtre* as the prosecutor calmly announced that he did not have any real proof concerning

31. *Combat*, August 12, 1945.

32. Pétain's silence was not absolute: in addition to brief statements at the beginning and end of the trial, he occasionally intervened to deny a particular charge. His senility was rarely admitted by either Vichyites or *résistants*. The former avoided mentioning it out of piety and because it would make them appear ridiculous for having followed him; the latter because it would tend to make him an object of pity rather than of righteous wrath.

33. *Mémoires*, III, 110, 248-49.

criminal responsibility for events before July 11, 1940; that all the testimony that had been heard should be regarded as "preface"; and that (on the ninth day of the trial) it was "time that the Pétain trial began".[34] Once the trial "had begun" it turned into a minute examination of the advantages and disadvantages of particular Vichy policies, a dreary procedure enlivened only by the flamboyant manner of Pierre Laval, who returned to France (unwillingly) in the middle of the trial and was called as a witness. The jury, after seven hours' deliberation, found Pétain guilty of intelligence with the enemy. He was sentenced to death, but with a recommendation from the jury – which General de Gaulle followed – that in view of Pétain's age the sentence not be executed.[35]

The real weakness of the Pétain trial, from the point of view of the Resistance, the Government, and public opinion at large, was the same as that which characterized so many of the trials, particularly those before the High Court. The prosecution played into the hands of the defense by placing the indictment on a material rather than a moral plane. Every time Mornet cited a concession granted the Germans, Pétain's lawyers could cite a concession wrung from them. For every pro-Axis public act the lawyers could show a pro-Allied private one. The testimony bogged down into a balancing of profit and loss – exactly the chosen terrain of the defense.[36]

If Pétain's trial was unsatisfactory, Laval's, which took place in early October, was a disaster. The *instruction* was concluded with indecent haste (in four sessions) – probably so that the trial could be completed before the October elections. Laval's lawyers stayed away from the first day's session in protest; there were several shouting matches between Laval and the President of the Court, but calm was eventually restored.

34. *Le Procès du Maréchal Pétain* (Paris: 1945), I, 427.
35. De Gaulle states that whatever the jury's recommendation he had been determined to commute the death sentence, and that in addition he had intended to release Pétain from prison after two years. (*Mémoires*, III, 250.) Long before then, of course, he had left power, and with it the opportunity to fulfill his vow. Most of the press was favorably disposed to the non-execution of the death sentence. *Humanité*, not surprisingly, was outraged (throughout August and September).
36. Prosecuting the men of Vichy on the charge of having preferred the lesser evil to a moral stand would have necessitated having a prosecutor who had not played his own "double game". Mornet had sworn the magistrate's oath to Pétain, volunteered to sit on the court at Riom, and served for years on Vichy's "denaturalization commission" (to brake its activity). These facts were frequently alluded to by the defense during the trials at which he served as prosecutor.

The calm lasted through the second day, at which Laval's lawyers were present, but on the third day Laval's manner – he was alternatively condescending and familiar, always ironic and witty – brought shouts of "scoundrel" and "twelve bullets in his hide" from the jury.[37] President Mongibeaux proved totally incapable of either keeping order in the tumultuous courtroom or controlling his own outbursts. At the end of the third day's session, Laval refused to remain any longer, and the rest of the trial was conducted in the absence of both Laval and his lawyers. The inevitable death sentence was pronounced on October 9. General de Gaulle, after receiving Laval's lawyers and soliciting the advice of his Minister of Justice, refused to either commute the sentence or order a new trial. The manner of Laval's death was a barbarous climax to the shabby proceedings. He attempted suicide just before his scheduled execution, and was dragged, retching and crying for water, to an impromptu firing squad. "Laval's trial", one observer wrote,

> is unpardonable because it made the French doubt the reality of French justice, so that none of our institutions, henceforth, will be immune from that disillusioned scepticism which finally renders a people ungovernable and drives men straight to anarchy. . . . Now the harm is done. French justice is discredited. Laval has won the last round and completed the demoralization of the country.[38]

Demoralized or not, France was committed to continuing the trials before the High Court until all Vichy ministers had been dealt with. Besides those cases already mentioned, the Court disposed of ten other cases in 1945. Joseph Darnand was sentenced to death and executed. Abel Bonnard and Marcel Déat were sentenced to death *in absentia*. In seven cases – including that of Robert Schumann – the Court decided not to prosecute; four prospective defendants died before the Court took action. There remained ninety cases on the docket.

The Court underwent several changes during its winter recess. Since there was now an elected Assembly, the dual system for selecting jurors was abandoned, and the Assembly chose a single list of ninety-six of its members, from whom the twenty-four jurors would be drawn by lot. Politically, the jury panel was a microcosm of the Assembly; each group named the number of candidates to which it was entitled, and the Assembly simply ratified their choices. So that the defense would not be able to alter the political composition of the jury, the right to challenge jurors was removed. Finally, it was decided to draw the

---

37. *Le Procès Laval* (Paris: 1946), p. 207.
38. Quoted in Pickles, *France*, p. 195.

judges as well as the jurors from the Assembly.[39] The Socialist deputy Louis Noguères became President of the High Court, assisted by two vice presidents – one a Communist, the other a Christian Democrat. Mornet was replaced as prosecutor by M. Frette-Damicourt, who, in addition to his other advantages, had a much less ambiguous record under the occupation: he had been removed from office by Vichy in 1940.

During most of 1945 the "résistantialiste" mood of the country had been waning, but the façade of Resistance unity had been maintained: there had been a formal moratorium on party politics; the parties continued to pay lip service to the C.N.R. Charter. Before the October 1945 elections all parties, uncertain of their own strength and of the popularity of General de Gaulle, had been fearful of an open breach with the General. Then, from October 1945 through November 1946, there was more concentrated political activity than in any year in French history before or since. There were three constitutional referenda and three general elections. It was a year of almost constant campaigning – a year in which the desire of the population for a "return to normalcy" found a distorted reflection in the revival of the political maneuvering and shifting alliances of the Third Republic. General de Gaulle's resignation from the presidency in January 1946 – and his replacement by a politician of the Third Republic (the Socialist deputy Félix Gouin) – was symbolic of the transition.

While the principal arena of maneuver was the constitutional commissions of the two Constituent Assemblies – the purge, and the High Court in particular, were complementary arenas. The Right – which had been hostile to the purge from the start – became more forthright in its criticisms. The Radicals for a time had found it advantageous to appear as implacable *épurateurs* in order to compensate for their thin Resistance record. But, as they could not hope to compete with the Socialists and Communists in an electoral appeal to "les durs", they directed their attention to "les mous". As their position on the press purge hardened, they became more and more openly hostile to the trials. The attitude of the M.R.P. was mixed. On the one hand, since the Liberation the Ministry of Justice had been in the hands of Christian Democrats: first François de Menthon, then P.-H. Teitgen; this inhibited their Party's ability to criticize government action in this field. At the same time, the M.R.P. was the inheritor of much of the Vichyite

39. Law No. 45-0146 of December 27, 1945.

clientele of the Right, and was also strongly influenced by the "reconciliationist" ideology of the Church. On the whole, the M.R.P. moved from lukewarm approval of the purge to a more and more critical attitude, and an emphasis on "binding up the nation's wounds".

The Socialists and the Communists were "les durs" on questions connected with the purge. The Socialists' support for the purge, though coupled with a commitment to equitable procedures, was zealous and consistent. Typical Socialist pronouncements called for the carrying out of the purge in the absence of "sterile thoughts of vengeance"; the purge was intimately linked in Socialist thought to "réformes de structure". They were the group most sincerely dedicated to the ideals of the C.N.R. Charter and to Resistance unity. At the same time, political strategy dictated a firm Socialist attitude on the purge. Throughout 1945 and 1946 – and indeed, throughout the Fourth Republic – the Socialists were competing with the Communists for the same share of the electorate; during the period when "résistantialisme" still had some appeal, they were afraid of being outflanked on the purge issue by greater Communist implacability.

For the Communists, the stance of "durs des durs" was not only temperamentally congenial and ideologically correct, but tactically advantageous, since it was part of their "image" as the most *résistant* of all the parties. The tone of Communist oratory on the purge was almost always frantic: verdicts which were considered overly lenient were never "ill-advised", "unfortunate", or "mistaken"; rather they were "outrageous", "shocking", or "unbelievable". "Hatred", the reader of *Humanité* were told, "is a national duty."[40] The address to the jury by a state prosecutor was attacked because it lacked "cette flamme vengeresse indispensable".[41] The Stalinist logic which made all collaborators equally guilty (and thus equally deserving of severe punishment) was summed up by Maurice Merleau-Ponty: "Good or bad, honest or venal, courageous or cowardly, the collaborator is a traitor in the eyes of the *résistant*, and thus objectively or historically a traitor the day the Resistance is victorious".[42] Not only collaborators, but also *résistants* who under torture gave information to the Germans, were "objectively" traitors and to be punished as such.[43] However, while the S.F.I.O. followed its policy of measured firmness more or less

40. January 11, 1945.
41. *Ibid.*, January 4, 1946.
42. "Le Yogi et le Prolétaire", *Temps Modernes*, II, 13 (October 1946), 28.
43. *La Vie du Parti*, June 1943, January 1944; Pierre Hervé in *Action*, January 5, 1945.

consistently, the Communist Party stressed or subordinated its "outraged implacability" according to the shifting tides of the war and of political necessity.

In the fall of 1944, when the Allied armies appeared capable of ending the war within a few months, the Communists were in the vanguard of those calling for vigorous action on the purge. When the "Von Rundstedt offensive" of December 1944 called into question the prospect of immediate victory, the Communists quickly switched their propaganda emphasis in line with their consistent policy of subordinating political goals to the war effort. In early 1945, when most of the Resistance press was raising its voice in protest against the slowness and incoherence of the trials, L'Humanité played down this theme; with very rare exceptions, every issue down to V-E Day devoted its major headline to the exploits of the Red Army.[44]

With the end of the war in Europe, the purge again became a dominant theme in Communist propaganda. Other parties were attacked for alleged Vichyism or for insufficient support of the purge. By using this tactic the Communists tried – unsuccessfully – to intimidate the Socialists into running joint slates with them in the October 1945 elections; failing this, they attempted to discredit their Socialist competitors by attacking the prewar and wartime activity of the S.F.I.O. After the elections, Communist policy switched to one of reconciliation with the Socialists, cooperation in drafting a "Marxist Constitution", and the development of a popular front coalition. The purge – and attacks on alleged Socialist softness toward Vichy – were played down in the Communist press.

The attitudes of the political parties toward the purge were reflected not only in their public pronouncements and their legislative behavior; they could also be seen at work in the conduct of the parties' representatives on the High Court. Except for the Communists, jurors did not function as disciplined, instructed agents. There were "hard" jurors

44. Two examples of P.C.F. policy in this period are worth noting. Maurice Thorez was extremely hostile to the spontaneous strikes in the coal mines which had as their object the removal of collaborationist supervisors; such stoppages interfered with "the battle of production". (August Lecoeur, Le Partisan [Paris: 1963], pp. 214-19.) In the case of the Army, P.C.F. policy in early 1945 was to caution against "unfair" sweeping purge measures which might impair fighting efficiency. (Cf. Maurice Thorez, Œuvres, XX [Paris: 1960], 171; J.O., A.C.P. Documents, Nos. 379, 415.) After V-E Day, Communist attacks on Vichyites in the Army brushed aside all considerations of equity.

in "soft" parties; Socialist jurors frequently split, or voted *en bloc* with those on their right.[45] Nevertheless, it became clear that representatives of the Radicals, the M.R.P., and the parties of the Right were in general disposed toward leniency, while Communist and Socialist jurors leaned toward severity. The procedure for the selection of High Court juries provided for proportionality only on the panel of ninety-six; the twenty-four sitting jurors were chosen from this panel by lot. Thus, by the luck of the draw, a defendant might face a jury with a lenient (Radical-M.R.P.-Right) or severe (Communist-Socialist) majority.[46] Fluctuation in the political composition of High Court juries was simply one among many factors which added to the impression of "incoherence" in High Court verdicts.

In the spring of 1946, High Court verdicts ranged from death to suspended national degradation. The verdicts were, in fact, roughly proportional to the seriousness of the offense of the minister involved. Those receiving heavy sentences had generally been zealous collaborationists, and had been personally responsible for deportations or bloody repressions: Hubert Lagardelle, who as Minister of Labor had cooperated with the S.T.O., was sentenced to life at hard labor. Those who got off lightly were those who had served briefly in the early days of Vichy in "technical ministries", and those who had used their influence to combat collaboration inside the regime: Jean Ybarnégaray, who was Minister of Family Affairs at the beginning of the Vichy Regime and later was deported to Dachau by the Germans, had his (automatic) sentence of national degradation immediately suspended by the Court. (No one who had been in Pétain's Third Republic cabinet after June 17 and left it by July 11, 1940, was prosecuted; they all received *non-lieux*.)

During the spring session of the Court, Communist policy once again swung toward a hard line. In the referendum of May 5 the voters had rejected the draft constitution supported by the two parties of the Left; the Communists blamed the defeat on Socialist unwillingness to conduct a joint campaign. In the campaign for the election of a new Constituent Assembly the Communists found themselves under Socialist attack. André Le Troquer accused the Communists of having become "patriots" in the 1930's only after the signing of the Franco-Soviet

45. Votes within juries were secret; this observation is based on what must have happened in order to explain moderate verdicts in cases where there was a Communist-Socialist majority, severe verdicts when there was a technically "soft" majority.

46. As it happened, there was never a jury with a purely Communist majority (i.e., thirteen jurors plus the Communist vice-president).

Treaty and of abandoning France in August 1939; Maurice Thorez' desertion in 1939 was invoked as a symbol of Communist conduct.[47]

The Communists were too astute to be drawn into a controversy on this terrain: instead they threw up a smokescreen of outraged patriotism and perfervid purging zeal. Immediately following Le Troquer's speech the Communists launched a violent campaign against Frédéric Dupont, a leader of the Parti Républicain de la Liberté; Dupont, they claimed, had been a shameless collaborator. A few days later Edouard Daladier also became a daily Communist target; his crimes were the Munich Agreement and repressive action against the Communists in 1939. Then Paul Reynaud joined the list – charged with responsibility for the 1940 defeat and having invited Pétain and Weygand into his cabinet. It was a campaign of unlimited vituperation and abuse. The Party demanded the invalidation of the election of the three men to the new Constituent Assembly, and secured resolutions to this end from trade-union and Resistance groups under its control. The Communists carried the issue to the floor of the Assembly, demanding that the elections in question be declared invalid, despite the fact that no formal irregularity was charged. They were completely isolated, and went down to crushing defeat.

The Communists seemed to be courting isolation – to be promoting the idea that they alone were patriots and *résistants*, while their competitors were all *munichois* and apologists for Pétain. This impression was heightened by their next move, which brought the 1946 session of the Court to a close amid dissension, acrimony, and – if this was still possible – even more public disillusionment with the trials than already existed.

On July 26 Pierre-Etienne Flandin was tried by the High Court. The charges against him hardly went beyond the fact of his brief tenure as Vichy Foreign Minister from December 1940 to February 1941. The prosecution called no witnesses, and admitted that Flandin had acted to brake collaboration during his term of office. The jury sentenced him to five years' national degradation, but immediately suspended the penalty for "faits de résistance".[48] The Communist press again broke out into a chorus of outraged protests. When, four days later, the Court

47. *Monde*, May 24, 1946.
48. The suspension of the penalty did not, as it turned out, restore Flandin's electoral eligibility. In October 1946 the A.N.C. adopted, by voice vote, a Socialist motion which called for the continued ineligibility of those whose sentences of national degradation had been suspended. (All other disqualifications were to remain suspended.) The Law – No. 46-2174 of October 4, 1946 – was popularly and aptly known as the "Loi Flandin".

convened again to consider its next case, the Communist vice-president and jurors were not present: they were "on strike". The Communist delegation to the Constituent Assembly introduced a motion to radically reorganize and "politicize" the High Court: both the *commission d'instruction* (made up of five judges and eight deputies) and the prosecuting staff (made up entirely of Ministry of Justice attorneys) should be composed entirely of deputies; both the meetings of the *commission d'instruction* and the deliberations of the jury should be open; the stenographic record of their deliberations and of all votes should be published in the *Journal Officiel*.

As in the validation debate, the Communists stood alone. Jacques Duclos attacked those who said that one should judge "without hatred and without fear". On the contrary, he said, it was necessary for a judge in these cases to have hatred "au fond de son coeur". Hatred of those who had betrayed France was "une haine sacrée". He was interrupted by shouts of "à bas la haine"; in the final vote the Communist proposal was swamped.[49] Raymond Aron commented:

> In the acquittal of M. Flandin, as in the validation of M. Daladier, the Communist Party purports to see a "rehabilitation" of Munich – a rehabilitation they then have a fine time denouncing. A good deal of fervor goes into these denunciations, because for them, Munich is ... the indispensable alibi. The French Government *must* have been betraying France in 1938, in 1939, before June 1940 – so that no one else could have been committing treason during those years. The Communist Party chases phantoms because they are themselves pursued by the phantom of their past, which will not leave them in peace.[50]

The Court, withouts its Communist members, went on to hear one more case, then suspended its work until 1947. By the time it reconvened, almost three years had elapsed since the Liberation. The High Court's work – and that of the *cours de justice* – was no longer part of an ambitious program for "renouvellement"; it was merely one of the incompleted chores of cleaning up wartime debris, and one of which everyone was heartily sick.

49. J.O., A.N.C. (II) Debates, August 8, 1946, pp. 3076-85, 3106-07.
50. *Combat*, August 2, 1946.

Chapter 10

IN CONCLUSION

The idea of justice is based on a fixed system of reference; the presence of the two variables of time and value turns the whole concept of 'historic justice' into a subjective and arbitrary one; in fact reduces it to a contradiction in terms. History cannot be judged by the application of any rigid code of ethics; it can only be represented in the manner of the Greek tragedy, where the antagonists are both right in their own terms of reference and in their own universe of discourse.

ARTHUR KOESTLER[1]

THE trials dragged on for years, with the High Court continuing to hear cases through the summer of 1949. Only one more High Court death sentence resulted in an execution – that pronounced against the arch-collaborationist Fernand de Brinon in early 1947. Later that year the procedure for the selection of High Court jurors was modified to make the juries themselves, as well as just the panels, proportional to voting strength in the Assembly. (Only the Communists voted against the ending of the "jury gamble"; the Socialists abstained.[2])

In all, 108 cases fell within the Court's competence during its four-year history. Eight men died before the Court could act; in forty-two cases the Court decided not to prosecute. Of the remaining fifty-eight cases, sixteen were heard *in absentia*, forty-two in the presence of the accused. Of the latter eight cases resulted in death sentences (three of which were executed), seventeen in "peines privatives de liberté" of various sorts; there were fourteen sentences of national degradation, seven of which were suspended; three men were acquitted.[3] (See Table 6 and Appendix F.)

1. *Promise and Fulfillment* (New York: 1949), p. 23.
2. The reform was unquestionably desirable and overdue, but the De Brinon trial – held under the old dispensation – showed that the political composition of juries was not decisive in the leniency or severity of High Court verdicts. His death sentence was voted by one of the furthest right juries in High Court history: 17 from the M.R.P.-Radical-Right bloc, 10 Communists and Socialists.
3. Law No. 54-288 of March 3, 1954, annulled that section of the ordinance setting up the High Court which provided for the execution of sentences pronounced *in absentia*. As a result, a number of *émigrés* returned

184

TABLE 6. – *Statistical summary of the work of the Haute Cour de Justice*[a]

Year	Cases tried in the presence of the accused										Cases tried *in absentia*[b]					Total of all trial verdicts	Decisions not to prosecute	Total of all decisions	Died before trial
	Death		Imprisonment				National degradation		Acquittals	Total	Death	Imprisonment		National degradation	Total				
	Executed	Commuted[c]	Life	Term			Penalty imposed	Suspended				Life	Term						
				10 years and over	5-10 years	Under 5 years[d]													
1945	2	2	1	—	—	—	—	—	—	5	2	—	—	—	2	7	7	14	4
1946	—	1	1	2	2	1	2	2	—	11	3	1	—	—	4	15	4	19	1
1947	1	2	—	3	1	—	3	1	—	11	3	—	3	—	6	17	18	35	—
1948	—	—	—	2	—	4	2	2	2	12	2	—	1	1	4	16	6	22	2
1949	—	—	—	—	—	—	—	2	1	3	—	—	—	—	—	3	7	10	1
Total	3	5	2	7	3	5	7	7	3	42	10	1	4	1	16	58	42	100	8

[a] For a complete list of High Court verdicts see Appendix F.
[b] Sentences *in absentia* were neither commuted nor suspended.
[c] As a rule death sentences were commuted to life imprisonment.
[d] Sentences of less than five years were usually made equivalent to the time the defendant had served while awaiting trial.

185

The *cours de justice* and *chambres civiques* finished the bulk of their work sooner than the High Court, although the last *cour de justice* did not cease operation until 1951. Most departmental *cours* and *chambres* were closed down in 1946 and their cases transferred to the principal courts at the seats of the judicial districts. These too were abolished in 1947, only the regional courts at Paris, Colmar, Toulouse, and Lyon remaining open. Eventually all were closed except the court at Paris; that jurisdiction finally stopped its work on January 31, 1951, and handed over its few remaining cases to the Military Tribunal of Paris. In all, the *cours de justice* and *chambres civiques* heard 124,751 cases. Death sentences in the presence of the accused totalled 2,853, of which 767 were carried out; 3,910 death sentences were handed down *in absentia*. There were 38,266 sentences involving "peines privatives de liberté": 2,702 sentences of life at hard labor; 10,637 terms of hard labor; 2,044 sentences to solitary confinement; 22,883 to terms of imprisonment. National degradation was visited upon 49,723 individuals: in 3,578 of these cases this was the principal penalty decreed by a *cour de justice*; the *chambres civiques* sentenced 46,145 individuals to national degradation, and in addition imposed the penalty and then immediately suspended it in 3,184 cases.[4]

Too harsh? Too lenient? Pointing to the experience of other western European countries is only begging the question, yet it is perhaps not without interest. There were, in absolute terms, more executions in France than anywhere else, though fewer relative to population than in Belgium.[5] (In Denmark, Holland, and Norway the death penalty had been abolished for many years, and was reintroduced – temporarily – to deal with collaborators.) The 38,000 prison sentences in France

---

for retrial before a temporarily reconstituted High Court. In all cases the new trials resulted in acquittals, suspended sentences, or sentences already having expired (e.g., a sentence handed down in 1960 calling for ten years banishment as of 1945). See *Bilans Hebdomadaires*, No. 421 (June 24, 1954); Yves-Frédéric Jaffre, *Les Tribunaux d'exception: 1940-1962* (Paris: 1962), pp. 145-46.

4. Emile Garçon, *Code pénal annoté* (Paris: 1952-59), I, 266. Cf. J.O., A.N. Debates, December 12, 1951, p. 9100; July 12, 1952, p. 3939; October 21, 1952, p. 4248; March 23, 1954, p. 1213; Ministère de la Justice, *Compte général de l'administration de la justice civile et commerciale et de la justice criminelle: 1944 à 1947* (Melun: 1951), pp. 262-64; and Appendix E below.

5. There were 25 executions in Norway. (Paul Sérant, *Les Vaincus de la libération* [Paris: 1964], p. 327.). As of the beginning of April 1948, 23 death sentences had been carried out in Denmark. (C. C. Givskov, "Danish 'Purge

meant that 94 out of every 100,000 Frenchmen were imprisoned for collaboration. The 14,000 prison sentences in Denmark meant that 374 out of every 100,000 Danes were jailed for this offense; the 40,000 in Holland hit 419 out of every 100,000 Dutchmen; the 50,000 in Belgium, 596 out of every 100,000 Belgians; the 20,000 in Norway, 633 out of every 100,000 Norwegians.[6]

In France, as elsewhere, figures concerning trial verdicts do not accurately reflect the severity of the punishment actually meted out to collaborators; presidential pardons and commutations were widely employed to soften overly harsh verdicts and bring some order out of the chaos of postwar jurisprudence. The process of equalization was, of course, a one-way street, since while overly harsh penalties could be reduced, overly lenient ones could not be increased. The aim of scaling down verdicts in more or less identical cases to the lowest common denominator produced a result not unlike that of the amateur carpenter who tries to even out the legs of a table with a saw: the general level became lower and lower.

As already noted, presidential commutations spared all but 3 of the 8 men sentenced to death by the High Court, and all but 767 of the 2,853 sentenced to death by the *cours de justice*.[7]

Presidents de Gaulle, Gouin, Bidault, and Auriol also used their powers to shorten prison sentences, or release prisoners altogether, and to suspend national degradation. Of the almost 40,000 persons imprisoned for collaboration, only 13,000 remained in custody by Decem-

---

Laws' ", *Journal of Criminal Law*, XXXIX [1948], 459-60.) In Holland, as of December 1950, 36 collaborators had been executed. (Henry L. Mason, *The Purge of Dutch Quislings: Emergency Justice in the Netherlands* [The Hague: 1952], p. 64.) In Belgium, 230 death sentences had been carried out as of December 1949. (Mason, p. 177 n. 20.) Considering that Belgium's population is one-fifth that of France, the relative incidence of executions in Belgium was, therefore, higher.

6. André Boissarie, *La Répression* (Paris: 1949), p. 8; *Monde*, April 14, 1949; J.O., A.N. Debates, October 28, 1952, p. 4499; Sérant, *Vaincus*, p. 168.

7. Verdicts *in absentia* not included, since they were never executed. General de Gaulle reports that, although in his view all but about 100 of the *cour de justice* death sentences pronounced during his term of office were justified, he commuted 1,303, including all those directed against women, almost all those involving minors, and most of those handed down against men acting under orders and at the risk of their own lives. (*Mémoires de guerre* [Paris: 1954-59], III, 107-08.) In Norway, 25 out of 30 death sentences were carried out, in Denmark, 23 out of 46; in Holland, 36 out of 130; in Belgium, 230 out of 4,170. (Sérant, *Vaincus*, p. 327; Givskov, 459-60; Mason, pp. 63-64; 177 n. 20, 181 n. 97, 187-88 n. 36.)

ber 1948, 8,000 by October 1949, and under 4,000 by early 1951 – the eve of the first important Amnesty Law. The overwhelming majority of those released had completed only a fraction of their original sentences. By mid-1948 presidential action had suspended over one-third of all sentences of national degradation.[8]

The first amnesty laws – passed in mid-1947 – were only secondarily concerned with collaboration, and were extremely limited in scope. Certain categories of minors and some Alsatians (who had been subjected to special pressures) were relieved of national degradation.[9] In 1951 a considerably broader amnesty law was enacted. It involved the end of national degradation for virtually all those who received this sentence as a principal penalty, either from a *cour de justice* or *chambre civique*, the list of penalties involved in national degradation was reduced. There were numerous provisions for the early release of prisoners. Those condemned by the High Court were excluded from the scope of the Law, as were informers, torturers, and those who worked with the German police.[10] By the time that the next (and final) amnesty bill was debated by the National Assembly in October 1952, the number of those still imprisoned for collaboration was down to 1,500.[11] Under the Amnesty Law of August 6, 1953, national degradation as a principal penalty was abolished. Electoral ineligibility was ended. Pension rights were restored to those who lost them in the administrative purge. Very broad provisions were made for the release of those still in prison. By 1956, only sixty-two men remained in prison; by 1958, nineteen; in 1964, twenty years after the Liberation, there were none.[12]

Frenchmen who agree on nothing else have joined in denouncing the purge, although, to be sure, for very different reasons. In the eyes of many *résistants* it was a series of timorous and half-hearted gestures which lost France her best chance for *renouvellement*. To others – mainly Vichyites – it was an orgy of vengeance and partisanship which deformed the Fourth Republic at birth. The passage of twenty years has brought few modifications in the judgments of those who believed

8. *Monde*, December 10, 1948 and April 14, 1949; Boissarie, *Répression*, p. 8; J.O., A.N. Debates, August 31, 1951, p. 6684.

9. Law No. 47-1504 of August 16, 1947, and Law No. 47-1622 of August 28, 1947.

10. Law No. 51-18 of January 5, 1951.

11. Memorandum from André Boissarie to General de Gaulle, October 15, 1957.

12. J.O., A.N. Debates, October 6, 1956, p. 4048; May 15, 1958, p. 2330; *Express*, December 14-20, 1964, 27-28.

themselves betrayed by the excessive indulgence of the purge, or those who felt themselves victimized by its excessive severity.

The failure of the purge to satisfy either of these groups – or indeed, to satisfy anyone – was inevitable. We have seen the moral dilemmas, material obstacles and political difficulties which faced the leaders of the Provisional Government in carrying out the purge. They dealt with them, I believe, as honestly, as conscientiously, and as well as any group of men could in the circumstances. They made mistakes and errors in judgment, but the inequities, inconsistencies and delays which characterized the purge were much less the result of human failings than of the impossible and contradictory demands of the task which they confronted. Even if the purge had progressed much more smoothly and serenely than it did, no one would have been – no one could have been – satisfied.

In the minds of *résistants* the purge was intimately and inextricably tied to their chiliastic vision of a "new France"; it was to be the first step in the construction of a "République pure et dure", based on the C.N.R. Charter. When the Provisional Government proved unable – or as some would have it, unwilling – to fulfill the extravagant expectations nurtured during the occupation, hope turned to despair, expectation to disillusionment. The inadequacies of the purge became the symbol of all the disappointed hopes of the Liberation period. It was *la justice révolutionnaire sans la Révolution* – a bitter mockery of their dreams, which would have been despised even had all its imperfections been absent.

The most violent attacks on the purge have, of course, come from the camp of its victims. Their criticism is not directed at procedural flaws or individual injustices; these are exploited, but only as a rhetorical device. For the *épurés* and their spokesmen the entire operation was, in its very conception, a monstrous injustice. On their premises – that Vichy was a legitimate regime, and collaboration a legitimate policy – their charge is unanswerable. Whatever the often-invoked "verdict of history" may be, these suppositions were not calculated to appeal to the victorious Resistance in 1944.

A third group, standing between *résistants* and *vichyssois*, speaks of the purge more in sorrow than in anger: they are the apostles of "reconciliation". Recognizing that a purge of some sort was inevitable after the Liberation, they blame the postwar regime for not having centered its attention on reconciling "les deux Frances" of 1940-44. They are deeply concerned over what they perceive to be a continuing malaise occasioned by the nation's failure to bind up its wartime wounds.

The wounds undeniably still exist: wartime antagonisms which divided Frenchmen have proved much more lasting than wartime alliances. But within a very few years, as new issues and new alignments appeared, these quarrels became more and more marginal to the political life of the nation. Vichy, the Resistance, the purge – passed into history. Historical quarrels have been politically important in France, but only when they have been the vehicle for contemporary struggles. Disputes concerning Vichy and the Resistance quickly became the concern not of competing politicians, but of those in both camps who could indulge in them because, excluded from active politics, they had nothing better to do with their time.

Appendix A

THE LEGITIMACY AND LEGALITY OF VICHY

The Gaullist attack on the legitimacy and legality of Pétain's Regime was noted in Chapter 2. The contention that Vichy was both illegitimate and illegal came to be the juridical foundation of the future Provisional Government, and also of the purge. Of course, it was the military victory of the Allies and the political victory of the Gaullists which determined the course of events, and not the strength or weakness of their legal arguments. Nevertheless, these arguments, and later glosses on them by legal scholars, are intrinsically interesting, and for that reason they are summarized in this Appendix.

For General de Gaulle, as we have seen, Pétain's Government was illegitimate from the moment it first assumed office because its purpose – the solicitation of an armistice – was illegitimate. De Gaulle's assertion, it has been noted, is sustained by the "supra-constitutional principle" enunciated in Article 121 of the Constitution of 1793:"The French people do not make peace with an enemy who occupies its territory."[1] The argument, whatever its merit in natural law, has no constitutional standing (i.e., in positive law). As Georges Vedel points out: "The legitimacy or illegitimacy of a government is independent of the benevolent or malevolent character of its policies."[2] (Indeed, in positive law it is doubtful whether one can even speak of an admittedly legal government being illegitimate, while a *de facto* government may or may not be legitimate, according to the criteria and the circumstances.[3]

Secondly, according to the General, "the Government at Bordeaux [was] in immediate and direct dependence on the Germans and Italians . . ."; there was "no longer on the soil of France herself any independent Government capable of upholding the interests of France and the French overseas".[4] Concerning this assertion Professor Vedel

1. M. Waline, *Manuel élémentaire de droit administratif* (Paris: 1946), p. 32.
2. *Manuel élémentaire de droit constitutionnel* (Paris: 1949), p. 279.
3. See Maurice Duverger, "Contribution à l'Etude de la Légitimité des Gouvernements de Fait", *Revue du Droit Public et de la Science Politique en France et à l'Etranger*, LX, 1 (January-March 1945), 76.
4. Speech of June 23, 1940, in Royal Institute of International Affairs (Margaret Carlyle, ed.), *Documents on International Affairs, 1939-1946*, Vol. II: *Hitler's Europe* (London: 1954), p. 166.

makes the interesting point that if you contend that no legitimate government can exist in a country partially occupied and in a state of armistice, then you attack the Government of National Defense and the National Assembly which founded the Third Republic.[5] Furthermore, the argument that the Pétain Government – up to November 1942 – was completely dependent on the occupying powers, is not unchallenged. That Government had, according to Otto Kirchheimer, "a margin of freedom for maneuvering . . . probably not much smaller than that held by many contemporary governments".[6]

Finally, for De Gaulle, Pétain's Government was illegitimate because, in accepting the Armistice, it was accepting "not just capitulation, but reduction to slavery". Honor demanded its rejection because of France's solemn commitments not to make a separate peace; good sense demanded its rejection, because in the long run the Allied coalition was stronger; the higher interests of *la Patrie* demanded its rejection because "if the forces of liberty eventually triumph over those of servitude, what would be the destiny of a France which had submitted to the enemy?"[7] By signing the Armistice, Pétain's Government was betraying the national interest, and was thereby illegitimate. De Gaulle himself, by cleaving to the national interest, automatically acquired legitimacy.[8]

The concept of legitimacy is an extremely slippery one, resting as it does on largely intangible factors. Most writers who have dealt with this question as it relates to Vichy accept the notion that legitimacy, at least in a country with democratic traditions, is somehow tied to the question of popular confidence and support. With this consideration in mind, it is often maintained that Pétain's Government was legitimate at the outset, but became illegitimate at some later date. The prosecutor at the trial of Angelo Chiappe fixed the time as October 1940, when Pétain met with Hitler at Montoire.[9] Pierre Pucheu's defense attorney suggested that the regime became illegitimate with Laval's return to power in April 1942 (when his

5. *Loc. cit.*

6. *Political Justice: The Use of Legal Procedure for Political Ends* (Princeton [N.J.]: 1961), p. 317.

7. Speech of June 22, 1940, in *Discours de guerre* (Fribourg: 1944-45), I, 18.

8. This theory is developed at length in Maurice Flory, *Le Statut International des gouvernements réfugiés et le cas de la France libre: 1939-1946* (Paris: 1952), pp. 91ff.; Joseph Vialatoux, *Le Problème de la légitimité du pouvoir: Vichy ou De Gaulle?* (Paris: 1945), *passim*.

9. *Combat*, December 23, 1944.

client left the cabinet).[10] Joseph Vialatoux admits that the bulk of the population may have rejected Pétain's legitimacy only after November 1942, but insists that they did so retroactively to June 1940.[11] Georges Vedel, in his review of the question, maintains that only two things are certain: "that at the moment of the Armistice Marshal Pétain was in accord with the majority of the country, and that at the moment of the Liberation he no longer was".[12]

But for De Gaulle, and later for the Provisional Government which he dominated, June 16, 1940, was the cut-off date: Pétain's Third Republic cabinet was as illegitimate as the Vichy Regime which followed; the Armistice which it negotiated was null; its servants, as well as those of Vichy, would later be called to account.

The doctrine of the nullity of the Armistice was important, among other reasons, because of its Article 10, which prohibited Frenchmen from bearing arms against Germany. De Gaulle was always particularly insistent on this point; in his negotiations with General Giraud in 1943 he made this doctrine ("the foundation of the national war effort") the first condition of unity.[13]

Purge legislation provided for the prosecution or removal from office of all those who had been members of Pétain's governments after June 16, 1940; however, as this related to men who left office immediately following the vote of July 10, 1940, the provision was honored only in the breach.[14] The (automatic) indictments against those of Pétain's ministers who were in this category were all quashed. Similarly, when Charles Frémicourt, who had been Minister of Justice in Pétain's Third Republic cabinet, was automatically removed from a high judicial post, the Conseil d'Etat annulled the action on the grounds that the Government constituted on June 16, 1940, was regular in every respect.[15]

For a variety of reasons, noted in Chapter 2, the Gaullists decided to charge the Vichy Regime with "illegality" as well as "illegitimacy". The definitive version of the charge was formulated by Professor René

10. Paul Buttin, *Le Procès Pucheu* (Paris: 1948), p. 107.
11. *Op. cit.*, p. 14.
12. *Op. cit.*, p. 280.
13. "Memorandum du Comité national français au général Giraud" (February 23, 1943), cited in Henri Michel, *Les Courants de pensée de la Résistance* (Paris 1962), p. 18.
14. See above, pp. 155, 177, and Appendix F.
15. Decision dated June 4, 1947, *Juris Classeur Périodiques*, 1947, II, 3673, concl. Célier.

Cassin in December 1940 in an article entitled "Un Coup d'Etat: La Soi-Disant Constitution de Vichy".[16]

Cassin's first point concerned the irregular circumstances in which the National Assembly met: it did not meet, as the Constitution stipulated, at Versailles; the senators and deputies were allegedly coerced by organized pressure; in any case the fact of partial German occupation made a free vote impossible. The force of these points is open to question. Fulfillment of the letter of the law requiring that the Assembly sit at Versailles would have meant violation of its spirit. As Cassin himself notes, the intention of the framers of this provision was to remove the Assembly from outside pressure. If Pétain had accepted the German invitation to move his government to the occupied zone (as he later considered doing), and had the Assembly met surrounded by German bayonets, it would hardly have been more independent. The extent of the coercion to which members of the Assembly were subject is an open question; Otto Kirchheimer has observed that

> the respective amounts of voluntariness and coercion in the 1940 change were certainly not much smaller than during the 1958 transition from the Fourth to the Fifth Republic. The threat of Massu's parachutists stood as much godfather to the Fifth Republic of De Gaulle as the proximity of German tanks did to the ascent of Pétain.[17]

In this connection Professor Vedel makes the pertinent point that, according to Article 1112 of the Civil Code, in order for duress to be established, it must be of such a nature as to "faire impression sur une personne raisonnable", taking into account the "condition" of the individual involved. This, he holds, implies that "un représentant de la nation doit être réputé moins facilement contraint qu'un simple citoyen", and he concludes that the charge that the vote was invalid

16. *La France Libre* (London), I, 2 (December 16, 1940), 162-76. (The second part of the article, which appeared in the issue of January 1941 (252-59), was devoted to the thesis that the establishment of Vichy was the culmination of a long-standing dream of overthrowing the Republic held by defeatists, fascists, Maurrasians, etc.)

17. *Loc. cit.* The analogy with the advent of Vichy was not lost on a number of Pétainists in June 1958, and there was a good deal of heavy-handed ironizing at the *renversement*. See Paul Faure, *Histoire d'un faux et de ses conséquences* (Paris: n.d.), pp. 5-11 and *passim*; Alexander Werth, *The De Gaulle Revolution* (London: 1960), pp. 165-66, 168; Philip M. Williams and Martin Harrison, *De Gaulle's Republic* (London: 1960), p. 79 n. 1.

because of duress is unacceptable.[18] (In 1946 the framers of the Fourth Republic Constitution locked the barn door after the horse had been stolen: Article 94 provided that "if the whole of Metropolitan France or part of it be occupied by foreign troops, no procedure of revision may be initiated or pursued".

Cassin's second point was that the National Assembly alone held the right to revise the Constitution; it had absolutely no right to delegate (or abdicate) its constituent power to another party, and acts by such a party were thus null. Interestingly, Cassin's position on this point was supported by a number of legal scholars writing openly in Vichy France, and by P.-H. Teitgen, future Minister of Justice in the Provisional Government, in his lectures at the University of Montpellier Law School.[19] Cassin's opinion is rebutted by Maurice Duverger and Georges Vedel. The former argues that the procedure followed by the National Assembly was completely analagous to the widespread use of decree laws during the inter-war period; if the Assembly's delegation of its legislative powers was legitimate, so was its delegation of its constituent power.[20] Vedel's argument is more subtle. He grants Cassin's contention that the Assembly could not delegate its constituent power, since this power is derived from the Constitution, and not original, as with a revolutionary constituent assembly. However, the Assembly unquestionably had the power to *revise the mode of revision*, and, following the doctrine that legislative enactments should receive the benefit of the doubt, it should be considered that this is what the Assembly did in the vote of July 10. Thus the Assembly acted within its competence.[21]

Cassin's final point was that Pétain's "Constitutional Acts", by abolishing the Republic, violated the constitutional law of 1884 which denied that right even to the National Assembly: thus the Vichy Regime was illegal and unconstitutional. Maurice Prélot accepts this contention of Cassin, and argues that by suppressing the Republic Pétain destroyed the foundation of his derived constituent power, and acted as if he had original constituent power – i.e., revolutionary

---

18. *Op. cit.*, p. 277. Cf. the similar conclusion arrived at by Maurice Prélot in his *Précis de droit constitutionnel* (Paris: 1950), p. 257.

19. J. Laferrière, *Le Nouveau gouvernement de la France* (Paris: 1942); G. Berlia, "La Loi Constitutionnelle du 10 Juillet 1940", *Revue du Droit Public et de la Science Politique*, 1944, 57ff.; Prélot, *loc. cit.*

20. *Manuel de droit constitutionnel et science politique* (Paris: 1948), pp. 294-97.

21. *Loc. cit.*

legitimacy.[22] Vedel accepts this doctrine, but differs in his appreciation of the fact situation. In his view the Republic was not in fact abolished, since a hereditary ruler was not established, the substitution of "Chef d'Etat" for "President" and "Etat" for "République" being legally meaningless.[23]

Those writers who deny the validity of all or part of Cassin's indictment do not necessarily grant legality to Vichy. Many base their assault on Pétain's behavior subsequent to July 10. The Constitutional Acts establishing the Vichy Regime were legal only if issued under the authority of the July 10 resolution, which required their ratification by the nation. Since the Regime immediately manifested its intention of ignoring the requirement of ratification, it was, they maintain, illegal almost – but not quite – from the beginning. Vichy was illegal because it failed to play by its own rules.[24]

Whatever the subsequent reservations of legal scholars, Cassin's conclusions were officially adopted by the Gaullist movement; the metropolitan Resistance, though less concerned than London with Vichy's juridical status, later also came to accept his thesis completely.[25] Belief in Vichy's illegality was (apparently) so universal among *résistants* of all political complexions that it could be taken for granted: in the extended debates of the Provisional Consultative Assembly in Algiers in 1943-44 – debates which frequently dealt with constitutional questions – it was simply assumed, and never discussed. Years later, however, some prominent wartime Gaullists indicated that they had been less than wholehearted in their acceptance of Cassin's thesis. François Quilici, editor of the Gaullist *La Marseillaise* in London and Algiers, remarked in the National Assembly that it was a "thèse d'opportunité", adopted in order to give the Free French a juridical basis in view of "le traditionalisme anglo-saxon". He himself, he reported, never considered Vichy illegal, though he did think it illegitimate.[26] Raymond Aron, another close wartime associate of the General, went further, saying that "Vichy was legal and probably legitimate".[27]

But these reservations were not to be voiced for many years. At the time, Cassin's thesis was unquestioned Resistance orthodoxy. Two

22. *Op. cit.*, pp. 260-63.
23. *Op. cit.*, p. 278.
24. Vedel, pp. 278-81; Prélot, pp. 259-60; Duverger, "Contribution", *passim*.
25. Michel, *Courants*, pp. 40-43, 168-69.
26. J. O., A.N. Debates, November 4, 1950, p. 7452.
27. *The Opium of the Intellectuals* (London: 1957), p. 130.

corollaries of this thesis – both explicitly contained in Cassin's December 1940 article – should be noted in conclusion. First, since Vichy was illegal from the moment of its birth, the Republic had never ceased to exist and the Constitution of 1875 remained in force. This conclusion was formally set down in the Ordinance of August 9, 1944, one of the fundamental enactments of the Provisional Government.[28] General de Gaulle was always very insistent on this point. When, on the day of the Liberation of Paris, he was asked to publicly proclaim the re-establishment of the Republic, he replied: "The Republic has never ceased to exist. Free France, Fighting France, the French Committee of National Liberation, each, in turn, incorporated it. Vichy always was, and remains, null and void. I myself am president of the Government of the Republic. Why should I proclaim it?"[29]

The doctrine of republican continuity meant, in turn, the applicability of the "Loi Treveneuc" which authorized the *conseils généraux* to meet and form a new Assembly if the old one was illegally dissolved and unable to meet. But by 1943-44, when this procedure might conceivably have been employed, it had been abandoned by the Gaullists as well as by the metropolitan Resistance, and it was never even seriously considered. (The idea was supported by P.-E. Flandin and some *conseillers généraux* in North Africa, but they were without influence.)

There were several practical difficulties: to base a government solely on the *conseils* in North Africa would have been not only ludicrous, but politically suicidal, since they were generally controlled by forces hostile to De Gaulle and the Resistance; before the Allied landings in June 1944 it could not be anticipated that within a few months almost the entire territory of the metropole would be liberated and provision had to be made for governing a few departments in the vicinity of a beachhead for an indefinite period; all the *conseils*, in any case, had been drastically purged by the Vichy Regime. Beyond this, there was a more compelling argument against using the Treveneuc procedure: neither De Gaulle nor any significant section of the Resistance had the slightest desire to go back to the Third Republic. Their plans for the sort of Fourth Republic they wanted differed, but all agreed on barring a return to the Third.[30]

28. J. O., August 10, pp. 688-89.
29. *Mémoires de guerre* (Paris: 1954-59), II, 308.
30. See Flory, p. 423; Michel, *Courants*, pp. 90-93, 322-23, 351-87.

PROGRAM OF THE CONSEIL NATIONAL DE LA RESISTANCE[1]

II. *Measures to be adopted after the Liberation*

United concerning our goals, united on the means to attain them – the swift Liberation of our land – the delegates from the movements, groups, parties and political currents represented in the C.N.R. proclaim their determination to remain united after the Liberation:

1. In order to establish the Provisional Government of the Republic formed by General de Gaulle to defend the political and economic independence of the nation and to reestablish French power, grandeur, and the universal mission of France.

2. In order to assure the punishment of traitors and the eviction from the administration and professional life of all those who have dealt with the enemy or have actively associated themselves with the policy of the governments of collaboration.

3. In order to see to the confiscation of the property of traitors and black marketeers, the establishment of a progressive tax on war profits and in general on all profits realized at the expense of the people and the nation during the occupation, as well as the confiscation of all enemy property, including the shares in French and colonial businesses that the Axis Governments and their nationals have acquired since the Armistice – these shares to become inalienable national property.

4. In order to assure:

> the establishment of the broadest possible democracy by allowing the people to voice their desires through the reestablishment of universal suffrage;
>
> full liberty of thought, conscience and expression;
>
> freedom of the press – an honest press, independent of the State, powerful economic interests and foreign influences;

1. The program was adopted unanimously at a plenary session of the C.N.R. on March 15, 1944. The first (and longer) portion was a "plan d'action immédiate" concerning underground activity; the second portion, translated here, is that generally referred to as the "C.N.R. Charter". My translation is based on the text appearing in Henri Michel and Boris Mirkine-Guetzévitch, *Les Idées politiques et sociales de la Résistance* (Paris: 1954), pp. 215-18. The first portion may be found in René Hostache, *Le Conseil National de la Résistance: Les Institutions de la clandestinité* (Paris: 1958), pp. 457-61.

freedom of association, freedom to meet and demonstrate;

the inviolability of the home and of private correspondence;

respect for the individual;

absolute equality of all citizens before the law;

5. In order to effect the necessary reforms:

   (*a*) Economic:

      the establishment of a true economic and social democracy, with the requisite eviction of the great economic and financial feudatories from the direction of the economy;

      rational organization of the economy, assuring the subordination of special interests to the general interest, and freed from the professional dictatorship installed in the image of the fascist states;

      the development of national production following a state plan, established after consultation with the representatives of all interested groups;

      the return to the nation of the great monopolies, fruits of the labor of all, of energy resources, of the underground riches of the country, of the insurance companies and the major banks;

      the development and support of producers', buyers', and sellers' cooperatives in both agriculture and manufacturing;

      the right of qualified workers to rise to administrative and management positions in businesses, and workers' participation in the running of the economy.

   (*b*) Social:

      the right to work and the right to leisure, in particular by the reestablishment and the improvement of labor contracts;

      a major readjustment of wages and the guarantee of a level of wages and working conditions which will assure every worker and his family security, dignity, and the chance of a decent life;

      guaranteed purchasing power through a policy of monetary stabilization;

      the reestablishment of the traditional liberties of an independent trade-union movement with broad powers in the organization and management of the economic and social life of the country;

a complete social security system, providing all citizens with the means of existence when they are unable to secure it themselves – a system whose management is shared by those concerned and by the State;

security of employment, regulation of hiring and firing, the reestablishment of shop delegates;

raising and guaranteeing the standard of living of agricultural workers by a policy of farm price supports, improving and extending the experience of the *Office du Blé*, by social legislation giving agricultural workers the same treatment as industrial workers, by a system of insurance against crop failures, by the establishment of fair rates for share-croppers and tenant-farmers, by facilitating access to farm-ownership by young farm families, and by the institution of a program of making farm equipment available;

a pension system permitting aged workers to end their days in dignity;

indemnification for war damages, payments and pensions for victims of fascist terror;

an extension of political, social and economic rights to native and colonial populations;

a meaningful opportunity for all French children to have the benefits of education and access to the best of French culture, whatever their family's financial status, so that the highest positions in society are truly open to all those with the capacity to fill them, thus bringing into being a real élite, of merit rather than of birth, constantly renewed from the people.

Thus a new Republic will be founded, which will sweep away the reactionary regime installed by Vichy and return to our democratic and popular institutions the effectiveness which they lost through the corrupting and treasonous activity that preceded the surrender. Thus we will make possible a democracy which brings together effective control by the representatives of the people and stable government.

The unity of the representatives of the Resistance, for present and future action, in the highest interests of the nation, should be a symbol of confidence and a stimulus to all Frenchmen. It should inspire them to banish all particularist sentiment, that divisiveness which can restrict their action and serve only the enemy.

Forward, then, in the union of all Frenchmen around the C.F.L.N.

and its president, General de Gaulle. Forward to battle. Forward to victory, so that France may live.

The Conseil National de la Résistance, comprising

le Mouvement de Libération Nationale (Combat, Franc-Tireur, Libération, France au Combat, Défense de la France, Lorraine, Résistance); le Front National; l'Organization Civile et Militaire; Libération zone Nord; Ceux de la Résistance; Ceux de la Libération; la Confédération Générale du Travail; la Confédération Française des Travailleurs Chrétiens; Parti Communiste; Parti Socialiste; Parti Républicain-Radical et Radical-Socialiste; Parti Démocrate Populaire; Alliance Démocratique; Fédération Républicaine.

Appendix C

SUMMARY EXECUTION STATISTICS

> There are in the world scholars whose good nature has worn itself
> out in seeking a middle ground between antagonistic statements.
> They are like the little chap who, asked for the square of the
> number two, when one neighbor whispered "four" and the other
> "eight", thought he had hit the mark in answering "six".
>
> MARC BLOCH[1]

Figures offered for the total of summary executions of collaborators in
France before and after the Liberation are of three orders of magnitude.
There are the "maximalist" estimates of over 100,000, the official
government estimates of approximately 10,000, and most recently, the
estimates of Robert Aron who believes that there were between 30,000
and 40,000.

The 100,000-plus figures come from *revanchiste* anti-Resistance
circles and from Vichy apologists. They are typically accompanied by
the allegation that France was in the grip of a red terror in 1944-45 and
that the executions were signs of a Communist attempt at a seizure of
power.[2] Three sources are produced in support of the view that executions totalled over 100,000.

The figure of 105,000, which frequently appears, stems from a remark allegedly made in November 1944 by Adrien Tixier, then Minister of the Interior. According to André Dewavrin ("Colonel Passy"),
Tixier told him that information from the prefects indicated that there
had been a total of 105,000 summary executions.[3] Tixier died in 1946
and there is no other supporting documentation for his remark aside
from Dewavrin's account.

Figures of 112,000 and 120,000, also frequently advanced, seem to
be derived from two sorts of extrapolation. One is the incontestable
fact that summary executions in the provinces continued for some

1. *The Historian's Craft* (Manchester: 1954), p. 112.
2. See, e.g., Maurice-Yvan Sicard ["St.-Paulien"], *Histoire de la collaboration* (Mayenne: 1964), pp. 533-41; Louis Rougier, "La France est-elle un
Etat de Droit?" *Ecrits de Paris*, February 1950, 77-96. *Ecrits de Paris* was
more or less the house organ of this point of view.
3. Dewavrin's account of the conversation was included in a speech he
delivered to a political meeting in March 1950. See *Ecrits de Paris*, April
1950, p. 35; *Paroles Françaises*, June 12-18, 1950.

months after Tixier's alleged estimate of 105,000 in November 1944. The other statistics taken as a point of departure for arriving at totals over 100,000 are government estimates of war casualties among the civilian population, which in 1946 listed 97,000 "due to various causes" and 36,000 dossiers not yet examined. "What could these 'various causes' be if not summary executions?" asks Jean Montigny, who adds that doubtless most of the 36,000 cases not yet examined are in the same category.[4]

The third major pillar on which "maximalist" estimates rest is an alleged "calculation by the Chief of the Historical Division of the American Army that approximately 50,000 persons were killed in the Mediterranean Zone during the years 1944-45 alone".[5] By extending the totals backward in time and northward in space it is easy to arrive at totals in excess of 100,000. Belief in the existence and dependability of this "impartial and reliable" official American estimate is not restricted to Vichy-apologists of the extreme Right; it is, for example, used as a prime source by Jean Paulhan, late of the Resistance, now of the Académie Française.[6] This source turns out to be not an American Army document at all, but a sensational article written in a lunatic-fringe American magazine by a Hearst journalist who served briefly during the war in the historical division of the civil affairs section of the Army. The figure of 50,000 is in any case not of American provenance, but represents what (unnamed) French officers suggested to the author in conversation.[7]

The extravagant figures of the extreme Right are important not

---

4. *Paroles Françaises, loc. cit.* Cf. the *Requête aux Nations Unies sur les violations des droits de l'homme* (Paris: 1951) published by the "Union pour la Restauration et la Défense du Service Public", pp. 24-32; Jean Pleyber, "L'Epuration Insurrectionnelle", *Défense de l'Occident*, Nos. 39-40 (January-February 1957), pp. 44-46.

5. Pleyber, *loc. cit.* Sometimes this estimate is described as applying only to the period from August to November 1944. (Sicard, p. 533.)

6. *Lettre aux directeurs de la Résistance* (Paris: 1952), p. 37.

7. Donald B. Robinson, "Blood Bath in France", *The American Mercury*, April 1946, pp. 391-98. So far as I know, critics of the inflated summary execution estimates have never discussed the origin of the "American Army calculations". Robert Aron discusses the estimate, and rightly dismisses it as a mere guess, but mistakenly believes – or writes as if he believes – that it is the guess of American officers. In Robinson's English text the officers are identified as French by the phrase "of the Sécurité Militaire". Aron translates the entire passage into French, and the fact that the officers' identification was in French in the English original is obscured. (*Histoire de la Libération de la France: Juin 1944-Mai 1945* [Paris: 1959], p. 649.)

because the numbers themselves are taken seriously by scholars; they never will be unless some real evidence is produced in their support. Their importance stems from the fact that, by their constant reiteration, the suspicion is created that "where there's smoke there must be fire"; they are a trap for serious and objective scholars who contrast them with the much lower government estimates and conclude that "the truth must lie somewhere in between". Whether this discounting phenomenon is in the minds of the marketers of the 100,000 estimate – whether like rug peddlers they offer their wares at a price of 100,000 in the hope of getting 50,000 – I cannot say.

At the other end of the spectrum there are the figures offered by the French Government.[8] There are two sets, both based on inquiries conducted among the prefects, in 1948 and 1952 respectively. In both cases the Government underlined the multiple difficulties attendant upon the collection of this data, and thus the approximate and tentative nature of the information given. The first figures on executions are as follows:[9]

A. Pre-Liberation Executions		5,234
B. Executions during and after the Liberation		
1. Without trial	3,114	
2. After a "de facto" trial	1,325	
	———	
	4,439	
		———
		9,673

The second set is broken down somewhat differently:[10]

A. Executions of persons suspected of collaboration with or without a "de facto" trial			
1. Pre-Liberation	5,143		
2. Post-Liberation	3,724		
	———		
		8,867	
B. Victims of murders or executions in which the motive is not established			
1. Pre-Liberation	1,532		
2. Post-Liberation (to January 1, 1945)	423		
	———		
		1,955	
		———	
		10,822	

8. Offered, it should be noted, on a take-it-or-leave-it basis; no access to archival material concerning this question has been allowed, even to customarily privileged researchers. (Aron, *Libération*, pp. 652-53.)

9. J.O., A.N. Debates, November 9, 1951, p. 7835.

10. J.O., A.N. Debates, January 7, 1954, p. 35. These are the figures used by General de Gaulle in his *Mémoires de guerre* (Paris: 1954-59), III, 38.

Assuming, as I do, that these figures are offered in good faith, what are we to make of them?[11] The most that I can suggest is that with respect to post-Liberation figures there may have been some "built-in under-reporting". If this is so, the post-Liberation figures for the execution of collaborators (B-1 and B-2 in the first set, A-2 and to some extent B-2 in the second) should be considered as minima rather than mean estimates.[12]

A middle position between that of the Government and that of the "maximalists" is held by Robert Aron. His estimate, based on various sources and calculations, is that there were between 30,000 and 40,000 summary executions, including those both before and after the Liberation. Aron's estimate has been accepted by serious scholars, and unless challenged, seems destined to be passed on as scholarly orthodoxy to future historians. It thus merits detailed examination.

Aron is skeptical of the highest claims, not only because of their lack of documentation, but on grounds of inherent improbability. But he finds the government figures equally improbable. He tells of asking Michel Debré his opinion of the government estimate of 4,500 post-Liberation executions. Debré's reply confirmed Aron's own view.

11. This assumption is of course not made by the "maximalists" for whom they represent the attempt of the accomplice to minimize the extent of his partner's crime. Their official sponsorship, instead of carrying a presumption of reliability, is for them *prima facie* evidence that they are dishonest.

12. Briefly, the reason to suspect possible under-reporting is as follows. While there may be assumed to be a real corpse for every statistical one, the converse is by no means necessarily the case. Unreported executions are most likely to have occurred in those regions and at those times when disorder and fear were general – at a time when sometimes those who had carried out the executions were installed in the *mairies* and headquarters of the *gendarmerie*. In these circumstances it is not improbable that there were a number of families that preferred to keep quiet rather than draw attention to themselves – particularly if in order to report the crime they had to walk into what was for them the lion's den. Jean Montigny claims that since local populations knew that the Provisional Government had "legitimized" all Resistance acts, they also knew that there was no point in reporting Resistance depradations. (*Paroles Françaises, loc. cit.*) Jean Pleyber alleges that victims of looting and arson on the part of the Resistance in 1944-45 preferred, when possible, to blame it on the Germans or *milice* and thus be eligible for compensation (p. 42). It is possible that the same held true for the reporting of executions. It is also at least theoretically possible that the procedure occurred in reverse under the occupation, and *milice* exactions and executions were reported as being the work of the Resistance. There is at least one authenticated case in which a *milice* assassination was officially laid at the door of the Resistance (that of Maurice Sarraut, cited above); there may have been others.

"That's absurd," the future premier said. "Two or three departments in the southwest had that many between them."[13]

Wanting to cast more light on this question, Aron determined on the following procedure, recognizing that the results it could yield would be at best partial and approximate. He took as his point of departure the few departmental statistics appended (as examples) to the overall estimates in the 1951 Ministerial statement. These he compared with the results of inquiries which he conducted in the provinces "among trustworthy individuals belonging to various camps". His findings were as follows:

1. There was no foundation for the "Tixier-Dewavrin estimate" of 105,000.

2. In those *départements* which had had few summary executions, his estimates were close to the official figures.

3. On the other hand, in those *départements* in which there had been the most popular violence, his figures were two, three and four times those of the Ministry. For example:

	Ministry	Aron
Dordogne	528	1,000 (minimum)
Bouches-du-Rhône	310	800
Rhône	294	800
Haute-Vienne	260	1,000 (approximate)

His conclusion is that while these are only samples, giving at best only an order of magnitude, they lead to the conclusion that the official estimate of 10,000 before and after the Liberation should be tripled or quadrupled. Thus the true totals would be 30,000 to 40,000.[14]

With respect to the above, two observations may be made.

1. On the basis of Aron's own examples, the difference is of the order of 2·5 to 1, not 3 or 4 to 1. The revised estimate, on the basis of the departments he cites, should be 25,000, not 30,000 or 40,000.

2. Aron found that some of the components of the Ministerial grand total were approximately correct; others were on the average 3 to 4 times (his assertion) or 2·5 times (his figures) too low. Then he multiplies the Ministerial grand total (made up of both accurate and allegedly deflated totals) by the factor which relates only to the latter. Assuming that half of the Ministry's grand total is derived from approximately accurate sub-totals, and half from underestimates (Aron gives no indication of the proportion), his estimate should either be

13. *Libération*, pp. 651-52.
14. *Ibid.*, pp. 654-55.

20,000 to 25,000 (using the 3 or 4 to 1 ratio) or 17,500 (using the ratio of 2·5 to 1).

Aron's estimate of 30,000 to 40,000 would seem, on internal evidence alone, to be double the probable total, based on his own observations. However, just before his book was published, Aron finally received a reply to a request he had made to the *gendarmerie* for information on summary executions. The document consisted of (here Aron quotes – presumably from the letter from the *gendarmerie* accompanying the statistics) a "statistical statement drawn up with the assistance of . . . objective . . . reports . . . received by units of the *gendarmerie*". Unfortunately the statement is not complete: the urban centers of Paris, Orléans, Limoges and Toulouse are missing altogether; reports from Metz, Dijon, Lyon and Marseilles are "fragmentary". (Aron notes that these areas were the scenes of some of the greatest Liberation violence.)

Aron reports that apart from these missing areas, the number of summary executions "carried out at the moment of the Liberation" and verified by units of the *gendarmerie* is given as 14,468. Taking the missing regions into account, something over 20,000 would be a fair estimate for all of France. And if the summary executions carried out before the Liberation – which the Minister's statistics state to be greater than the number carried out at the moment of the Liberation – are included, we come up with at least the figure that Aron suggested: between thirty and forty thousand. This is confirmed for Aron by the fact that the figures of the *gendarmerie* are approximately four times those of the Minister of the Interior "for executions contemporaneous with the Liberation", thus corresponding to the results of the sampling which Aron carried out, and which he used in arriving at his conclusions.[15]

Here we would seem to have, "for the first time", as Aron remarks in presenting it, "a document emanating from an official service bear-[ing] within it the elements of a real solution to the problem posed by the summary executions". Curious about the document, I asked M. Aron if I might see it. His assistant, who was present at our meeting, offered to make and send me a photocopy, which I now have in my possession. Aron's report on the *gendarmerie* document in his book contains one flat misstatement and one equally important distortion.

First, the document does not consist of statistics concerning executions *at* the Liberation, but rather is entitled "Exécutions sommaires en Métropole de 1942 à 1945". The report's total figure, which Aron, after adjusting, doubles to arrive at a figure for both pre- and post-

15. *Ibid.*, p. 723.

Liberation executions, already includes those carried out before the Liberation.

Second, the total given by the *gendarmerie* is not 14,468 as Aron states, but 15,110. Why are 642 "summary executions" omitted in Aron's version? Because opposite the total of 3,483 for the "Fourth Region" (which includes 850 in Haute-Vienne) there is the comment "Victimes d'Oradour-sur-Glane (642) incluses". The report, far from referring to the execution of collaborators, either before or after the Liberation, gives every indication of having reference to all extra-legal executions, carried out by the Germans, the *milice*, the Resistance, and anyone else operating outside the law in France from 1942 to 1945.[16] M. Aron drew the line at including the 642 victims of the German massacre at Oradour in the total of "summary executions carried out at the Liberation", but not at including every other execution – whatever its date or author.

What then can be said concerning the number of summary executions? With certainty: nothing. All that we can do is note that up to this point the revisionist attacks on the Minister of the Interior's estimates – whether the attacks are patently outrageous or pseudo-scholarly – must be thrown out of court. The official figures (5,200-6,700 before the Liberation, 4,100-4,400 after), while perhaps representing minima rather than mean figures, must provisionally stand.

There are two methodological problems which will plague any future research into this question. Any verified additions to the present figures will have to rest on the identification of bodies. But are the newly discovered bones of a long-dead corpse those of a *milicien* shot by the Resistance, or a *résistant* shot by the *milice*? The second problem is one of definition, and so far as I know it has never been dealt with. Both before and after the Liberation there were pitched battles between small (and sometimes large) bands of *miliciens* and *résistants*. Are those of the former who were killed to be classed among those "summarily executed"? It was not legal for C.D.L.'s and other local Resistance groups to try and execute collaborators; on the other hand, under certain circumstances it was legal for these groups to arrest them. If a collaborator was killed resisting arrest (in reality, not police-blotter fiction) was this a "summary execution"?

16. The *gendarmerie* figures – restricted as they are to irregular executions – do not appear to include the over 20,000 French men and women "legally" shot by the Germans after arrest or internment. (In addition, 163,000 out of 200,000 political and racial deportees did not return from Germany.) See J. O., C.R. Debates, October 28, 1947, p. 2087.

Appendix D

COMPARATIVE PURGE LEGISLATION AND COURT SYSTEMS[1]

All of the Western European countries found their existing treason legislation inadequate to deal with the unanticipated phenomenon of lengthy occupation and widespread collaboration.[2] All had to repair this lack by one form or another of retroactive legislation.

In Norway, Holland and Denmark, retroactive laws were introduced in the most striking fashion imaginable; capital punishment, absent from their penal codes for as long as seventy-two years, was reintroduced after the Liberation for the punishment of crimes committed under the occupation. (Belgium, like France, had never abandoned it.[3]) In Norway (where the last death sentence had been carried out in 1876) capital punishment was decreed by the Royal Ordinance of October 3, 1941. The decision was announced in the occupied territory

1. Italy, because its experience was *sui generis*, has been omitted from this survey, which is restricted to Belgium, the Netherlands, Denmark and Norway. I have relied principally upon the following studies: Holland, Henry L. Mason, *The Purge of Dutch Quislings: Emergency Justice in the Netherlands* (The Hague: 1952); Denmark, C. C. Givskov, "Danish 'Purge Laws'", *Journal of Criminal Law*, XXXIX (1948), 447-60; Belgium, W. J. Ganshof van der Meersch, *Réflexions sur la répression des crimes contre la sûreté extérieure de l'Etat belge* (Brussels: 1946) and Jean Dupréel, "Aperçu Général des Déchéances de Droits Frappant les Personnes qui, en Temps de Guerre, ont Contribué à Mettre le Pays en Danger", *Revue de Droit Pénal et de Criminologie* (Brussels), XXVII, 4 (January 1947), 347-56; Norway, Johs Andenoes, "La Répression de la Collaboration avec l'Ennemi en Norvège", *ibid.*, XXVII, 7 (April 1947), 587-606; comparative treatments in J. M. van Bemmelen, "The Treatment of Political Delinquents in some European Countries", *Journal of Criminal Science* (London), I (1948), 110-26 and Pierre Vermeylen, "The Punishment of Collaborators", *Annals of the American Academy of Political and Social Science*, CCXLVII (September 1946), 73-77.

2. Van Bemmelen (112) found that countries which had participated in World War I (France and Belgium) had adapted their penal codes to the needs of war and occupation better than those which hadn't (Holland, Norway, Denmark).

3. However, the Belgian Decree-Law of December 1, 1942 (enacted by the Government-in-Exile), extended the death penalty to offenses previously punished by lesser sanctions. (Ganshof van der Meersch, p. 23.)

by means of leaflets and radio broadcasts.[4] The Dutch Government-in-Exile decided on the reintroduction of the death penalty (abolished in 1870) by an Ordinance dated December 22, 1943, but it was not announced until September 1944 when the first Dutch territory was liberated.[5] In Denmark, where there was no exile government which could legislate during the war, capital punishment for treasonous acts going back to the beginning of the German occupation was introduced by a Law of June 1, 1945.[6]

But apart from the question of the death penalty, there was the fact that the forms of treason provided for in prewar legislation, even in previously occupied Belgium, were not the only ones with which the courts would have to cope. If the prewar treason legislation were used to punish the new and widespread forms of petty collaboration, the rigid penalties called for by that legislation would result in a double disadvantage; it would be unjustly harsh to treat men who were merely

4. Mason, p. 130. The decree, issued by the King in London under the plenary powers given him by the Storting in May 1940, was ratified by that body in July 1945. It instituted the death penalty for those offenses against existing treason legislation which had previously been punishable by life imprisonment. Those under 18 when they committed their offense were not subject to it. The decree was not formally retroactive, since it did not extend to offenses committed before the date it was issued. The Norwegian Supreme Court refused to accept an appellant's contention that it should be struck down as unconstitutionally retroactive because it was only officially promulgated after the Liberation. (Andenoes, 587-91.)

5. Because of the date of its introduction its effect was perforce formally retroactive: it could be used to punish offenses going back to the beginning of the war. In October 1945 a public opinion poll showed 73 per cent favoring its use for the worst collaborators, and 22 per cent opposed. Several leading criminologists opposed it on the grounds that, particularly in this area, where the passage of time and fading memories would make for lighter sentences later on, "irrevocable" sentences should not be applied. (Mason, pp. 61-64, 130.)

6. Givskov, 448-51. In the parliamentary debates preceding adoption of the law there were some who spoke out for making it applicable only to offenses committed after August 29, 1943 (the date of the replacement of the Danish Government by direct German rule). There were also a few – but only a few – who opposed the death penalty on grounds of conscience. The majority opinion was expressed by the Social Democratic spokesman who said that while normally opposed to capital punishment, "Recalling the relief we felt when an informer was liquidated, we accept the death penalty for traitors". Another speaker remarked that the introduction of the death penalty legitimized the summary executions carried out under the occupation. (*News Digest*, No. 1769 [May 28, 1945]. See also Nos. 1772 and 1774 [May 31 and June 2, 1945].)

APPENDIX D

weak or venal in the same manner as avowed traitors; at the same time, the very harshness of the sentences would inhibit their application, and many guilty men would escape.[7]

In each of these four countries, the solution adopted was some form of "National Indignity". In Holland, not only membership in Nazi or Fascist groups, but sympathy for Nazism or a "Nazi state of mind", as well as friendly relations with Germans, were punishable offenses.[8] In Belgium the categories of "incivique" behavior declared punishable were analogous to those listed in the French Ordinance of August 26, 1944.[9] Norway, while not drawing up a list of specific offenses entailing national indignity, enacted a new lower scale of penalties – usually involving the equivalent of national degradation – for lesser offenders against the prewar code.[10] The Danes, without establishing separate legislation, achieved the same effect in practice by sentencing minor offenders to as little as thirty days in prison, but accompanying all sentences with an extremely rigorous list of civic disqualifications.[11]

The penalties attached to national indignity varied widely. In Belgium they were roughly the same as in France, but included also a ban on performing the duties of clerical office. However in Belgium the list of penalties was not necessarily to be applied *en bloc*, but could be meted out with discretion.[12]

In Holland they were considerably stiffer, including internment for

7. Cf. Dupréel, 349; Mason, pp. 128-29; Andenoes, 592-94; Givskov 450-51; *News Digest*, No. 1769 (May 28, 1945).

8. No specific proof of intent (as in the French ordinances) was required. The Tribunal Decree of September 17, 1944, made Dutchmen liable for having committed any of the enumerated offenses provided that "*he must be supposed to have known* that by so doing, he has acted against the interests of the Dutch people, or that he has done damage to the resistance against the enemy and his allies". (Italics added.) (Van Bemmelen, 116-17; Mason, pp. 74-75.)

9. Decree Laws of May 6, 1944; June 20, 1945; September 19, 1945. Belgium alone of the five Western European countries occupied during the Second World War had, on the basis of her experience twenty-five years earlier, an already existing body of legislation concerning "anti-national conduct" during enemy occupation. It proved inadequate, however. (Dupréel, 348-352.)

10. Penalties in the new scale did, however, go up to a maximum of three years imprisonment; the minimum sentence under the regular code was four years imprisonment. The new scale, contained in the Ordinance of December 15, 1944, was based on the work of a Resistance Committee which sent its recommendations to London. (Andenoes, 594-97.)

11. Givskov, 451.

12. Van Bemmelen, 117-18; Dupréel, 351-52.

up to ten years.[13] There were the usual provisions for civic disqualification and fines, but for 60,000 Dutch citizens there was a further and
all-embracing disqualification: all those who had been members of
certain German-sponsored military and police organizations were
judged to have entered the service of a foreign power, and were consequently deprived of Dutch nationality.[14] Among the many consequences
of this action was the confiscation of the property of the condemned,
since it became that of an "enemy alien".[15]

In Norway, in addition to short prison terms, lesser offenders were
subject to disqualifications so broad that they included a prohibition
on virtually all independent economic activity, including operating a
farm, workshop or store. In practice, however, these were rarely applied and only political rights were removed. Fines were heavy, and
most wealthy collaborators found the bulk of their property confiscated.[16]

Each of the four countries under consideration adapted its judicial

13. The original tribunal decree, cited above, made ten years' internment
mandatory for those guilty of national indignity, but in May 1945 the
tribunals were given discretionary power. Three-quarters of the tribunal
sentences provided for some period of internment, but usually under five
years. One interesting distinction between internment and imprisonment,
which dated from before the war, was that while the wife of a man sentenced
to prison for more than four years could sue for divorce on those grounds, the
wife of an internee could not.

14. Twenty thousand of these were wives who automatically lost their
citizenship when their husbands did. If a woman entered foreign service she
did not lose her citizenship unless her husband independently lost his.
Minors too could not lose Dutch nationality through their own actions since
their citizenship, like that of wives, was derivative.

15. Mason, pp. 64-79. Belgium provided for deprivation of citizenship for
those who fled to avoid prosecution for infractions against the external
security of the state (Decree Law of May 6, 1944) and those who were
directors of German-created political organizations or active pro-German
propagandists (Decree Law of June 20, 1945). (Dupréel, 349.) Léon Blum
reported that during their imprisonment in Buchenwald Georges Mandel
told him that he favored denaturalization and deportation to Germany for all
French collaborators not shot at the Liberation. (*Populaire*, July 5, 1949.)

16. Andenoes, 594-602. The fiscal measures were calculated on two bases,
one looking to the past, the other to the future. Members of the Norwegian
Nazi Party were regarded as collectively financially responsible for the
physical damage wrought by that Party, and were subject to confiscation
proportionate to their degree of activity. At the same time fines were levied
against them in proportion to their wealth in such a way as to see that "no
member of the N.S. can be a powerful economic factor".

machinery to the new and massive task in a different way. Belgium used military courts, but their composition was altered so as to consist of two civil judges and three officers.[17] Dutch practice was the mirror image of Belgian – thirty-five Special Courts, closely resembling ordinary criminal courts, were established, but two of the five judges were required to be serving officers in the armed forces. They dealt with the most serious cases of collaboration.[18] For lesser offenders, over 100 Tribunals were set up, consisting of a judge and two laymen from the Resistance.[19]

For major cases, the Norwegians modified their Assize Courts in a way reminiscent of French practice. Customarily these courts consisted of ten lay jurors who decided guilt or innocence, and three judges who deliberated on the sentence. The modified courts were made up of four jurors and three judges who deliberated together on both. Since the fact of guilt was not usually in dispute, this revision allowed popular participation in what became the crucial question: the sentence. Lesser cases were heard before regular cantonal or town tribunals.[20] In Denmark very minor procedural changes were introduced.[21]

Brief mention should be given to a novel procedure widely employed in Belgium, Holland and Norway. In these three countries "negotiated settlements" were introduced to reduce the huge backlog of cases. (In Holland, at the time that the system was introduced there were 250,000 persons awaiting trial, including 100,000 internees. It was estimated that the Special Courts and Tribunals could handle a maximum of 30,000 of these a year.)[22] In Belgium and Norway the settlement took place before a court; in Holland it was handled privately by the regional

17. Vermeylen, 74-75.

18. The death penalty, ordinary penal sanctions, as well as deprivation of citizenship, could be pronounced only by these courts. Following the practice of the French *cours de justice*, national degradation customarily accompanied whatever other penalties were pronounced.

19. Mason, *passim*. Dutch courts do not customarily employ lay jurors, and their use came in for a certain amount of criticism. The Minister of Justice, speaking at the inauguration of the first tribunal, defended the practice on the grounds that while "the administration of penal justice . . . presupposes a very carefully defined punishable deed . . . there are ten thousand and more forms of unpatriotic behavior" which patriotic Dutchmen could judge as well as jurists. (*News Digest*, No. 1669 [January 29, 1945].) After the Tribunals had been dissolved, a poll among the jurists who had presided over them disclosed that 90 per cent thought that the experiment with lay judges had proved successful. (Mason, p. 79.)

20. Ordinance of February 16, 1945 (Andenoes, 602-03).

21. Law No. 260 of June 1, 1945 (Givskov, 448-49).

22. Mason, pp. 79-80.

Solicitors General.[23] In all three countries the state prosecutor would "propose" a penalty to the accused which might include a short prison sentence, a fine, a period of probation, the loss of certain rights, or any combination of these. If the accused accepted, further court action would not be necessary; if he declined the settlement, he would face trial.[24] The procedure was very widely employed in all of these countries, and was a major factor in bringing their programs of punishing collaborators to a speedier, if not happy conclusion.[25]

In every country the complex of solutions arrived at was the resultant of all the different forces and pressures brought to bear; legal traditions, popular clamor, political divisions, and many more. In no country were the solutions found satisfactory.[26]

23. The private nature of the proceedings in Holland, coupled with the fact that settlements were not published, allowed the individuals concerned to claim that they had got off very lightly (i.e., were "virtually acquitted") which led to widespread public suspicion that collaborators were escaping justice. As a result, when an extension of the procedure was proposed in 1946 it had to be withdrawn because of popular opposition. (Mason, pp. 80-83.)

24. Mason, pp. 79-84; Van Bemmelen, 117-20. In Belgium a panel made up of a judge and two members of the Resistance had to approve the settlement in more serious cases. (Mason, pp. 180-81, n. 95.)

25. In Holland roughly 60 per cent of all suspects received settlements; 20 per cent were tried before Special Courts or Tribunals; 20 per cent were released without trial. (Mason, p. 84.) In Norway about half of the cases settled in 1945 were handled in this way; the extension of the system in 1946 to include negotiation of brief prison sentences was expected to result in the out-of-court settlement of 40,000 of the over 60,000 other cases outstanding. (Van Bemmelen, 119-20.)

26. In Holland, Professor van Bemmelen thought that the wider interpretation of pre-war legislation (à la française) would have been preferable to the frankly retroactive Dutch procedure; a Belgian commentator noted that while his countrymen "pretended" to adhere to the principle of non-retroactivity, the Dutch system "is more honest than ours". (Both quoted in Mason, p. 130.)

APPENDIX E

Appendix E

COUR DE JUSTICE VERDICTS BY
JUDICIAL DISTRICTS

This Appendix consists of (1) a map showing the judicial districts into which the *cours de justice* were divided; (2) a table which presents statistics showing the work of the *cours de justice*, by district, through the end of 1948; and (3) a table presenting computations which I have made using these statistics concerning the relative severity of the *cours de justice* in the various districts.

FIG. 1. – The Judicial Districts of France.

1. Agen	10. Chambéry	19. Nîmes
2. Aix	11. Colmar	20. Orléans
3. Amiens	12. Dijon	21. Paris
4. Angers	13. Douai	22. Pau
5. Bastia	14. Grenoble	23. Poitiers
6. Besançon	15. Limoges	24. Rennes
7. Bordeaux	16. Lyon	25. Riom
8. Bourges	17. Montpellier	26. Rouen
9. Caen	18. Nancy	27. Toulouse

TABLE 7. – Statistical summary of the work of the cours de justice and chambres civiques to December 31, 1948[a]

Judicial district		Cours de justice			Death sentences		Hard labor					Chambres civiques			
		Cases not prosecuted[b]	Cases heard[c]	Acquittals	In absentia[d]	Contradictory[e]	Life	Term	Solitary confinement[f]	Prison	National degradation[g]	Cases heard[c]	Acquittals	National degradation	National degradation suspended[h]
Colmar	Besançon	452	1,174	185	118	47	71	244	77	552	85	1,328	159	1,209	48
	Colmar	7,286	3,870	288	—	81	58	518	321	2,611	362	8,403	2,342	6,953	261
	Nancy	557	1,346	232	70	54	71	261	75	778	—	1,582	462	1,062	79
Lyon	Aix	3,745	4,080	649	490	209	200	1,184	105	1,960	—	2,783	750	1,864	276
	Bastia	49	76	35	10	3	5	19	3	30	—	328	144	83	23
	Bourges	701	796	96	82	30	44	185	—	234	—	1,026	244	759	32
	Chambéry	315	685	106	122	26	49	160	55	227	—	425	114	207	17
	Dijon	730	859	112	108	190	51	247	30	488	—	1,193	245	1,041	61
	Grenoble	702	1,463	238	370	106	112	209	9	462	—	722	166	420	82
	Lyon	1,505	2,400	391	513	180	211	451	37	786	—	3,884	894	3,073	86
	Nîmes	808	1,730	147	466	54	108	274	49	545	90	1,144	157	902	124
	Riom	564	1,093	206	165	137	221	318	17	365	—	1,753	429	1,485	67
Paris	Amiens	845	1,482	181	128	39	31	225	52	660	—	1,599	549	1,252	21
	Angers	320	847	127	59	35	25	172	57	542	—	1,451	427	1,024	15
	Caen	569	1,362	450	39	43	74	365	82	756	—	2,418	450	2,051	90
	Douai	4,826	5,362	1,094	371	82	104	872	135	2,704	—	2,082	710	1,331	41
	Orléans	455	1,118	256	82	95	43	240	69	522	—	2,807	553	2,230	119
	Paris	11,500	8,340	2,088	123	241	416	1,965	484	5,531	—	14,123	6,320	8,245	6,320
	Poitiers	2,726	2,236	479	—	272	207	372	125	837	—	1,924	608	1,330	59
	Rennes	791	1,586	255	111	90	93	423	102	562	—	3,768	550	3,165	22
	Rouen	1,828	1,176	162	78	31	71	208	45	595	91	3,040	1,170	1,886	57

Agen	364	1,276	252	172	59	65	174	19	535	—	654	153	460	41
Bordeaux	534	1,542	204	134	84	107	392	62	476	—	2,729	740	1,992	211
Limoges	1,052	613	57	138	81	25	151	15	146	—	300	93	201	6
Montpellier	1,119	1,525	102	51	221	180	388	51	498	31	2,740	578	1,905	257
Pau	199	518	—	62	23	45	122	31	224	6	825	208	469	108
Toulouse	475	1,540	211	335	127	90	295	66	490	—	2,934	666	1,887	406
Totals	45,017	50,095	8,603	4,397	2,640[f]	2,777	10,434	2,173	23,816[j]	692[k]	67,965	19,881	48,486	8,929

[a] Statistics are taken from *Cahiers Français d'Information*, March 15, 1949.

[b] Includes "affaires classées" in both *cours de justice* and *chambres civiques*.

[c] "Cases heard" total less than the total number of individual verdicts, since some cases involved several defendants, while the figures for verdicts are individual.

[d] Cases heard *in absentia* had to be retried when the accused was apprehended or surrendered himself. The effect of such verdicts was thus largely moral; one practical consequence was that it permitted the government to seize the property of the accused. There are no available statistics concerning the number of lesser penalties pronounced *in absentia*.

[e] I.e., in the presence of the defendant.

[f] This penalty was customarily employed when a defendant who otherwise would be sentenced to hard labor was too old or too ill for such a punishment.

[g] National degradation was a complementary penalty automatically added to any other sentence by a *cour de justice*. Figures in this column refer to those instances in which a *cour de justice* sentenced a defendant *only* to national degradation.

[h] *Chambres civiques* could immediately suspend application of a sentence of national degradation on the grounds of Resistance activity. Verdicts appearing in this column are in addition to those listed in the previous column.

[i] Only 791 of these sentences were actually carried out.

[j] The correct total for this column is 24,116. The original total is given since it is possible that the error lies in the transcription of one of the district totals.

[k] The correct total for this column is 665. (See previous note.)

TABLE 8. – *Comparative severity of cours de justice and chambres civiques by judicial district*[a]

Region	Judicial district	1946 population in 1000's[b]	Number of all cases per 1000 population[c]	Cour de justice cases per 1000 population[d]	All guilty verdicts per 1000 population[e]	Cour de justice guilty verdicts per 1000 population	Contradictory death sentences per 1000 population[f]	Contradictory death sentences as a percentage of all cour de justice guilty verdicts[f]	Cour de justice acquittals as a percentage of all cour de justice verdicts	Chambre civique acquittals as a percentage of all chambre civique verdicts	Cour de justice prosecutions as a percentage of all cases[g]
Colmar	Besançon	803·9 (8)	3·4 (8)	1·7 (5-6)	3·0 (5)	1·5 (4)	0·06 (12-13)	4·4 (19-20)	13·4 (10)	11·6 (1)	72·2 (5-6)
Colmar	Colmar	1767·1 (1)	7·7 (1)	2·4 (2)	6·2 (1)	2·2 (1-2)	0·05 (14-16)	2·1 (26-27)	6·8 (3)	25·2 (12)	34·7 (27)
Colmar	Nancy	1305·2 (19-20)	2·3 (19-20)	1·2 (15-17)	1·8 (17-20)	1·0 (17-19)	0·04 (17-19)	4·4 (19-20)	15·1 (17)	30·3 (18)	70·7 (8)
Lyon	Aix	1875·0 (3)	4·0 (3)	2·6 (1)	3·2 (3)	2·2 (1-2)	0·11 (4-7)	5·7 (14)	13·5 (11)	28·7 (16)	52·1 (21)
Lyon	Bastia	267·9 (26-27)	1·2 (26-27)	0·4 (27)	0·1 (27)	0·0 (27)[h]	0·01 (27)	5·0 (17)	33·3 (27)	63·4 (27)	60·8 (17)
Lyon	Bourges	786·8 (21-23)	2·1 (21-23)	0·9 (21-23)	1·7 (21-22)	0·7 (23-24)	0·04 (17-19)	6·1 (13)	14·3 (15)	24·3 (10)	53·2 (19)
Lyon	Chambéry	506·5 (10)	2·1 (21-23)	1·5 (10)	1·7 (21-22)	1·3 (8-9)	0·05 (14-16)	5·1 (15-16)	14·2 (14)	35·5 (24)	68·5 (10)
Lyon	Dijon	1024·1 (16)	2·5 (16)	1·2 (15-17)	2·1 (13-16)	1·1 (13-16)	0·19 (1-2)	18·9 (2)	9·1 (5)	19·1 (5)	54·1 (18)
Lyon	Grenoble	927·1 (19-20)	2·3 (19-20)	1·6 (7-9)	1·8 (17-20)	1·4 (5-7)	0·11 (4-7)	11·8 (7)	15·8 (20)	28·3 (15)	67·6 (12)
Lyon	Lyon	1857·3 (7)	3·5 (7)	1·4 (11-13)	2·8 (5)	1·2 (10-12)	0·10 (8-11)	10·8 (8)	15·2 (18)	22·5 (8)	61·5 (16)
Lyon	Nîmes	975·7 (12-13)	2·9 (12-13)	1·8 (4)	2·5 (10)	1·6 (3)	0·06 (12-13)	4·8 (18)	8·5 (4)	14·8 (2-3)	68·2 (11)
Lyon	Riom	1207·3 (15)	2·6 (15)	1·1 (18-19)	2·1 (13-16)	1·0 (17-19)	0·11 (4-7)	12·9 (5)	14·4 (16)	22·4 (7)	66·0 (14)
Paris	Amiens	1291·5 (17-18)	2·4 (17-18)	1·0 (20)	1·8 (17-20)	0·9 (20)	0·03 (20-26)	3·9 (22)	13·8 (12)	30·5 (19)	63·7 (15)
Paris	Angers	1164·6 (21-23)	2·1 (21-23)	0·9 (21-23)	1·6 (23)	0·8 (21-22)	0·03 (20-26)	4·2 (21)	12·5 (7)	29·4 (17)	72·6 (4)
Paris	Caen	1108·7 (4)	3·9 (4)	1·6 (7-9)	3·1 (4)	1·2 (10-12)	0·04 (17-19)	3·3 (23)	24·8 (26)	18·0 (4)	70·5 (9)
Paris	Douai	3086·0 (17-18)	2·4 (17-18)	1·7 (5-6)	1·8 (17-20)	1·4 (5-7)	0·03 (20-26)	2·1 (26-27)	20·4 (24)	34·8 (23)	52·6 (20)
Paris	Orléans	939·0 (2)	4·4 (2)	1·4 (11-13)	3·5 (2)	1·1 (13-16)	0·10 (8-11)	9·8 (9)	19·6 (22)	19·9 (6)	71·1 (7)
Paris	Paris	7743·9 (9)	3·3 (9)	1·4 (11-13)	2·2 (11-12)	1·1 (13-16)	0·03 (20-26)	2·8 (25)	19·2 (21)	43·4 (26)	42·0 (24)
Paris	Poitiers	1436·7 (12-13)	2·9 (12-13)	1·6 (7-9)	2·2 (11-12)	1·3 (8-9)	0·03 (20-26)	2·8 (25)	20·9 (25)	31·4 (21)	45·1 (23)
Paris	Rennes	3001·9 (24)	1·8 (24)	0·5 (26)	1·5 (24)	0·5 (26)	0·19 (1-2)	15·0 (4)	15·6 (19)	14·8 (2-3)	66·7 (13)
Paris	Rouen	1162·0 (5-6)	3·7 (5-6)	1·1 (18-19)	2·6 (8-9)	1·0 (17-19)	0·03 (20-26)	3·0 (24)	12·6 (8)	38·3 (25)	39·1 (25)

Toulouse { Agen	610·8	3·1 (10-11)	2·1 (3)	2·1 (13-16)	1·4 (5-7)	0·10 (8-11)	6·9 (12)	19·7 (23)	25·0 (11)	77·8 (1)
Bordeaux	1557·1	2·7 (14)	0·9 (21-23)	2·1 (13-16)	0·8 (21-22)	0·05 (14-16)	7·5 (10)	14·0 (13)	27·1 (14)	74·3 (3)
Limoges	779·6	1·2 (26-27)	0·8 (24)	1·0 (26)	0·7 (23-24)	0·10 (8-11)	19·4 (1)	9·3 (6)	31·6 (22)	36·8 (26)
Montpellier	1266·5	3·1 (10-11)	1·2 (15-17)	2·6 (8-9)	1·1 (13-16)	0·17 (3)	16·1 (3)	6·7 (2)	23·3 (9)	57·7 (22)
Pau	866·2	1·4 (25)	0·6 (25)	1·1 (25)	0·6 (25)	0·03 (20-26)	5·1 (15-16)	0·0 (1)^i	30·7 (20)	72·2 (5-6)
Toulouse	1124·1	3·7 (5-6)	1·3 (14)	2·9 (6)	1·2 (10-12)	0·11 (4-7)	11·9 (6)	13·1 (9)	26·1 (13)	76·4 (2)
FRANCE	40502·0	3·1	1·4	2·4	1·2	0·07	6·1	15·5	29·1	52·7

[a] Judicial statistics are based on Table 7. The numbers in parentheses refer to the ranking of the twenty-seven districts according to these indices of severity. Since the incidence of acquittals is an index of leniency, rather than of severity, in the two columns which refer to acquittals the numbers in parentheses are – for the sake of a consistent and comparable standard – in inverse ratio to the percentages given.

[b] Population figures are taken from the report of the "Haute Comité Consultatif de la Population et de la Famille", *La Population française* (Paris: 1955), I, 144-46.

[c] "Cases" here refers to the number of dossiers opened, whether or not prosecution followed.

[d] "Cour de justice cases" here refers to the number of individuals who were prosecuted before the *cours de justice*.

[e] I.e., guilty verdicts handed down by both the *cours de justice* and *chambres civiques*.

[f] Since death sentences *in absentia* were often pronounced for "moral effect", with full knowledge that they would not be carried out, only contradictory death sentences have been employed as an index of the frequency with which the death penalty was pronounced.

[g] I.e., as a percentage of all dossiers opened – the remainder having been "classées" or turned over to the *chambres civiques*.

[h] Less than 0·05.

[i] The statistics published in the *Cahiers Français d'Information* list no acquittals in the Pau judicial district. I have been unable to determine whether this is an oversight.

Appendix F

VERDICTS OF THE *HAUTE COUR DE JUSTICE*

Date	Name	Disposition of Case
March 15, 1945	Estéva, Jean-Pierre	Life imprisonment
April 20, 1945	Dentz, Henri	Death (commuted)
May 2, 1945	Chatel, Yves	Died before trial
June 13, 1945	Barthélemy, Joseph	Died before trial
June 19, 1945	Déat, Marcel	Death (*in absentia*)
July 4, 1945	Bonnard, Abel	Death (*in absentia*)
August 15, 1945	Pétain, Philippe	Death (commuted)
September 5, 1945	Bichelonne, Jean	Died before trial
September 5, 1945	Février, André	Not prosecuted
September 5, 1945	Pinot, Maurice	Not prosecuted
September 5, 1945	Rivière, Albert	Not prosecuted
September 19, 1945	Debeney, Victor	Not prosecuted
September 19, 1945	Platon, Jean	Died before trial
October 3, 1945	Darnand, Joseph	Death (executed)
October 9, 1945	Laval, Pierre	Death (executed)
November 28, 1945	Cayrel, Antoine	Not prosecuted
December 5, 1945	Schumann, Robert	Not prosecuted
December 12, 1945	Leroy-Ladurie, Jacques	Not prosecuted
March 12, 1946	Chevalier, Jacques	20 years' hard labor
March 12, 1946	Gibrat, Robert	10 years' national degradation
March 13, 1946	Gabolde, Maurice	Death (*in absentia*)
March 15, 1946	Dayras, Georges	Death (commuted)
March 18, 1946	Ybarnégaray, Jean	National degradation (suspended)
March 28, 1946	Colson, Louis	Not prosecuted
April 12, 1946	Frossard, Louis	Died before trial
May 6, 1946	Weygand, Maxime	Not prosecuted
June 13, 1946	Archard, Louis	Not prosecuted
June 13, 1946	Pomaret, Charles	Not prosecuted
July 10, 1946	Berthelot, Jean	2 years' imprisonment
July 11, 1946	Charbin, Paul	10 years' national degradation
July 17, 1946	Lagardelle, Hubert	Life at hard labor
July 18, 1946	Bonnefoy, René	Death (*in absentia*)
July 18, 1946	Rochat, Charles	Death (*in absentia*)
July 19, 1946	Cayla, Léon	5 years' imprisonment
July 26, 1946	Flandin, Pierre-Etienne	5 years' national degradation (suspended)
August 14, 1946	Abrial, Jean	10 years' hard labor
August 14, 1946	Auphan, Paul	Life at hard labor (*in absentia*)
August 14, 1946	Marquis, André	5 years' imprisonment
January 23, 1947	Mireaux, Emile	Not prosecuted
January 23, 1947	Rivaud, Albert	Not prosecuted

Date	Name	Disposition of Case
January 30, 1947	Moreau, Robert	Not prosecuted
February 18, 1947	Frémicourt, Charles	Not prosecuted
March 3, 1947	Baudouin, Paul	5 years' hard labor
March 6, 1947	De Brinon, Fernand	Death (executed)
March 7, 1947	Alibert, Raphaël	Death (*in absentia*)
March 7, 1947	Hilaire, Georges	5 years' imprisonment (*in absentia*)
March 14, 1947	Jardel, Jean	National degradation
March 14, 1947	Robert, Georges	10 years' hard labor
March 19, 1947	Caziot, Pierre	National degradation
March 21, 1947	Annet, Armand	National degradation
March 21, 1947	Brévié, Jules	10 years' imprisonment
March 22, 1947	Lémery, Joseph	5 years' national degradation (suspended)
March 25, 1947	Chautemps, Camille	5 years' imprisonment (*in absentia*)
March 25, 1947	Guérard, Jacques	Death (*in absentia*)
March 28, 1947	De Laborde, Jean	Death (commuted)
May 2, 1947	Michelier, Félix	Not prosecuted
May 2, 1947	Ripert, Georges	Not prosecuted
May 8, 1947	Musnier de Pleignes, F.	Not prosecuted
May 22, 1947	Di Pace, Vincent	Not prosecuted
June 6, 1947	Benoist-Méchin, Jacques	Death (commuted)
June 19, 1947	Du Paty du Clam, Charles	Not prosecuted
June 19, 1947	Portmann, Georges	Not prosecuted
July 4, 1947	De l'Epine, Amaury	Not prosecuted
July 4, 1947	Fatou, Pierre	Not prosecuted
July 11, 1947	Carcopino, Jérôme	Not prosecuted
July 11, 1947	Prouvost, Jean	Not prosecuted
July 25, 1947	Lamirand, Georges	Not prosecuted
November 18, 1947	La Porte du Theil, J. de	Not prosecuted
November 18, 1947	Gait, Maurice	Not prosecuted
November 28, 1947	Noguès, Charles	20 years' hard labor (*in absentia*)
December 10, 1947	Darquier de Pellepoix, L.	Death (*in absentia*)
December 10, 1947	Vallat, Xavier	10 years' imprisonment
December 18, 1947	Grasset, Raymond	Not prosecuted
January 28, 1948	Marquet, Adrien	10 years' national degradation
January 29, 1948	Boyez, Emile	Not prosecuted
January 29, 1948	Roujou, Frédéric	Not prosecuted
January 29, 1948	Weinmann, Robert	Not prosecuted
May 25, 1948	Pascot, Joseph	5 years' national degradation (suspended)
May 27, 1948	Mathé, Pierre	5 years' national degradation
June 1, 1948	Bléhaut, Henri	10 years' imprisonment (*in absentia*)
June 3, 1948	Delmotte, Georges	2 years' imprisonment
June 4, 1948	Piétri, François	5 years' national degradation (*in absentia*)
June 24, 1948	Creyssel, Paul	4 years' imprisonment
June 29, 1948	Lemoine, Antoine	5 years' national degradation (suspended)

Date	Name	Disposition of Case
July 1, 1948	Laure, Emile	Acquitted
July 2, 1948	Cathala, Pierre	Died before trial
July 2, 1948	Masson, André	Death (*in absentia*)
July 8, 1948	Bouthillier, Yves	3 years' imprisonment
July 16, 1948	Chasseigne, François	10 years' hard labor
July 22, 1948	Bruneton, Gaston	4 years, 6 months' imprisonment
November 25, 1948	Bergeret, Jean	Not prosecuted
November 25, 1948	Pujo, Pierre-Louis	Not prosecuted
December 2, 1948	Bonnafous, Max	Not prosecuted
December 14, 1948	Marion, Paul	10 years' imprisonment
December 16, 1948	Boisson, Pierre	Died before trial
December 18, 1948	Bridoux, Eugène	Death (*in absentia*)
December 22, 1948	Peyrouton, Marcel	Acquitted
January 27, 1949	Barnaud, Jacques	Not prosecuted
January 27, 1949	Belin, René	Not prosecuted
January 27, 1949	Jannekeyn, Jean	Not prosecuted
February 17, 1949	Decoux, Jean	Not prosecuted
February 17, 1949	Gastin, Paul	Not prosecuted
February 17, 1949	Lehideux, François	Not prosecuted
February 17, 1949	Moniot, Paul	Not prosecuted
June 21, 1949	Moysset, Henri	Died before trial
June 23, 1949	Bousquet, René	5 years' national degradation (suspended)
June 28, 1949	Olivier-Martin, Félix	Acquitted
July 1, 1949	Parmentier, André	5 years' national degradation (suspended)

SUGGESTIONS FOR FURTHER READING

A list of the sources on which this study is based – and much fuller documentation in footnotes – may be found in my doctoral dissertation, "The Purge in Liberated France: 1944-46", submitted to Columbia University in 1965. In revising the dissertation for publication it seemed to me more useful to offer what follows: suggestions for the reader who is interested in further exploring specific topics discussed or mentioned in the text.

I

With the possible exception of July 1914, no month in history has been more thoroughly discussed than June 1940. John C. Cairns, "Along the Road Back to France 1940", *American Historical Review*, LXIV, 3 (April 1959), is an excellent introduction to the historiography of the defeat. There is an extensive bibliography in Jacques Benoist-Méchin, *Soixante jours qui ébranlèrent l'occident*, 3 vols. (Paris: 1956); the *Revue d'Histoire de la Deuxième Guerre Mondiale* (R.H.D.G.M.) regularly publishes reviews and bibliographies which note everything of consequence appearing on the subject. Among the French political and military leaders who have published their memoirs or diaries of this period are Paul Baudouin, Georges Bonnet, Camille Chautemps, General de Gaulle, Pierre-Etienne Flandin, General Gamelin, Pierre Laval, Albert Lebrun, Paul Reynaud and General Weygand. Also of great interest are the accounts of two British participant-observers, Sir Winston Churchill and Major General Sir Edward Spears, and the testimony of participants in *Le Procès du Maréchal Pétain*, 2 vols. (Paris: 1945) and in *Les Evénements survenus en France de 1933 à 1945* [a two-volume report of, and nine volumes of testimony heard by, a parliamentary commission of inquiry] (Paris: 1947ff.). Among the most useful of the secondary accounts are Philip C. F. Bankwitz, "Maxime Weygand and the Fall of France: A Study in Civil-Military Relations", *Journal of Modern History*, XXXI, 3 (September 1959); Marc Bloch, *L'Etrange défaite* (Paris: 1957); Colonel A. Goutard, *1940: La Guerre des occasions perdues* (Paris: 1956); Albert Kammerer, *La Vérité sur l'Armistice* (Paris: 1944); and two special numbers of the R.H.D.G.M.: No. 3 (June 1951), "Autour de l'Armistice de Juin 1940", and Nos. 10-11 (June 1953), "La Campagne de France: Mai-Juin 1940".

All the existing accounts of the events surrounding the vote of July 10 are polemical. On the side of the "yes-voters": Jean Castagnez, *Précisions oubliés: Vichy, 9 et 10 juillet 1940* (Sancerre: 1945), and Jean Montigny, *De l'Armistice à l'Assemblée nationale, 15 juin-15 juillet 1940: Toute la vérité sur un mois dramatique de notre histoire* (Clermont-Ferrand: 1940).

For the "no-voters": Louis Noguerès, *Un défi à la Résistance: M. Jules Jeanneney, Ministre d'Etat* (Rodez: 1945), and Jean Odin, *Les Quatre-vingts* (Paris: 1946). There are important documents and testimonies relating to the vote in *Les Evénements survenus en France*.

The best brief account of the Vichy Regime is Alfred Cobban's essay "Vichy France" in Arnold and Veronica M. Toynbee (eds.), *Hitler's Europe* [*Survey of International Affairs: 1939-1946*] (London: 1954). There is as yet no satisfactory full treatment; Robert Aron's *Histoire de Vichy* (Paris: 1954), often cited as the "standard work", should be used with the greatest reserve. Two American doctoral dissertations shed much-needed light on important aspects of the regime: Adrienne Hytier's *Two Years of French Foreign Policy: Vichy 1940-1942* (Geneva: 1958), and Robert O. Paxton's *Parades and Politics at Vichy: The French Officer Corps Under Marshal Pétain* (Princeton: 1966). Useful insights are to be found in the Marquis Marc Pierre d'Argenson's *Pétain et le pétinisme: Essai de psychologie* (Paris: 1953); Paul Farmer, *Vichy: Political Dilemma* (New York: 1955); Louis R. Franck, "The Forces of Collaboration", *Foreign Affairs*, XXI, 1 (October 1942); Stanley Hoffmann, "Aspects du Régime de Vichy", *Revue Française de Science Politique*, VI (1956); J. Lacroix and J. Vialatoux, "Le Mythe Pétain", *Esprit*, November 1951; André Siegfried, *De la IIIᵉ à la IVᵉ République* (Paris: 1956); Alexander Werth, *France: 1940-1955* (New York: 1956) [the chapters on Vichy are by far the best part of this uneven volume]; and Gordon Wright, "Vichy Revisited", *Virginia Quarterly Review*, XXXIV (1958).

There is no adequate biography of Pétain, but for the war years see Louis Noguerès, *Le Véritable procès du maréchal Pétain* (Paris: 1955); on Laval there is the friendly *Pierre Laval*, 2 vols. (Paris: 1955), by Alfred Mallet. Laval's daughter collected hundreds of depositions favorable to her father which the Hoover Institution irresponsibly published under the title *France during the German Occupation: 1940-1944*, 3 vols. (Stanford [Cal.]: 1958). There is an angry rejoinder by P. Arnoult *et al.*, *La France sous l'Occupation* (Paris: 1959). Interesting material on the doctrine of Vichy is to be found in Eugen Weber, *Action Française: Royalism and Reaction in Twentieth-Century France* (Stanford [Cal.]: 1962); H. du Moulin de Labarthète, *Le Temps des illusions: Souvenirs, juillet 1940-avril 1942* (Geneva: 1946); J. Plumyène and R. Lasierra, *Les Fascismes français: 1923-1963* (Paris: 1963). I am not convinced by Stanley Hoffmann's attempt (*In Search of France* [Cambridge (Mass.): 1963]) to establish parallels between the ideologies of Vichy and the Resistance. It is true that technocratic ideas were common to some resistance groups, such as the Organisation Civile et Militaire, and to some Vichyites. But the O.C.M. was far from typical of the Resistance, and technocracy at Vichy coexisted with (and was subordinate to) narrow nationalism, reactionary clericalism and fascism.

On the Riom Trial, see Pierre Mazé and Roger Génébrier, *Les Grandes journées du procès de Riom* (Paris: 1945), and Maurice Ribet, *Le Procès de Riom* (Paris: 1945). Vichy anti-semitism is treated in Léon Poliakov, "Lois de Nuremberg et Lois de Vichy: du Racisme Intégral au Racisme de Compromis", in Max Beloff (ed.), *On the Track of Tyranny* (London: 1960), and Joseph Billig, "La Condition des Juifs en France: Juillet 1940-Août 1944 ', R.H.D.G.M., No. 24 (October 1956). Robert J. Soucey's "The Nature of Fascism in France", *Journal of Contemporary History*, I, 1 (1966), is the most sensible introduction to the subject. The collaborationist milieux are also discussed by Plumyène and Lasierra, and in Michèle Cotta, *La Collaboration: 1940-1944* (Paris: 1964); Paul Sérant, *Le Romantisme fasciste: Etude sur l'œuvre politique de quelques écrivains français* (Paris: 1959); "Saint-Paulien" [Maurice-Yvan Sicard], *Histoire de la Collaboration* (Mayenne: 1964). The psychology of the individual collaborator is a subject that deserves much more serious treatment than it has so far received. Jean-Paul Sartre's essay "Qu'est-ce qu'un Collaborateur?" in his *Situations, III* (Paris: 1949) contains some penetrating psychological suggestions. Vichy's sordid epilogue is dealt with in Louis Noguerès, *La Dernière étape: Sigmaringen* (Paris: 1956).

For De Gaulle, the most important source is his *Mémoires de guerre*, 3 vols. (Paris: 1954-59), with extensive documentary appendices, together with his *Discours de guerre*, 3 vols. (Fribourg: 1944-45). Some speeches not included in the *Discours* are to be found in his *La France n'a pas perdu la guerre: Discours et messages* (New York: 1944). The best biography to date is Paul-Marie de la Gorce, *De Gaulle entre deux mondes: Une vie et une époque* (Paris: 1964). On the Gaullist milieu in London (and later in Algiers) the memoirs of Jacques Soustelle, *Envers et contre tout*, 2 vols. (Paris: 1947-40), are extremely helpful. See also Maurice Flory, *Le Statut international des gouvernements réfugiés et le cas de la France Libre* (Paris: 1952), and Nicholas Wahl's 1956 Harvard dissertation, "De Gaulle and the Resistance: The Rise of Reform Politics in France". There is a short *Histoire de la France Libre* (Paris: 1963) by Henri Michel.

There is as yet no satisfactory history of the Resistance. The Comité d'Histoire de la Deuxième Guerre Mondiale, with which most of the scholars in the field are associated, has decided that such a project is premature, and instead has concentrated on monographic studies of particular aspects of the Resistance. Many short studies appear in the R.H.D.G.M.; the Comité also sponsors a series of monographs, "Esprit de la Résistance", of which one, René Hostache, *Le Conseil National de la Résistance: Les Institutions de la clandestinité* (Paris: 1958), gives a comprehensive picture of the organization of the Resistance. M. Michel, who is President of the Comité and Editor of the *Revue*, has produced a very full *Bibliographie critique de la Résistance* (Paris: 1964) as well as an extremely brief overall *Histoire de la Résistance en France*, 3rd ed. (Paris: 1962).

There is a fairly extensive literature on the wartime history of the French Communist Party. Alfred J. Rieber's *Stalin and the French Communist*

Party: 1941-1947 (New York: 1962) is a valuable study – noteworthy for using Russian as well as French sources – but occasionally is somewhat uncritical in its use of French sources. The second volume of Jacques Fauvet's *Histoire du Parti communiste français* (Paris: 1965) covers the war years. Angelo Tasca (writing under the pseudonym of Angelo Rossi) has produced a number of polemical works whose careful documentation is a great embarrassment to Communist apologists: *La Physiologie du Parti communiste français* (Paris: 1948); *Les Communistes français pendant la drôle de guerre* (Paris: 1951), *Les Cahiers du Bolchevisme pendant la campagne 1939-1940* (Paris: 1951); *La Guerre des papillons: Quatre ans de politique communiste, 1940-1944* (Paris: 1954). The anonymous *Histoire du Parti communiste français*, 2 vols. (Paris: 1960-62), is the product of a group of dissident Communists and contains much of value, as does the writing of another dissident, Auguste Lecoeur: *L'Autocritique attendue* (St. Cloud: 1955) and *Le Partisan* (Paris: 1963). For the earlier period, Germaine Willard's *La Drôle de guerre et la trahison de Vichy* (Paris: 1960) is the orthodox P.C.F. account; the most recent comprehensive Party history is *Histoire du Parti communiste français: Manuel* (Paris: 1964) edited by Jacques Duclos and François Billoux. Maurice Thorez' *Œuvres* have been published in many volumes: XIX, XX and XXI are relevant to the present study.

II

The Gaullist attack on Vichy's legality and legitimacy is stated in systematic fashion by René Cassin in "Un Coup d'Etat: La Soi-Disant Constitution de Vichy", *La France Libre* (London), I, 2 (December 16, 1940). (The second part of the article, which appeared in the issue of January 1941, is devoted to the thesis that the establishment of Vichy was the culmination of a long-standing dream of overthrowing the Republic, held by defeatists, fascists, Maurrasians, etc.) In my view the most subtle and convincing critique of Cassin's views is that of Georges Vedel, *Manuel élémentaire de droit constitutionnel* (Paris: 1949). But see also G. Berlia, "La Loi Constitutionnelle du 10 juillet 1940", *Revue du Droit Public et de la Science Politique en France et à l'Etranger* (1944); Maurice Duverger, *Les Constitutions de la France* (Paris: 1944); Duverger, "Contribution à l'Etude de la Légitimité des Gouvernements de Fait", *Revue du Droit Public . . .*, LX, 1 (January-March 1945); Duverger, *Manuel de droit constitutionnel et science politique* (Paris: 1948); Maximilian Koessler, "Vichy's Sham Constitutionality", *American Political Science Review*, XXXIX, 1 (February 1945); J. Laferrière, *Le Nouveau gouvernement de la France* (Paris: 1942) and *Manuel de droit constitutionnel*, 2nd ed. (Paris: 1947); Maurice Prélot, *Précis de droit constitutionnel* (Paris: 1950); Joseph Vialatoux, *Le Problème de la légitimité du pouvoir: Vichy ou De Gaulle* (Paris: 1945); M. Waline, *Manuel élémentaire de droit administratif* (Paris: 1946).

228

Resistance thought is embodied in the underground press – most of which is preserved in the collection of the Bibliothèque Nationale; its holdings are detailed in the library's *Catalogue des périodiques clandestins diffusés en France de 1939 à 1945* (Paris: 1954). A few journals have been reprinted: *Les Cahiers* [of the Organisation Civile et Militaire] in Maxime Blocq-Mascart, *Chroniques de la Résistance* (Paris: 1945); *Défense de la France* in Marie Granet (ed.), *Le Journal "Défense de la France"* (Paris: 1961); *Les Lettres Françaises* in George Adam, *L'Album des Lettres Françaises clandestines* (Paris: 1947); and *Bir-Hakeim* (somewhat expurgated) in André Jacquelin, *Quatre ans de Résistance à l'intérieur: Toute la vérité sur le journal clandestin gaulliste Bir Hakeim* (Paris: 1945). The Resistance press as a whole is surveyed in Claude Bellanger, *Presse Clandestine: 1940-1944* (Paris: 1961); see also the Introduction to the Bibliothèque Nationale's *Catalogue* by R. and P. Roux-Fouillet. Henri Michel and Boris Mirkine-Guetzévitch have put together an anthology which illuminates *Les Idées politiques et sociales de la Résistance* (Paris: 1954). Finally, there is the exhaustive and penetrating *Les Courants de pensée de la Résistance* (Paris: 1962) by Henri Michel, which examines the thought of all sections of the Resistance on a variety of subjects.

III

For the background of the Allied landings in North Africa see William L. Langer's defense of American policy, *Our Vichy Gamble* (New York: 1947). On the military side there is George F. Howe, *Northwest Africa: Seizing the Initiative in the West* (Washington: 1957), a volume in the official series, "United States Army in World War II". Many of the participants in the events of November 1942 have published their memoirs. On the French side see Henri Giraud, *Un seul but la victoire* (Paris: 1949), which reveals his political incapacity; Alphonse Juin's self-justificatory *Mémoires*, Vol. I (Paris: 1959); "Crusoe" [Jacques Lemaigre-Debreuil], *Vicissitudes d'une victoire: 1940-1943* (Paris: 1946). American memorialists include Harry C. Butcher, *My Three Years with Eisenhower* (New York: 1946), a perceptive insider's view; Mark W. Clark, *Calculated Risk* (New York: 1950); Dwight D. Eisenhower, *Crusade in Europe* (New York: 1948). Robert Murphy's *Diplomat Among Warriors* (New York: 1964) reveals perhaps more of the author's prejudices than he realizes; Kenneth Pendar's *Adventure in Diplomacy* (New York: 1946) is a spiteful anti-Gaullist work by one of Murphy's bright young men. Among the most important secondary studies is Albert Kammerer, *Du débarquement africain au meurtre de Darlan* (Paris: 1949); General Schmitt's "Le Général Juin et le Débarquement en A.F.N.", R.H.D.G.M., No. 44 (October 1961), is highly critical of his subject's selective recollections.

Arthur Layton Funk's misleadingly titled *Charles de Gaulle: The Crucial*

Years, 1943-1944 (Norman [Okla.]: 1959) is a fair, careful, and perceptive study of North African politics from the Allied landings to the Liberation of France. Yves-Maxime Danan covers more ground in his *La Vie politique à Alger de 1940 à 1944* (Paris: 1963), and he includes a good deal of material not found in Funk, but the author's prejudices (which are my own) sometimes get in his way. Henri Michel's *Courants* includes a chapter on "Giraudisme"; for a view from the inside of Giraud's administration see Robert Aron, *Le Piège où nous a pris l'histoire* (Paris: 1950). The memoirs of De Gaulle and Soustelle devote a great deal of space to the conflicts with Giraud; also interesting in this connection is General Georges Catroux, *Dans la bataille de Méditerranée* (Paris: 1949).

Marcel Peyrouton has recounted how he went *Du service public à la prison commune* (Paris: 1950). Churchill's memoirs deal with the case, and from the American side there is a valuable collection of documents in *Foreign Relations of the United States, Diplomatic Papers: 1943, Vol. II: Europe* (Washington: 1964). Emmanuel d'Astier of the C.F.L.N. discusses conflicts with Churchill on the affair in *Sept fois sept jours* (Paris: 1947) and *Les Dieux et les hommes* (Paris: 1952). There is a posthumously published and dishonest *Ma Vie* (Paris: 1958) by Pierre Pucheu; Paul Buttin contributes a defense counsel's view of *Le Procès Pucheu* (Paris: 1948); General Schmitt provides the best account in what he tells us is *Toute la vérité sur le procès Pucheu par un des juges* (Paris: 1963).

IV

The study by René Hostache on the C.N.R., cited above, is indispensable for De Gaulle's military and civil preparations for the Liberation. The only work dealing with the Liberation as a whole is Robert Aron's *Histoire de la Libération de la France: Juin 1944-Mai 1945* (Paris: 1959). It is full of picturesque anecdotes and contains many shrewd observations, together with a number of serious errors and distortions. The official U.S. Army volume on military government contains much that is relevant: Harry L. Coles and Albert K. Weinberg, *Civil Affairs: Soldiers Become Governors* (Washington: 1964). For Normandy, see Marcel Baudot, *L'Opinion publique sous l'Occupation: L'Exemple d'un département français (1939-1945)* (Paris: 1960), together with Crane Brinton, "Letters from Liberated France", *French Historical Studies*, II, 1 (Spring 1961). Madeleine Baudoin's *Histoire des Groupes Francs (M.U.R.) des Bouches-du-Rhône de septembre 1943 à la Libération* (Paris: 1962) is helpful in getting a picture of developments in southern France. There is no shortage of accounts of terror, violence and summary executions. The fullest collection of these stories appeared monthly in the late 1940's in *Ecrits de Paris*. Yves Farge, *Rebelles, soldats et citoyens* (Paris: 1946) recounts the efforts of a *commissaire de la République* to restore order in the Lyons area; it should be supplemented with Petrus Faure, *Un témoin raconte* (St Etienne: 1962). On Communist policy and activity at the time of the Liberation, the anonymous *Histoire du P.C.F.* and the works by Rieber and Lecoeur cited above are enlightening. Among the most informed brief discussions of the subject is Pierre Hervé, "Le Parti Communiste depuis 1944", *Crapouillot*, No. 55 (January 1962). In *L'Affaire Marty* (Paris: 1955), André Marty defends himself against the charge of *blanquisme* in 1944.

V

Most of what has been written on the administrative purge falls into two categories. First of all, there are polemics from the camp of its victims. Jacques Isorni's "L'Epuration Administrative" in *Défense de l'Occident*, Nos. 39-40 (January-February 1957), summarizes this point of view. It receives more extended treatment in the *Requête aux Nations unies sur les violations des droits de l'homme* submitted by the Union pour la Restauration et la Défense du Service Public (Paris: 1951); the Association also published a *Bulletin Mensuel*. There are also a number of studies which discuss the program from a procedural point of view: André Basdevant, "L'Epuration Administrative sous la Contrôle du Conseil d'Etat" (unpublished *thèse en droit*, University of Paris, 1955); Robert Foucqueteau, "Epuration Administrative et Répression Disciplinaire" (unpublished *thèse en droit*, University of Paris, 1947); Elijah Ben-Zion Kaminsky, "An Anti-Subversive Program in the French Public Service: The French Epuration Administration of 1944-53" (unpublished Ph.D. dissertation, Harvard University, 1962); Georges E. Lavau, "Le Contrôle Juridictionnel de l'Epuration Administrative et Professionnelle" and "De Quelques Principes en Matière d'Epuration Administrative" (*La Semaine Juridique*, 1946, 1st part, No. 501 and 1947, 1st part, No. 584 respectively). Also relevant are the remarks concerning the administrative purge in René Bourdoncle, *Fonction publique et liberté d'opinion en droit positif français* (Paris: 1957). Among those works which discuss the purge in the armed forces are Paul Auphan and Jacques Mordal, *The French Navy in World War II* (Annapolis [Md.]: 1959); Raoul Girardet (ed.), *La Crise militaire française, 1945-1962: Aspects sociologiques et idéologiques* (Paris: 1964); Paul-Marie de la Gorce, *The French Army: A Military-Political History* (New York: 1963); and Robert Paxton's *Parades and Politics at Vichy*, cited above.

VI

Works already cited are valuable for Resistance opinions concerning the Third Republic and the future of French politics (Michel, *Courants* and Michel and Mirkine-Guetzévitch, *Idées politiques*); and also for the attitude of "les quatre-vingts" toward "yes-voters" (Noguerès, *Un défi* and Odin,

Quatre-vingts). The *Livre d'or des quatre-vingts* (n.p.: n.d.) contains useful information on the postwar careers of "no-voters". A number of men whose ineligibility was not suspended by the *Jury d'honneur* defended their record in manifestos addressed to their ex-constituents: Fabien Albertin, *A mes véritables juges* (Marseilles: 1946); Georges Boully, *Mémoire à mes juges* (St Valerien [Yonne]: 1945); Charles Pomaret, *Lettre aux lozériens* (Marseilles: 1947). Many ineligibles joined the Association des Représentants du Peuple de la IIIᵉ République, which published an account of its *Banquet des "Mille" du 14 mars 1948* (Paris: 1948) and also issued a periodical *Lettre aux adhérents*.

On the prewar split in the Socialist Party and its relation to later wartime conduct see the detailed and scholarly study by Georges Lefranc, *Le Mouvement socialiste sous la Troisième République: 1875-1940* (Paris: 1963), and Daniel Ligou, *Histoire du socialisme en France: 1871-1961* (Paris: 1962), which covers more ground. There are three accounts of the S.F.I.O. during the war years, all by postwar leaders of the Party: Jules Moch, *Le Parti socialiste au peuple de France* (Paris: 1945); Jean Pierre-Bloch, *Mes jours heureux* (Paris: 1946); Robert Verdier, *La Vie clandestine du Parti socialiste* (Paris: 1944). Apologias of excluded Socialists include André Février, *Expliquons-nous* (Malakoff: (1946), and Sabinius Valière and Marcel Vardelle, *N'oubliez pas trop* (Limoges: 1949). *Le Socialiste* was the official organ of the short-lived *fauriste* Parti Socialiste Démocratique ("Vieux Parti Socialiste S.F.I.O."). The only account of the Radicals during the War is the official Party pamphlet, *Patrie et liberté: Le Parti Radical-Socialiste pendant la Résistance* (n.p.: n.d.). For the Communists, see the various accounts previously cited.

An excellent handbook of the parties in the wake of the Liberation is Paul Marabuto, *Les Partis politiques et les mouvements sociaux sous la IVᵉ République* (Paris: 1948). The first postwar national elections receive detailed treatment in Raoul Husson, *Élections et referendums des 21 octobre 1945, 5 mai et 2 juin 1946* (Paris: 1946); see also *Année Politique*, 1944-45. There are tables showing comparisons between prewar and postwar party strength in *Encyclopédie politique de la France et du monde*, 2nd ed. (Paris: 1950). On the extent of the political revolution, by far the most enlightening study is Mattei Dogan, "Political Ascent in a Class Society: French Deputies, 1870-1958" in Dwaine Marvick (ed.), *Political Decision Makers* (Glencoe [Ill.]: 1961).

VII

Nationalizations – punitive and otherwise – are discussed in Mario Einaudi *et al.*, *Nationalizations in France and Italy* (Ithaca [N.Y.]: 1955); Harold A. Fletcher, "The Nationalization Debate in France: 1942-1946" (unpublished Ph.D. dissertation, Harvard University, 1957); L. Julliot de la Morandière and M. Bye, *Les Nationalisations en France et à l'étranger*

(Paris: 1948), Vol. I. The abortive program for the confiscation of illicit profits is discussed from a legal and procedural point of view in Gilbert Bevin, "Le Commerce avec l'Ennemi et l'Ordonnance du 29 mars 1945", *La Semaine Juridique*, 1946, 1st part, No. 546; Georges Capdeville and Jean Nicolay, *La Confiscation des profits illicites résultant du commerce avec l'ennemi ou de violation de la réglementation économique* (Paris: 1945); Jean Castagnez, *Les Profits illicites: Leur confiscation* (Paris: 1946); Maxime Chrétien, "La Confiscation des Profits Illicites", *La Semaine Juridique*, 1945, 1st part, Nos. 458 and 463; Pierre H. Doublet, *Commerce avec l'ennemi pendant l'occupation; épuration des entreprises: Commentaires suivis des ordonnances du 29 mars 1945 et des textes antérieurs* (Paris: 1945); René Floriot, *Les Profits illicites et la confiscation* (Paris: 1945).

The press establishment of Occupied France is dissected in Jean Quéval, *Première page, cinquième colonne* (Paris: 1945); "La Presse Autorisée sous l'Occupation Allemande: 1940-1944", *Notes Documentaires et Etudes*, No. 218 (January 14, 1946); and the work by Cotta cited above. The organization of underground discussions concerning the press is treated in the previously mentioned studies by Bellanger and Hostache. See also the underground manifesto of the Fédération Nationale de la Presse Clandestine, *Pour une presse patriote, honnête et libre* (n.p.: n.d. [early 1944]). In *Le Vent souffle sur l'histoire* (Paris: 1949), Jean Pierre-Bloch gives some information on the Liberation takeover. By far the best discussion of the press controversy is Jean Mottin's informed and reliable *Histoire politique de la presse: 1944-1949* (Paris: 1949). Noel Jacquemart's *Quatre ans d'histoire de la presse française: 1944-1947* (Paris: 1948) is very critical of the press revolution, but his strictures seem mild compared to the invective of Claude Hisard in his *Histoire de la spoliation de la presse française* (Paris: 1955). The continuing anxiety of the Fédération Nationale de la Presse Française about the status of the new press is reflected in its monthly, *La Presse Française*, and in such pamphlets as *La Presse de Pétain va-t-elle chasser la presse de la Résistance?* (Paris: n.d.). The various legal imbroglios surrounding the Law of May 11, 1946, are discussed in detail by Gérard Lyon-Caen, *L'Application de la loi du 11 mai 1946 sur la dévolution des biens des entreprises de presse* (Paris: 1950); Marguerite Richard, "La Société Nationale des Entreprises de Presse" (unpublished *thèse en droit*, University of Paris, 1959); Pierre Terrou, "Le Statut Juridique de l'Entreprise de Presse en France", *Etudes de Presse*, No. 8 (Winter 1953). Jacques Kayser surveys the postwar French press from several angles in *Le Quotidien français* (Paris: 1963).

Everything of interest on the writers' purge is cited in footnotes to the discussion in the text. Georges Duhamel's *Tribulations de l'espérance* (Paris: 1947) and *Eclaircissements* (n.p.: 1947) together with Henri Bordeaux, *Quarante ans chez les quarante* (Paris: 1959), shed light on the French Academy's attitude toward its "compromised" members. Also of interest is the anonymous [André Siegfried?] "Les Elections à l'Académie

Française: Analyse d'un Scrutin Significatif, l'Echec de M. Paul Morand", *Revue Française de Science Politique*, VIII, 3 (September 1958). The role of the Church under Vichy is still a matter of dispute. For the prosecution, see Jean Cotereau, *L'Eglise a-t-elle collaboré?* (Paris: 1946) and *L'Eglise et Pétain* (n.p.: n.d.); for the defense, Mgr. Emile Guerry, *Le Rôle de l'episcopat français sous l'occupation allemande* (Lille: 1945) and *L'Eglise catholique en France sous l'occupation* (Paris: 1947). On the removal of bishops, by far the best account is that of André Latreille, advisor to the Ministry of the Interior for religious affairs in early 1945: "Les Débuts de Mgr. Roncalli à la Nonciature de Paris: Souvenirs d'un Témoin, Décembre 1944-Août 1945", *Revue de Paris*, August 1963.

The two best accounts of this critical period in the history of the French labor movement are those by Georges Lefranc (himself "épuré"), *Les Expériences syndicales en France de 1939 à 1950* (Paris: 1950), and Henry W. Ehrmann, *French Labor from Popular Front to Liberation* (New York: 1947). They should be supplemented with Edouard Dolléans and Gérard Dehove, *Histoire du travail en France: Mouvement ouvrier et législation sociale* (Paris: 1953-55); Val R. Lorwin, *The French Labor Movement* (Cambridge [Mass.]: 1954). René Belin's long deposition in *Les Evénements survenus en France* is worth consulting, as is Rieber's study of the P.C.F. and Kaminsky's thesis (all cited above). *La Révolution Proletarienne* carried many articles on the trade-union purge in the years after the Liberation. The subsequent careers and activity of excluded Belinists can be followed in *La Revue Syndicaliste*, which was more or less their alumni magazine.

Some prominent theatrical performers touched by the purge discuss their experiences in memoirs: Sacha Guitry, *Quatre ans d'occupation* (Paris: 1947) and *Soixante jours de prison* (Paris: 1949); Maurice Chevalier, *With Love* (Boston: 1960); Corinne Luchaire, *Ma drôle de vie* (Paris: 1949).

VIII

The prewar changes in the French Penal Codes with respect to treason are discussed in "Wartime Collaborators: A Comparative Study of the Effect of their Trials on the Treason Law of Great Britain, Switzerland and France", *Yale Law Journal*, LVI, 7 (August 1947). Jacques Charpentier, head of the Paris bar, relates some of the underground discussions preceding the establishment of special courts in *Au service de la liberté* (Paris: 1949). Probably the most judicious and perceptive comments on the new legislation are in Emile Garçon, *Code pénal annoté*, 3 vols. (Paris: 1952-59). See also René Floriot, *La Répression des faits de collaboration* (Paris: 1945), and Pierre H. Doublet, *La Collaboration, l'épuration, la confiscation, les réparations aux victimes de l'occupation: Exposé et commentaire suivis des principales ordonnances* (Paris: 1945). On the *cours de justice*, see also Albert Colombini, "Les Cours de Justice: Commentaire de l'Ordonnance du 28

Novembre 1944", *Les Lois Nouvelles*, No. 3 (March 5-15-25, 1945), 1st part, and No. 5 (May 5-15-25), 1st part; René Vigo, "Les Cours de Justice" (unpublished *thèse en droit*, University of Paris, 1950). On another aspect of the Government's judicial program, see Henri Faucher, "L'Indignité Nationale", *La Semaine Juridique*, 1945, 1st part, No. 454; Germaine Fauvet, "L'Indignité Nationale" (unpublished *thèse en droit*, University of Paris, 1947). The history of "High Courts" is recounted in Raymond Lindon, *La Haute cour de justice en France* (Paris: 1945) and in *Bulletin Hebdomadaire d'Informations Judiciaires*, No. 3 (April 28, 1945). The one with which we are concerned is discussed from an organizational and procedural point of view in Louis Noguerès, *La Haute cour de la Libération: 1944-1949* (Paris: 1965). For a systematic attack on the new legislation and institutions, see Louis Rougier, "La France est-elle un Etat de Droit", *Ecrits de Paris*, February 1950.

IX

Many trial records have been published, usually in somewhat abbreviated form. A number appeared in a series edited by Maurice Garon: *Le Procès du maréchal Pétain*, 2 vols. (Paris: 1945); *Le Procès Laval* (Paris 1946); *Le Procès de Charles Maurras* (Paris: 1946); *Les Procès de collaboration: Fernand de Brinon, Joseph Darnand, Jean Luchaire* (Paris: 1948); *Les Procès de la Radio: Ferdonnet et Jean Hérold-Paquis* (Paris: 1947). Other published trials include: Jean-Louis Aujol, *Le Procès Benoist-Méchin* (Paris: 1948); Jacques Isorni, *Le Procès Robert Brasillach* (Paris: 1946); Maurice Ribet, *Le Procès Georges Claude* (Paris: 1946); Geo London, *L'Amiral Estéva et le général Dentz devant la Haute cour de justice* (Lyons: 1945); *Le Procès Flandin devant la Haute cour de justice* (Paris: 1947); Robert Dufourg, *Adrien Marquet devant la Haute cour* (Paris: 1948); *Le Procès de Xavier Vallat présenté par ses amis* (Paris: 1948). Typescripts of others are available at the Bibliothèque Nationale and the B.D.I.C.

Jacques Isorni, principal defense attorney at the Pétain trial, has written of the case in *Je suis avocat* (Paris: 1950), *Souffrance et mort du maréchal Pétain* (Paris: 1951), and *Témoignage sur un temps passé* (Paris: 1953). See also Jean Schlumberger, *Le Procès Pétain* (Paris: 1949), for the perceptive comments of a spectator. All three of Laval's lawyers have written about his trial: Jacques Baraduc, *Dans la cellule de Laval* (Paris: 1948); Yves-Frédéric Jaffre, *Les Derniers propos de Pierre Laval* (Paris: 1953); and Albert Naud, *Pourquoi je n'ai pas défendu Pierre Laval* (Paris: 1948). Simone de Beauvoir comments on the trial in "Oeil pour Oeil", *Les Temps Modernes*, I, 5 (February 1, 1946).

The volumes of *L'Année Politique* for 1944-45 and 1946 are indispensable for the politics of the Liberation period. The best general treatments are Dorothy Pickles, *France Between the Republics* (London: 1946); Gordon Wright, *The Reshaping of French Democracy* (New York: 1948); and André

Siegfried, *De la IIIe à la IVe République* (Paris: 1956). For the Communists see the works cited above; B. D. Graham discusses *The French Socialists and Tripartisme: 1944-1947* (London: 1965); Francis de Tarr analyses *The French Radical Party from Herriot to Mendès-France* (London: 1960).

X

The provisions of the successive amnesties are discussed in Jean-René Bricaut, "Présentation Méthodique des Principales Dispositions de la Loi d'Amnistie du 16 Août 1947", *La Semaine Juridique*, 1948, 1st part, No. 681; Henri Faucher, "Amnistie et Collaboration avec l'Ennemi (Loi du 16 Août 1947)", *La Semaine Juridique*, 1947, 1st part, No. 658; Albert Colombini, "La Loi du 5 Janvier 1951 Portant Amnistie et Modifiant les Effets de la Degradation Nationale", *Les Lois Nouvelles*, 1951, No. 6 (March 20-April 5), 1st part; René Tunc, "L'Amnistie, la Collaboration et les Activités Antinationales (Commentaire de la Loi du 5 Janvier 1951)", *La Semaine Juridique*, 1951, 1st part, No. 904; Jean Copper-Royer, *L'Amnistie loi du 6 août 1953* (Paris: 1954); René Tunc, "La Loi d'Amnistie du 6 Août 1953", *La Semaine Juridique*, 1953, 1st part, No. 1123. There are some interesting remarks on the politics of their passage in Otto Kirchheimer, *Political Justice: The Use of Legal Procedure for Political Ends* (Princeton [N.J.]: 1961).

INDEX

INDEX

Duclos, Jacques, 183
Ducreux, Jacques, 161n
Duhamel, Georges, 10, 126, 128-9 173
Dumesnil de Gramont, 146
Dunkirk, 4, 9
Dupont, Frédéric, 182
Duverger, Maurice, 195

l'Echo du Nord, 162
Ehrmann, Henry W., 133n
Eisenhower, Gen. Dwight D., 42, 55-6, 63, 170
Elections, ineligibility question, 98-101; communes (1945), 110; Communists, 182
l'Epoque, 114
Estéva, Adm. Jean-Pierre, 2n, 172

Fabre-Luce, Alfred, 127
Farge, Yves, 76-7, 83
Faure, Paul, 10, 107, 112
Faÿ, Bernard, 127
Fédération Nationale de la Presse Clandestine, 116-17
Fédération Nationale de la Presse Française, 121, 123
Fédération Républicaine, 201
le Figaro, 114-15, 166
Flandin, Pierre-Etienne, in Vichy government, 11, 50; arrest and trial, 55-6, 182; elections, 104n
Fleet *See* Navy
Forces Françaises de l'Intérieur, 63, 68, 71, 77
Franc- Tireur, 19, 26, 117; retitled *Paris-Jour*, 124; purge trials, 167
le Français, 33
France au Combat, 201
la France Combattante, 50, 169
la France Libre, 124
la France Socialiste, 115
France-Soir, 124
Franco-Soviet Treaty, 181-2
Francs-Tireurs et Partisans français, 25n, 26, 31, 63, 71-3, 201
Frémicourt, Charles, 193
Frenay, Henri, 14

French Occupation Army (in Germany), 54
Frette-Damicourt, Proc.-Gen., 178
Froideval, Raymond, 133
Front National, 19, 25n, 26, 73, 201
Front National (journal), 124
Front National des Juristes, 27
Funck-Brentano, Christian, 33

Galimand, Lucien, 97
Gamelin, Gen. Maurice-Gustave, 8
Gaulle, Gen. Charles de, Armistice, 3, 175; popularity, 6; Free French leader, 14, 19-21, 24, 44-5, 96, 128; N. African purge, 21, 30, 49, 50, 56; Vichy legality, 21-3, 80, 141-2, 191-4, 196-7; N. African government, 43-9, 51-2; C.F.L.N., 52, 54; Allies, 54, 56, 67; Pucheu trial, 58; Liberation authority, 60, 62-7; recognized, 67; Paris liberated, 69, 131; disorder, 70, 72n, 77; Communism, 61, 65, 73, 75; purge of administration, 61-2, 79, 92-3, 95; 5th Republic, 112; Press, 120n; Academy, 129-30; 'sword and shield', 153; purge trials, 157, 163n, 169, 172, 186; Pétain trial, 172-3, 175-6; Laval trial, 177; resignation, 178; C.N.R. Charter 198, 201
Gay, Francisque, 117
Gazier, Albert, 56
Georges, Gen. Alphonse, 47-8
la Gerbe, 115
Giacobbi, Paul, 96
Gide, André, 127
Giraud, Gen. Henri, N. African government, 42-8; N. African purges, 50-6, 59; Pucheu, 58; Eisenhower, 170; De Gaulle, 193
Giraudoux, Jean, 129
Gorce, Paul Marie de la, 3
Gouin, Félix, 7n, 96, 112, 178, 186
Gouvernement Provisoire de la République Française. *See* Provisional Government of the French Republic

INDEX